G000081113

SCHUBERT
AND THE SYMPHONY
A New Perspective

SCHUBERT
AND THE
SYMPHONY
A New Perspective

BRIAN NEWBOULD

Symphonic Studies
No. 1

TOCCATA
PRESS

First published 1992 by Toccata Press
© Brian Newbould, 1992

Music examples by Barry Peter Ould

British Library Cataloguing in Publication Data

Newbould, Brian
  Schubert and the symphony : a new perspective
  1. Austrian music. Schubert, Franz, 1797-1828
  I. Title
  780.92

ISBN 0-907689-26-4
ISBN 0-907689-27-2 pbk

Typeset by York House Typographic Ltd, London
Printed and bound by Short Run Press Ltd, Exeter

Contents

List of Illustrations

Preface

The celebration in 1978 of the 150th anniversary of Schubert's death stimulated research activity over a wide front. These researches, conducted both in anticipation of the anniversary and in its wake, had a particular impact on the understanding of the composer's symphonic career. After the re-dating of the 'Great' C major, always thought to be Schubert's last symphony but now brought forward from his last year, 1828, to 1825–6, it was discovered that a 'Tenth' Symphony was begun in the last weeks of his life. Other sketches from the middle years were re-examined and have appeared in performing versions which are widely performed and recorded. These include a large-scale Seventh Symphony, which throws light on the previously puzzling stylistic leap from the Sixth Symphony to the Eighth.

This study reviews Schubert's symphonic career in the light of these developments. From his first known attempt at symphonic composition (D2B, begun in 1811 at the age of fourteen), I have set out to examine each symphony for its individuality and to see it in relation to the total *œuvre*, giving special attention to the sketched works that have emerged more recently as well as to the two familiar masterpieces of Schubert's maturity, the 'Unfinished' and the 'Great'. Schubert's relationship to his symphonic forebears has been a particular concern, and I point to several new internal indications of the importance of Haydn and Mozart as models for the youthful Schubert.

This is the first full-length study of Schubert as symphonist, and the opportunity has been taken to explore

7

several specific aspects of his approach to the symphony. An attempt is made to elucidate, with corrective analysis as appropriate, formal procedures which have been the subject of some misunderstanding. The problems which confronted Schubert as an orchestral writer in the Classical period are explained, with special reference to the limitations of the brass instruments, with the intention of clarifying various facets of his orchestral treatment and symphonic outlook. Evidence about the manner in which he set about committing his planned symphonies to paper is examined, and a new hypothesis presented which it is hoped will help to establish the role of the piano sketch in Schubert's evolution as a symphonist. In the case of unfinished symphonies, the possible causes of abandonment are considered.

The book is offered as a companion to the symphonies for all who have an acquaintance, deep or casual, with the riches they contain, whether as ordinary listeners or as professional musicians or students. Where I adopt an analytical stance, I do so with the aim of illuminating the heartfelt response which, whether it be my reader's or my own, must come first. Those who prefer to use my commentary in conjunction with recordings or scores are not ignored; at the same time, I hope that where I have found that only by means of a modicum of technical explanation can one come to grips with the subject I shall not lose the reader whose enthusiasm for Schubert is not matched by a love of technicalities. The music examples are chosen less as adornments or samples than as illustrative aids in support of the text, and I make no apology for leaving some well-loved movements un-illustrated or for giving a more generous allowance of music examples to the works which have come to public notice only in recent years.

I dedicate my book to all friends of Schubert, whether long-standing, incipient or prospective, and especially to those around the world who are known to me either personally or by letter, to whom I feel a spiritual closeness that shrinks the miles between. It is written in self-evident debt to all who have researched and written on Schubert over a century and a half. They, and I, and all who read on are in turn indebted to the performers and interpreters who keep this repertory alive and will continue to do so as long as the world in its wisdom has an ear for it. Guy Rickards generously offered help with the proofreading. And not least, I acknowledge and thank Ann and Fiona, who have daily enriched the soil in which my Schubert studies took root and bore their modest fruit.

BRIAN NEWBOULD
Hessle
July 1988

I

The Lure of the Symphony

The symphony held a lifelong fascination for Schubert. He was only fourteen when he first tried to compose one, and a final attempt absorbed him in the last few weeks before his death. In all he set about writing a symphony at least thirteen times. How is this commitment on Schubert's part to be explained, when of all his many compositional pursuits the symphony was the least marketable and least likely to gain public performance in his home city?

To answer that question it is necessary to examine both the genre and the man. Those aspects of Schubert's musical personality which made him susceptible to the lure of symphonic composition will, I hope, emerge in the chapters that follow. As for the genre, the symphony was already an established four-movement medium long before Schubert's father was born in 1763. In the hands' of its early proponents, like Sammartini, Wagenseil, Johann Stamitz and Cannabich, some of the numerous Italian, Bohemian, German and Austrian composers who were busy producing symphonies in the middle of the eighteenth century, it had become an arena in which two essential and interdependent elements could fruitfully evolve: a 'modern' self-sufficient orchestra capable of serving the new 'sonata style', and a language capable of sustaining extended musical arguments without dependence on extra-musical factors such as a verbal text or on the concerto principle intrinsic to Baroque musical thought. Self-sufficiency, for the orchestra, entailed the development of the wind section not merely as a reservoir of timbres for distinctive solo use or effective opposition to or blending with the strings but as a constituent in all manner of *tutti* and semi-*tutti* textures. If the old continuo had not been abandoned because the burgeoning wind section could provide textural layers which rendered a keyboard superfluous, it would have disappeared eventually as the composer came to exert and require a more precise control over details of his scoring than was compatible with the presence of extemporised keyboard support. In short, the orchestra became, during the first 75 years of the concert-room symphony (c. 1725–1800), a distinctive instrument in its own right, adding up to much more than the sum of its multifarious parts.

If the emergence of a 'language capable of sustaining extended musical arguments' is cited as a complementary development, the term 'language' should be clarified as embracing vocabulary, phraseology and, indeed, architecture. The symphony imposed on is composer the necessity of thinking profoundly, yes; engagingly, yes; but increasingly in terms of a big canvas. Accordingly, within a continuum lasting from say, five to fifteen minutes the thematic material had to be effectively deployed, and the colours of the orchestra aptly applied, to specify two obvious requirements. Less obviously to the casual listener, but most importantly to the composer, long-term planning depended on a coherent and telling key-structure and on skill in the distribution and timing of harmonies. Such tonal and harmonic procedures were at the core of the Classical style, and treatises on composition written in the second half of the Classical period (c. 1790–1830)[1] tend to emphasise the role of tonality, or key-schemes, in

[1] Heinrich Christoph Koch, *Versuch einer Anleitung zur Composition*, Leipzig, 1782–93; Johann Gottlieb Portmann, *Leichtes Lehrbuch der Harmonie*, Darmstadt, 1789; and August F. C. Kollmann, *Essay on Practical Musical Composition*, London, 1799.

the construction of long movements at the expense of the thematic content.

Orchestrations, harmonic planning, tonal structure and thematic deployment: these were the essential nuts and bolts of symphonic writing. But a symphony did not merely test the composer's technique: as the genre developed, it came more and more to challenge the human spirit. An attractive context for the exercise of vision, breadth and integration, it appeared to offer limitless potential. For Schubert there was perhaps no more congenial framework for the projection of a range of spiritual and emotional states. The scheme would enable a variety of basic compositional attitudes to be struck, their relationship being characterised by contrast and by symmetry or other purposeful design, the outer movements perhaps providing a unifying frame by sharing similar tonal, temporal, rhythmic or spiritual issues. The scale of construction would permit cumulative power to be attained by means of an 'argument', an argument more variegated and expansive than the Baroque genres had allowed,[2] and the impact of poetry or lyricism to be intensified by being set within a context of some size and complexity. The oppositions of intensities of volume, of densities of scoring, of dynamism and tranquillity, of tension and relaxation, might interact to produce almost infinite shades of 'meaning', given the time-scale of events and the richness of the orchestral medium.

For Schubert the appeal of the symphony was so strong that he never lost his commitment to it, no matter how many attempts he abandoned in the face of creative or personal dilemmas. Not even in his especially troublesome early twenties was the appetite thwarted by the difficulties of completion that beset him.

[2] The Baroque 'ritornello form', although unitary in essence, was sufficiently prophetic of Classical principles of construction for Mozart to adopt it without incongruity as a basis on which to superimpose Classical variegation (for instance, the ideal of contrasting themes) in his piano concertos.

During those middle years Schubert was anxious to succeed as an operatic composer. There is no evidence that for him opera and symphony were incompatible, even if in a mundane sense urgent work on operatic projects in late 1821 prevented him finishing his Seventh Symphony. Nor could the operatic associations of the symphony have enticed him towards the genre, for although the origins of the symphony lay in the old opera overture (*sinfonia*), it had long since shed all traces of them, or at least they had been submerged by the growing independence of the symphonic stock itself. The historical connection between opera and symphony had become a remote genealogical link by Schubert's time: indeed, it is largely peripheral to our appreciation of any symphony written since the middle of the Classical period.

The division to which I refer falls in the early 1790s. The faint echoes of the opera house to be discerned in Mozart's final symphonic triptych (Nos. 39–41, 1788), more in No. 39 than in No. 41 (the 'Jupiter') and hardly at all in No. 40 in G minor, derive not so much from the old connection between symphony and opera as from Mozart himself and his parallel interests. By nature, Mozart was more an operatic composer than was any other of the principal Classical symphonists, and his instrumental music bears frequent testimony to the fact. While Haydn gave himself wholeheartedly to composing operas for the Esterháza palace from time to time, his later string quartets, piano sonatas and symphonies (the last of which appeared in 1795) are products of purely instrumental thinking by a composer who remains true to whatever medium he is working in, and is recognisably Haydn in all of them. No composer is more obviously or effortlessly a 'composer for all media' than Haydn. Ten years after Mozart's last symphony and five years after Haydn's, Beethoven had begun his pioneering cycle of symphonies, furthering the vigorous growth of a musical species which had well and truly declared its independence. Indeed, if the opera overture had failed to produce this progeny, the symphony would probably have developed from other sources – possibly as a direct transfer from the keyboard sonata or string quartet – well before Beethoven commandeered the medium; and its subsequent history would not have been very different.

Song, rather than opera, was the vocal genre in which Schubert achieved success. This success must have brought him solace and confidence, but it did not satisfy his creative aspirations. When, in 1828, the publisher Schott wrote to him to express interest in his works, Schubert replied with a list of works he could offer to Schott. It included many songs, and at the end of it he added: 'I have also written three operas, a Mass, and a symphony.[3] I mention these, though, only to acquaint you with my efforts in the highest forms of musical art'. That Schubert regarded the symphony as one of the 'highest forms' accords not only with the fact that it beckoned his attention thirteen times in eighteen years but also with the desire he expressed[4] in the early 1820s to write his '*grosse Symphonie*', which became something of an obsession in the years leading up to its composition.

Those who think of Schubert as a song composer, perhaps because they know the songs better than his other works, suffer a graver misconception than those who regard Chopin as a piano composer. Schubert was as likely to compose a symphony as a song, a piano sonata as a string quartet, Mass, or piano trio. In this respect he was a typical Classical composer. The tendency for composers to specialise, or at least to narrow their field of interest, was a development of the Romantic period. Haydn, Mozart, Beethoven and Schubert were men of all media, even if by inclination or circumstance they gave themselves to some more than to others. Why, then, has Schubert been neglected as an instrumental composer? The

[3] He probably refers to his most recent symphony, No. 9 in C (the 'Great'). The letter is dated 21 February 1828.

[4] *Cf.* p. 208.

question is not mine, but Alfred Brendel's. Brendel gives
eight answers to it. None of them apportions blame to the
composer himself, but collectively they imply that successive generations have been too ready to inherit the blink-
ered attitudes and narrow horizons of his contemporaries.[5]

Schubert enjoyed the frequent company of a fairly
regular circle of friends: literary men, a singer, lawyers,
artistic *dilettanti*. Their 'Schubertiads' (as they are now
called), social evenings in members' homes, were a forum
for songs, piano impromptus and the like, but hardly for
Masses and symphonies. Outside the 'Schubertiads',
Vienna offered little scope to a symphonist. The Viennese
were 'careless, pleasure-seeking and frivolous', suggests
Hans Gál: 'they preferred dancing to thinking, a joke to
a sermon, the coffee-house to the library, a waltz to a
symphony'.[6] It is probable that only half of Schubert the artist was known to his friends. His was a circle in
the social sense, but artistically there was more likely a
cluster of overlapping circles, but with that part of Schubert entertaining symphonic visions well removed. One
hopes for the composer's sake that he was able to touch
some contemporary souls as a symphonist, whether they
responded to performances (which, few as they were,
were largely private ones) or were shown and were able
to read and discuss the scores. Michael Holzer, the choir-
master at Liechtental Parish Church where the young
Franz Schubert was a choirboy, and who gave the young
composer early encouragement, may have heard and responded to the first few symphonies; so may Salieri, his
teacher at the City Seminary, where the orchestra performed the First Symphony and possibly another one or
two, even though Salieri as a composer himself was
almost exclusively occupied with vocal composition. The

[5] *Musical Thoughts and Afterthoughts*, Robson, London 1976, pp. 73–74.

[6] *The Golden Age of Vienna*, M. Parrish, London/New York, 1948, p. 70.

resident of Vienna best able to make true contact with this side of Schubert's artistry was Beethoven; but when the two met, it was only briefly, in Beethoven's last weeks and Schubert's penultimate year. Each is known to have admired the other, and one could imagine them exchanging artistic intimacies with enthusiasm, for composers' styles and aspirations were broadly unified at this time (in a way which has not obtained, for example, throughout the twentieth century) and few pairs of composers of any era could have shared as much common ground as Beethoven and Schubert.

Anyone who knows Schubert as a song composer may regard him as a Romantic. Those who see him in the round can regard him only as a Classical composer. Classicism implies a certain balance between intellect and emotion, a close interdependence between form and content. Such principles may operate in any musical medium, without compromise. Whatever the essence of Romanticism, it exalts different ideals and favours some media more than others. The string quartet may not be a medium hospitable to Romantic thought; the piano is. Schubert, a true Classical artist, seems to anticipate the Romantic movement in the sheer success and volume of his *Lieder*, the *Lied* being a meeting-ground between musical and literary art-forms and an obvious avenue for the infiltration into music of concrete, non-musical ideas, which was to be a prime facet of the Romantic ideal. Yet for Schubert the *Lied* ultimately remains one of his many media, and he remains the last great Classical composer.

Although Romanticism was born before Schubert died, it was given substance by others more than by Schubert. *Der Freischütz* (1821) was a case in point, and the imaginative musical evocations which its subject prompted from Weber seem to find an echo in some late examples of Classical genres – in the introduction to the finale of Schubert's Octet, for example. Even the string quartet seems capable of inhabiting the new Romantic world when we listen to Schubert's last exemplar, the G major

(D887). If the horn melody which opens the 'Great' C major Symphony seems to be imbued with similar resonances, that is an understandable illusion in that this, the last great Classical[7] symphony, exudes a vividness of imagination as well as an almost self-conscious confidence that presses Classical constraints virtually to their limit.

Without the dazzling glare of Beethoven the splendour of the 'Great' C major would be seen in sharper relief, as would that of the B flat Piano Sonata (D960) and the G major String Quartet (D887) – as pinnacles of the Classical era. The vista of late Schubert is obscured by the presence of Beethoven, the rival giant in instrumental music, for twentieth-century scholarship has tended to emphasise Schubert's distinctive un-Beethovenian feature – his achievement in song – and allowed it to characterise him to an exaggerated extent.

The relationship between the work of the two contemporaneous symphonists will naturally claim some attention in a survey of the achievement of the younger one, for he chose to strive for mastery in the still-bubbling wake of the older composer. Schubert's period of symphonic activity, in the same city as Beethoven's, can be chronologically located about a dozen years after Beethoven's by comparing the dates of their first symphonies (1800, 1813) and their eighth (1812, 1822). This is a convenient simplification, of course, and one of the facts it conceals is that Schubert was in truth more prolific a symphonist than Beethoven. Beethoven's nine symphonies amount to 13,162 bars of music (bars are a crude measure but reasonably valid over so large a sample). Schubert's seven-and-a-half finished symphonies contain 10,241 bars, but whereas Beethoven's total represents the accumulated *œuvre* of a 54-year-old (to take the date of completion of No. 9), Schubert's is the product of a 29-year-

[7]'Classical' here means 'Classical within the Classical period'. The extent to which the symphonies of, for example, Brahms may be 'Classical' is therefore not an issue.

old. The resultant ratio of productivity is: Beethoven, 234 bars per annum; Schubert, 321 bars per annum. This figure excludes the 3,421 bars[8] additionally sketched by Schubert. Schubert was, indeed, by this measure not only more prolific than Beethoven but more productive than any of the well-known nineteenth-century symphonists, including Bruckner and Dvořák.

How far the symphonic attitudes of Schubert and Beethoven have diverged by the time they reached their ninth symphonies will be seen later, although the divergencies in mid-career are no less fascinating. But neither could begin his exploration of the genre by doing anything other than building on eighteenth-century models.

[8] Including No. 7, No. 8 (third movement only), No. 10, D615, D708A and D2B.

II

First Steps

The symphonies of Haydn and Mozart were the natural models for Beethoven and Schubert. But Schubert could learn from another potential model – Beethoven himself, who had begun to blaze the trail of the nineteenth-century symphony eleven years before Schubert took his first tentative steps in the medium (on the evidence available at present) at the age of fourteen. When Schubert entered the choir of the Imperial *Kapelle* in 1808, as an eleven-year-old, he was enrolled at the school attached, which was part of the Vienna *Stadtkonvikt*, a boarding school in the old university quarter of Vienna, run by the Piarists, a Roman Catholic teaching order. Being an able violinist, he was taken into the school orchestra. The leader of the second violins was Josef von Spaun, a law student nine years older than Schubert, who was henceforward his lifelong friend. Spaun recalled, in the year after Schubert's death (1829), that every day 'the evening was devoted to the performance of a complete symphony and several overtures, and the young orchestra's forces sufficed for the successful performance of Haydn's, Mozart's, and Beethoven's masterpieces'.[1] Later, in 1858, Spaun recalled that Schubert would stand immediately behind him and play from the same copy. He was

[1] *Österreichisches Bürgerblatt für Verstand, Herz und gute Laune*, Linz, 27 and 30 March, 3 April 1829; reprinted in translation in O. E. Deutsch, *Schubert – A Documentary Biography*, J. M. Dent, London, 1946.

thus able to observe the spirit and commitment with which the otherwise quiet and serious little boy performed, and the remarkable sureness of his beat.[2] In this memoir Spaun stated that the school possessed the performance material of over thirty symphonies by Haydn, and several by Mozart and Beethoven, though he later deleted this statement in his manuscript, perhaps uncertain of its accuracy almost half a century later. But when his memory was fresher, in the 1829 note, he had referred to particular favourites of Schubert in the repertoire they played: 'Above all the glorious Symphonies in G minor[3] by Mozart and in D major by Beethoven made the profoundest impression on young Schubert every time, and even shortly before his death he still spoke of how greatly these compositions had moved and touched his youthful soul'.

It would therefore have been natural enough for Mozart's Fortieth and Beethoven's Second to affect Schubert's own early efforts at writing symphonies. Spaun refers to several works having been composed in these first years at the *Stadtkonvikt*, and some of them may have been symphonies. Certainly no fewer than five overtures were written between 1811 and 1813, and the symphony known as No. 1 in D (D82) was completed on 28 October 1813. At least one earlier attempt was made. All that survives of it is a fragment; indeed, that may be all that was ever composed. The fragment (D2B) dates from 1811 and amounts to 30 bars in all, comprising a slow introduction and the opening of an *Allegro*. It is in orchestral score, and the fact that Schubert has to work out on a spare stave at the foot of his first page[4] how to notate the

[2]'Notes on my Association with Franz Schubert', published in *Der Merker*, Vienna, February–March 1912, and reprinted in translation in O. E. Deutsch, *Schubert: Memoirs by his Friends*, A. and C. Black, London, 1958.

[3]No. 40 is doubtless referred to, rather than No. 25.

[4]*Cf.* p. 25.

upward-rushing scale of the first bar implies that he was
composing into orchestral score and not working from a
preliminary piano sketch. The question at issue was how
many beams were required for the short notes following
the long first note. If he had first sketched the work as
though for piano, on two staves, he would probably have
solved this notational problem at that stage. (He could
have adopted a temporary solution, of course, and postponed a final decision until he orchestrated the sketch,
but that appears unlikely.) It was nothing extraordinary
for a composer to compose directly into orchestral score
at this time in the history of music, though in later periods it became unusual. One could never imagine Beethoven doing so, but Beethoven was a creator *sui generis*. The
possibility of Schubert, like Mozart, composing in this way
is one to which I shall return later in connection with
other works.[5]

The *Adagio* which begins D2B contains nothing that
Haydn might not have done, though it must be said that
the fourteen-year-old has absorbed from his experience
of playing the Haydn symphonies, coupled no doubt with
glances at the scores, a basic competence in conceiving an
effective orchestral texture, not to mention an understanding of the principles of harmonic and thematic procedure appropriate to a slow introduction. When
Schubert begins his *Allegro*, it is to Beethoven and Mozart
that the listener's mind involuntarily turns. He opens (Ex.
1) with a repeated D in the violins, over an arching
broken chord in the violas. A flurry of violin semiquavers
in the second bar leads to the first change of harmony at
the third. A comparison with the opening of the *Allegro*
which follows the slow introduction of Beethoven's
Second Symphony (Ex. 2) is revealing. Beethoven, writing in 1802, has the repeated Ds in the violins, a rather
more spacious and decorated arching broken chord in
the cellos (his 'theme' indeed, announced in the bass),

[5] *Cf.* especially pp. 249–56.

Ex. 1

Ex .2

and a flurry of semiquavers in the fourth bar leading to
the first change of harmony at the fifth. Schubert's first
change of harmony is to the same chord as Beethoven's,
although the supertonic seventh now appears in a different inversion. Schubert has in fact compressed Beethoven's four-bar model into a two-bar one. Where he then
gives a pretty exact sequence of that model, complete
with the semiquavers (bar 4), Beethoven gives a freer
sequence which substitutes for the semiquavers an engag-
ing touch of *legato* woodwind colour. The following chord
in each case (in Schubert's fifth bar and Beethoven's
ninth) is what modern theory calls a V^7 of IV, or dominant seventh of the subdominant.

It is not often that one composer appears to emulate
another so obviously (though probably subconsciously) as
to reproduce melodic contours, rhythmic patterns and

harmonic scheme (and here, all in the same key of D major). But youth is impressionable, and as one *in statu pupillari* Schubert could hardly do better than learn from the greatest composer alive. Spaun vouched for his special attachment to Beethoven's Second Symphony. The most inspired feature of the master's opening was, however, something that eluded the pupil. That was the difference between a 32-year-old with some sixty full-blown multi-movement instrumental works to his name and a novice less than half his age who had barely ventured upon large-scale composition. Moreover, two of the overtures written at about the same time share this debt to Beethoven's Second. Both D4 and the unfinished D2A are likewise in D major, and have a triadic theme in the bass accompanied solely by an oscillation between tonic and leading-note in the violins.

There are two important aspects of the symphonic fragment, which are not unrelated. One is Schubert's choice of key; the other is his inclusion of trombones in the score. An examination of the full list of Schubert's symphonies, finished and unfinished, reveals that of thirteen attempts to compose a symphony six were in the key of D major. Moreover, all five of the overtures written between 1811 and 1813 were in that key. Was it that Beethoven's Second Symphony had shown the beginner what an effective key D major was for orchestral composition, and the lesson stayed with him? This factor was doubtless an influential one, though it should be borne in mind that Haydn wrote more symphonies in D major (23) than in any other key, as did Mozart (13).

It is true that D major suits the compass of the majority of orchestral instruments fairly well. But much depends on what kind of music the composer writes – on how, for instance, the thematic ideas 'lie' in the scale. With material of an appropriate kind, a Classical composer could just as effectively write a symphony in A – Beethoven did. But Schubert, although he admired Beethoven's Seventh,

The first page of the D2B *fragment in Schubert's autograph score.*
Trombones are placed at the foot of the score, immediately below the
strings (University Library, Lund, Sweden).

would probably never have attempted a symphony in
A himself. Another consideration is that all the stringed
instruments of the orchestra have a string tuned to the
note D. Moreover, the only string in the entire string
section of the orchestra not tuned to one of the diatonic
scale-notes of D major is the lowest string of the violas
and cellos, a C natural. Accordingly, in music with a
strong diatonic basis, which is true of the Classical period,
the key of D will enable 'open' strings to be used extensively, making possible a bright sonority harder to achieve
in, say, E flat or F. Yet G major actually suits the tuning-
structure of the string section even better than D. But
Schubert wrote no symphonies in G; and if he loved
Mozart's Fortieth as much as Beethoven's Second, might
it not have had as strong an influence? He must have
played some or all of Haydn's 'Military', 'Surprise', and
'Oxford' Symphonies, and possibly No. 88 too, and these
all demonstrate for the player as for the listener that G
major is an effective and practical key. Also, Beethoven
returned to D only once after the Second Symphony, for
the D minor/major Ninth. He relied on D as a symphonic
key less than others in this group of four composers
(Haydn, Mozart, Schubert), while Schubert chose it more
frequently than any of the group.

A new factor still to be taken into account will throw
light on the popularity of D at this point in music history,
and on Schubert's abnormal fidelity to it, and on Beethoven's less partial attitude. To present this hypothesis I
shall have to lumber my reader with some technical
explanation, which I shall do as succinctly and readably as
I can in the following chapter. These technicalities will
help in the understanding of aspects of symphonies other
than those in D, and will be a factor in the consideration
of the question 'Why did Schubert leave some of his symphonies unfinished?'.

The second of my final two observations on the 1811
fragment was that Schubert included trombones in the
score. This inclusion is surprising to those who already

know Schubert's symphonies well enough to recall that Nos. 1–6 make no use of trombones at all. One may see as a natural step, in view of later stylistic development, the addition of trombones for the symphonies from No. 7 onwards. But why should Schubert have used them in the 1811 work and then abandoned them until 1821?

Neither Haydn nor Mozart used the trombone in symphonies, but Mozart used it in certain of his operas (*King Thamos, Don Giovanni* and *The Magic Flute*) and Schubert may well have played overtures from these operas. If he admired the sonority achieved with the help of trombones in, say, the Overture to *The Magic Flute*, he may well have thought it reasonable to use them in a symphony. As was more to be expected, he used them in all the stage works he wrote from 1813 to 1820, and in most of the church music (both shorter pieces and Masses) of this same period contemporaneous with the first six Symphonies. Trombones were a standard resource of Roman Catholic church music. Although in the 1811 symphonic fragment, which is probably the earliest of all his compositions employing an orchestra, he makes an error in notating their part at one point, he seems to understand the function of trombones in an orchestral texture. But having made his experiment, he may have decided that they were too cumbersome for the athletic, transparent 'early Classical' style he aspired to practise at this time, so he omitted the instruments from his Symphony No. 1, and liked the result enough to exclude them from further symphonies after that. But such considerations represent only a part of the case for or against the use of trombones in a symphony at this time, and other factors will emerge from our study of the background to Schubert's choice of keys for his symphonies.

III

Problems
of Orchestral Resource
and their Solution

What sort of symphony orchestra was it that Schubert inherited? It had long possessed a pliable and resourceful string section. With the establishment of the clarinet's regular place in the orchestra in late Haydn (Nos. 99, 103 and 104) and early Beethoven, the woodwind section was a sizable ensemble of four pairs (ideal for the Viennese Classical style with its emphasis on leading or subsidiary part-movement in parallel thirds or sixths, as a study of any Beethoven score and especially Schubert's 'Great' will show) offering a wealth of solo timbres and adequate potential for blending, in skilled hands. That leaves, in the early Classical orchestra, three other instruments – horns, trumpets and drums – which are perhaps best thought of as one group, in that they are often used as such, although when the horns are required to work independently the trumpets and drums are frequently yoked together in a common role. This group (horns, trumpets and drums), for the early nineteenth-century melodist, harmonist, and explorer of keys distantly or even quite closely related, was the underdeveloped territory of the orchestral world.

When wishing to make use of the clarinet, or for that matter any of the woodwind instruments, the composer could ask it to play any note he wished, provided that it lay between the lower and upper limits of its compass. But he could not use the horn or trumpet with this same freedom. The horn, for example, which like the trumpet was valveless at this time, could produce only a fixed series of notes in relation to its 'fundamental' note. Ex. 3 shows a 'fundamental' low C (numbered 1) followed by the notes which could be produced. These notes constitute the so-called harmonic series. The notes indicated in black would be out of tune according to the equal-tempered scale.

Ex. 3

Within the range enclosed between double bars in Ex. 3 (harmonics 2 to 12 inclusive), the viola or clarinet could produce any note of the major (or minor) scale, and any of the chromatic notes between – a total of 32 notes.[1] The valveless horn can play only 11 of these notes. This restriction is clearly a severe limitation for the composer, and must either impede his musical invention or affect the way in which that invention is distributed among the instruments of the orchestra.

Fortunately, if a composer chose to write a piece in, say, E flat major, he was not restricted to those notes which appear in Ex. 3, thanks to a device known as a 'crook'. The crook was an extra length of tubing inserted in the instrument which had the effect of lowering the

[1] In fact, the clarinet in A cannot produce the very bottom note, nor the clarinet in B flat the lowest two, because they are beyond the lowest extreme of its compass.

fundamental note and accordingly all the other notes of
the series by the same degree. There were several different crooks available, lowering the pitch of the entire series by various amounts, and the composer would select
the crook to be used according to the key in which the
music was to lie.

For his Seventh Symphony, which is in A, Beethoven
duly chose the A crook and marked his horn parts 'in A'.
The effect of this was to bring the entire series of available notes (as seen in Ex. 3) down by a minor third.[2]
Thus the twelfth note of the series would now be an E,
not a G as in Ex. 3. Obviously, since the harmonic series
is based on the major chord whose root is the fundamental note, the transposition of that series to the key of the
symphony one was writing made it possible to use the
instrument much more extensively. Of course, if the
music modulated to other keys, the instrument could not
be given such an active part at these places. But the horn
could usually play at least occasional notes during an
excursion to another key, and this possibility became a
test of the craft (and judgement) of the composer, as a
study of Classical scores reveals.

Shortly before the end of his Seventh Symphony
Beethoven momentarily abandons his A major and
writes, several times in succession, something like a standard cadence-formation in F major (Ex. 4). The horns in
A can provide only one note in each chord; likewise the
trumpets, which have the same built-in limitation as the
horns. Beethoven uses these notes, but with somewhat
grotesque effect, since the resulting line (E to A, Ex. 5)
flouts the normal conventions of voice-leading, conventions which Beethoven would normally observe and does
observe in this same passage in the string parts (Ex. 4),
where the quasi leading-note E goes to its normal destination F, while the A in the second chord is the resolution

[2] That the player still reads from a part written in C is not relevant to
this discussion.

of the previous 'seventh', B flat. (The two timpani are tuned, in the conventional way, to the keynote and fifth (A and E) and Beethoven used them here to double the second horn one octave lower.)

Ex. 4

Ex. 5

This grotesqueness is such a characteristic feature of Beethoven's orchestral writing that even a listener unversed in the technicalities that lie behind it would probably hear it as 'Beethovenian'. If the brass parts in the above passage were rewritten using modern instruments, which have a complete chromatic range of notes, the result would not sound like Beethoven. Necessity has suggested, here as in countless other instances, a sound or contour (or, sometimes, a dissonance) which has become a hallmark of Beethoven's style. To some extent this phenomenon enters the style of all composers of the Classical period.

One characteristic of the harmonic series (Ex. 3) is that the gaps between successive notes decrease in size as the distance from the fundamental note increases. The valveless horn can therefore play nothing resembling a scale until the eighth note of the series is reached. It goes without saying that the scalic part of the series, from the eighth note upwards, is of most use to the composer. But at this point it has to be borne in mind that the harmonic series is a theoretical formulation of a natural law, and practical exigencies may make even some of the theoretically available notes unobtainable. There is, for instance, a more or less absolute limit to the altitude at which a horn player can play, irrespective of the structure of the harmonic series or of the crook being used. In Beethoven's Seventh the highest note given to the horn is an E, equivalent to the tenth note of Ex. 3 (e″). It is hardly used except for climaxes near the end of both of the outer movements, where the exhilarating brilliance imparted is memorable. Thus the potentially very useful notes 11 to 16, which are available in theory, cannot be employed in this symphony because their altitude puts them out of range.

Schubert is considerably more cautious than any of the other Classical composers in his use of the brass instruments. For one thing, his upper working limit for the horn is about half an octave lower than the Beethoven E. (In truth, the e″ is somewhat extreme even for Beethoven. The d″ ventured by Schubert in his First Symphony is untypical: the upper limits of b′ in the 'Unfinished' and a′ in the 'Great' are more characteristic of him.) But Schubert is cautious in another important sense. It had for some time been an accepted practice for horn players to 'find' extra notes not strictly available in the harmonic series by inserting the hand into the bell of the instrument, the effect of which could be (if properly done) to lower an existing member note of the harmonic series by a semitone, or by anything up to a whole tone. These notes were of inferior quality, and much softer than the 'natural' notes. (They are referred to as 'stopped notes' as distinct from 'open notes'.[3]) Composers other than Schubert used these stopped notes with some freedom,

[3]'Stopped notes' were not available on the trumpet, the bell not being within easy reach of the player's hand.

especially Mozart and Beethoven, despite the loss of quality. Schubert made relatively little use of them – another
aspect of his caution.

Schubert was therefore denying himself a form of compensation available to Mozart and Beethoven when the
adjacent notes or portions of scale in the harmonic series
were too high for use. Those composers widened their
choice of pitches available within the lower, available
range by employing 'false' or stopped notes. Schubert was
reluctant to do this; so what else could he do to remedy
the situation? The answer is that the longer the crook one
fitted to the horn, and the lower the 'key' into which one
shifted the harmonic series, the lower came the scalic portion of the harmonic series. Thus from a horn in D (that
is, fitted with a D crook) one could obtain the harmonic
series at this pitch (Ex. 6). It will be seen that this brings
most of the upper scale of the series down to a usable
pitch. With the thirteenth of the series, which Schubert
uses occasionally, there is almost one complete octave of
scale-steps obtainable.

Ex. 6

It was to secure this remedy, I suggest, that Schubert
used the key of D for so many symphonies. It was around
and just above middle C, in the alto voice range, that
Classical composers liked to 'centre' their horn parts; thus
the key of D – for the horns and for the symphony – was
of optimum convenience.

Schubert may have first discovered this remedy by
using Beethoven's Second as a model, as was seen above.
He began six symphonies in its key. How many did he
write in the key of his other boyhood favourite, Mozart's
No. 40 in G minor? None, because a G crook is only half

as curative a remedy as a D crook. So which keys *did*
Schubert use? All the Symphonies but two have D, C, or
B flat as their keynote. The advantages of C and B flat
were in one sense even bigger than those of D, for the
available notes on the horn were lowered one or two
degrees further still.[4] But there were some minor disadvantages in the effect on other instruments, and D was
found to be the best compromise. For the B minor Symphony (No. 8) Schubert used D horns. There were no B
crooks in existence; except as workshop curiosities,[5] and
in any case it was conventional and useful to pitch the
horns in the key of the third degree in a minor-key symphony, as will be explained in the case of the Fourth Symphony.[6] In the Seventh Symphony, horns in E are
used.[7] Horns in E are almost as advantageous as horns
in D.

Schubert, then, could use horns in D or lower for every
symphony except one. The keys used by the less cautious
Beethoven are, in ascending order, B flat (1), C (2), D(2),
E flat (1), F (2), and A (1).

This discussion has concentrated on the horn rather
than the trumpet, because the horn plays a more essential
part in Schubert's symphonic style than the trumpet.
It plays for longer periods, fulfilling a valuable 'bind-
ing' role in string-and-woodwind textures. Nevertheless,
what has been said about horns applies in large part to
trumpets too. But none of it applies to the trombones:
there were no 'gaps' within the range of the alto trombone, the tenor trombone, or the bass trombone. These

[4] Schubert used 'C basso' and 'B flat basso' rather than 'C alto' or 'B flat
alto' horns. These were pitched on the low C or B flat rather than the
C or B flat an octave higher.

[5] Cecil Forsyth, *Orchestration*, Macmillan, London, 1914, p. 79; *cf.* also
pp. 188–89.

[6] *Cf.* pp. 88–89.

[7] This remark will be amplified in the chapter on Schubert's manuscripts, p. 252.

instruments were therefore a boon to Schubert, as they were able to do all that he might have wished the horns to – that is, to provide harmonic filling in the middle register without restriction of choice of notes. They provide this service where the horns cannot in the third bar of the 1811 fragment, as can be seen in the facsimile on p. 25. It is therefore all the more surprising that Schubert then omitted the trombones from the Symphonies Nos. 1 and 6; but the reasons given earlier[8] for this omission still stand.

This point may be better understood by considering first the Fifth Symphony, which is unique in Schubert's *œuvre* in that it dispenses with clarinets, trumpets and drums and requires something like a middle-period Mozart orchestra (oboes, bassoons, horns and strings, with – in Schubert's case – one flute). Trombones would be as unimaginable in this context as in Mozart's Symphony No. 29 in A. Symphonists employed trombones only when a full complement of woodwind was present, with horns, trumpets, and timpani too. Trombones had no place in a 'chamber symphony'. Among Schubert's other symphonies, the nearest approach to the chamber orchestra of the Fifth is found in the Third. For all the moments of weighty resolve in the first and third movements of the Fifth, the qualities of litheness, grace and clarity abound, and where *gravitas* is required it is achieved by rhythmic means and by compressing the pitch-spread of the chamber orchestra resources to produce a concentration of unison and octave doublings. There could be no role here, not even in the noisy *tutti*s of the First Symphony, for the trombones. It is marginally less obvious that the trombones are alien to the worlds inhabited by the even-numbered Symphonies, because the Second and Fourth contain more earnest thoughts than any of the others, while the Sixth looks forward to the symphony in which, above all, trombones are

[8]*Cf.* p. 27.

central to Schubert's musical thought – the 'Great'. But
there is in fact nothing in these works that demands a
fuller ensemble than Beethoven's Fourth does. Before
Beethoven admitted trombones into the symphony he
had already written the *Marcia funebre* of the *Eroica* and
the first three movements of the Fifth; so it can hardly be
claimed that Schubert's Second, or his *Tragic*, is orchestrally underpowered. The Sixth Symphony is to some
extent a by-product of Rossini's advent to Vienna and
Schubert's liking for elements of his style. The crisp,
bright style favoured in No. 6, with its touch of prettiness,
is not worlds apart from that of the two *Overtures in the
Italian Style*, Schubert's earlier homage to Rossini, written
in the year before the Symphony (1817) and not requiring trombones.

It is not absolutely certain that the orchestra at the
Stadtkonvikt had trombonists as regular members. If the
First Symphony was composed for performance there, it
could be argued that such a gap in the establishment of
players caused Schubert to conceive that work for an orchestra without trombones. Meanwhile there was apparently no difficulty in securing players for ecclesiastical or
theatrical performances. But whatever the fluctuations in
the availability of players, it remains true that for a student composer patently modelling his early symphonic
writing on eighteenth-century practice, the orchestral
resource of that time was a *sine qua non*.

It is nevertheless unthinkable that Schubert did not,
while using trombones in so many non-symphonic works
up to 1820, come more and more to recognise their value
to the orchestrator faced with the severe limitations of the
other brass. It may be significant in this connection that
when he began his *Stabat Mater* (D175) in 1815, he
intended to use a pair of horns, but changed his mind
and used three trombones, perhaps realising that they
would be more serviceable in the chromatic excursions he
was planning to make in the course of the work. ('Corni'

is deleted on the first page of the autograph score,[9] and 'Tromboni' substituted.)

When the time did come for Schubert to re-introduce the trombones into the symphony, in the Seventh of 1821, there is no doubt that the new, grand, sonorous and exploratory style here ventured by him on his path to symphonic maturity justified the step.

[9] The autograph is in the Wiener Stadt- und Landesbibliothek, shelfmark MH 15/c.

IV

Building on the Past:
The First Symphony

When Schubert set about composing his Symphony No. 1 in D, which he completed on 28 October 1813, he had little experience of large-scale composition. It is not known if he finished the first movement, or more than that, of the symphony of 1811 of which a fragment (D2B) survives. Nor is it known if there were other early symphonic ventures, now lost. What is known is that he wrote, before October 1813, five overtures – an overture being roughly equivalent in scale to one movement of a symphony. He also embarked on fantasias for piano duet and string quartets in this period. The earliest of these works exhibit an unorthodox approach to key-structure: the fantasias begin in one key and end in another and tend towards extreme sectionalisation, while the First Quartet has five movements from which an unusual tonal plan emerges, as though by accident (I – C minor to G minor; II – G minor; III – Minuet in F major with Trio in C; IV – B flat major; V – B flat major). At the same time there is a certain boldness, almost fearlessness, in the way one thought yields to another. Clearly the youngster's head bristled with music, and he was determined to set it down, to give rein to his undoubted fluency, to develop the instincts and techniques that would make him a confident musical architect.

It is only to be expected that the ideas in these early

quartets reflect an acquaintance with Haydn and Mozart. As Schubert's brother Ferdinand later recalled when sketching a biography of himself,[1] Franz played the current repertoire in a family quartet:

> It was a great pleasure for him [Ferdinand] to play quartets with his brother Franz in company with his father and his brother Ignaz. This happened mostly in the holiday months, when Franz was still at the *Stadtkonvikt*, or when he came to his father's house each fortnight.

The music played presumably included quartets of Haydn and Mozart, in addition to early Beethoven (Op. 18) perhaps. What is particularly striking, though, is that while there are general resemblances from time to time between the early Schubert quartets and those of Haydn and Mozart, when one is reminded of specific works by those composers it is orchestral models that are concerned. Westrup[2] has drawn attention to unmistakable echoes of Mozart's *Magic Flute* Overture, 'Paris' Symphony (No. 31),[3] and Symphony No. 34 in C. There is also a hint of the *Prague* Symphony behind the opening of the slow movement of the D major Quartet, D74 (August/September 1813), and this particular homage was more openly paid in the Symphony No. 1 a month or so later.

That Schubert's early chamber music carries clear

[1] Ferdinand Schubert, *Skizzen zu Ferd. Schuberts Biographie*, Vienna, 1841 (manuscript).

[2] J. A. Westrup, 'The Chamber Music', in Gerald Abraham (ed.), *Schubert – A Symposium*, Lindsay Drummond, London, 1947, p. 89.

[3] The finale of D74 in D is obviously indebted to the finale of the 'Paris' Symphony in the same key. Einstein, having not observed this connection, states that the finale of the First Symphony 'proves that Schubert was well acquainted with the finale of Mozart's *Paris* Symphony'. If such proof be sought, the finale of the quartet comes closer to providing it than the finale of the symphony: in the latter case the relationship is 'once removed' (*cf.* Alfred Einstein, *Schubert*, Cassell, London, 1951).

reminiscences of the orchestral music of others rather than of their chamber music suggests that the symphonies and overtures he played as daily duty at the *Stadtkonvikt* had made an especially strong impression on him. However faithful to and successful in the media of chamber music and song he was in later life, the symphony always remained a prime influence and motivation in his artistic career. The reminders of earlier orchestral works, by Haydn, Mozart and Beethoven, in the First Symphony are more numerous still, and they are almost entirely specific rather than general ones.

Schubert's inclusion of a slow introduction is a Haydnesque strategy only in the sense that this feature was a more regular part of Haydn's symphonic thinking than of Mozart's. In its procedure Schubert's introduction is more clearly indebted to Mozart than to Haydn. The ear that follows the slow descent of the bass will find that a series of semitone steps soon leads to the fifth note of the scale; this note is extended for twelve bars as a basis for 'dominant preparation' for the *Allegro vivace*. This scheme, at least, is the foundation of the edifice, and it reflects Mozart's fundamental procedure in his 'Linz' Symphony, No. 36, and 'Dissonance' Quartet, к465, to name but two examples. The superstructure, based on the rise and fall of arpeggio notes, with double-dotted rhythms, is not dissimilar to that of the 'Linz', either. But the function of this material is not purely introductory: Schubert recalls it later in the movement to initiate his recapitulation. Thus, twice in the movement the listener has the sensation of introduction leading to first subject proper; but the second time is appreciably different from the first, since Schubert does not resume the *Adagio* tempo of the opening – instead, he re-states the opening material within the prevailing *Allegro vivace* tempo. Naturally, if the conductor has managed things rightly, one hears a double tempo here. The original *Adagio* can be discerned, in illusory recall, as well as the current *Allegro vivace*. An urge for unified wholeness is fulfilled without the momentum of the fast tempo being sacrificed. A similar integration, achieved by the same means, was sought some twelve years later in the Ninth Symphony.

No-one who knows the theme from the *Prometheus* Ballet which Beethoven re-used in the finale of his *Eroica* Symphony can fail to be reminded of it on hearing Schubert's second subject for the first time. Schubert cannot rid his mind of its obsessive contour even in the finale, whose own second subject presents a further reincarnation of it. For clarity of illustration, Beethoven's tune is shown in Ex. 7 (a) transposed to Schubert's key and transcribed into equivalent rhythmic notation. Below it are Schubert's second subjects, of the first movement (b) and finale (c).

Ex. 7

What happens on either side of Schubert's second subject (in the first movement) is less obviously derivative. The first subject deploys Haydnesque material, first in a statement-and-response pattern favoured more by Mozart (Symphonies Nos. 39 and 41) and Beethoven (early piano sonatas, Piano Concertos Nos. 1 and 2) than Haydn, the response reversing the harmonies of the statement. This grows into an energetic would-be transition which, however, fails to make the expected transition to the second-subject key. That transition follows, abruptly, in a soft four-bar link in the woodwind. The link does

something to alleviate the brusqueness of what is otherwise a typical early-Mozart 'transition-that-isn't' – to
which Mozart reverted as late as the *Figaro* Overture, and
which Beethoven accepted for the purposes of his First
Symphony, but only the First. After the second subject
has been stated, Schubert immediately treats it in
sequences which he doubtless would have looked back on
in later life as being too long-limbed as well as too relentlessly worked out. He did, indeed, have second thoughts,
and pruned his exposition by some twenty bars. This cut
is clearly indicated in the composer's hand in the autograph score and is fully explained in an appendix to the
Eulenburg score,[4] and in the New Schubert Edition.[5]

The spinning-out of the exposition, from the point
where a 'second subject' is first stated, was a recurrent
problem for Schubert, though not an insoluble one. What
the sixteen-year-old had not yet learned from the first
two symphonies of Beethoven is how beneficial a combination of succinctness and contrast can be in these closing
stages of an exposition. But one useful thing he had assimilated from Beethoven. The second half of an exposition, or of a recapitulation for that matter, is not obliged
to travel outside its own key: by tradition it ends in the
key in which the subject arrived. As the scale of the first
movements increases, with the growth of scale of the symphony as a whole in the late Classical period, and the
second half of the exposition or recapitulation grows
commensurately, how can sufficient variety be written
into this section if key-change is denied to the composer
and he is obliged to proceed on a tonal plateau? Beethoven found two solutions. One was to introduce the second
subject at first in a key other than that in which the exposition would eventually, and conventionally, end. The
works in which he did this include one symphony, the

[4] No. 504.

[5] *Neue Schubert-Ausgabe*, Series V, Vol. 1, *Sinfonien 1–3*, Bärenreiter,
Kassel, 1967.

Eighth. Schubert in later years did something similar, creating expositions on three tonal planes. Beethoven's other solution, which Schubert tentatively adopts in the First Symphony, is to venture a bold tonal excursion late in the course of the section concerned. It is hard to resist the feeling that one such instance in Beethoven lurked at the back of Schubert's mind as he moved towards the climax of his exposition here. The Beethoven passage (given in skeletal form in Ex. 8(a)) appears in the Second Symphony, after recapitulation has merged into coda, and generates the final climax of the movement.[6] Schubert's excursion (Ex. 8(b)) is mild by comparison, not touching on so many remote tonal areas as Beethoven's, but the harmonic starting-point is virtually identical.

Ex. 8

(a)

Beethoven Symphony No. 2/I/bars 326–9

(b)

Schubert Symphony No. 1/I/bars 183–92
(transposed)

Schubert's development section is concerned solely with the second subject, which he first re-states in its original form – as though rehearsing the topic for discussion. There are delightful touches, although the limitation self-imposed by confining the discourse to one theme which has already been extensively treated in the exposition, cannot quite be overcome, especially as Schubert works almost entirely in four-bar modules (with just one 'spare'

[6] The passage begins at bar 326.

pair of bars). Since much of this is strenuous music, he aptly separates it from the powerful reprise of the introduction (at the beginning of the recapitulation) by a leisurely *pianissimo* lead-in, assigned to the woodwind alone over a conventional dominant pedal. The debt here is to Mozart, and it will be discussed when the equivalent passage in the finale is considered.[7]

Mosco Carner[8] is less than fair to the recapitulation, which, he says, except for a short coda, is a mere repetition of the exposition. The differences are not confined to the coda, nor are they only those necessitated by the tonal adjustment required to close the recapitulation in the tonic key, where the exposition ended in the dominant. Still, the dominance of the second subject is again not quite vindicated, although in principle it is not itself a fault. When the movement closes no reference to the first subject has been heard outside its appointed place at the beginning of the exposition and recapitulation, and with hindsight one is tempted to imagine the fulfilling effect of a reference to its scale-ascent inserted perhaps ten bars before the end.[9]

For his slow movement Schubert evidently took the second movement of Mozart's 'Prague' Symphony, No. 38, as a model. Both composers chose to write an *Andante* in G major and in $\frac{6}{8}$ time; the themes, similar in outline, are set for strings and supported by like harmony and texture, involving a tonic pedal in the bass. Ex. 9 shows Schubert's opening below Mozart's. Schubert's deviations from Mozart's model are sufficient to give his opening its own character and life. A notable difference is that he

---

[7]*Cf.* p. 49.

[8]'The Orchestral Music', in G. Abraham (ed.), *op. cit.*, p. 41.

[9]Indeed, one could transpose a passage from the equivalent place in the Fifth Symphony for this purpose, beginning at the fifth note of bar 276, when Schubert coincidentally recalls and extends to an apt climax this same scale.

Ex. 9

jettisons Mozart's very characteristic chromatic ascent in short notes to the final tonic of the phrase.

But that figure stays in Schubert's mind, and eventually surfaces to provide the last cadence of his movement (Ex. 10). Is it a boy with a guilt complex who changes Mozart's D sharp to an E flat (the same note written in a different way), to salve his conscience?

Ex. 10

Schubert does not treat the 'Prague' movement as a model in any other respect. His *Andante* is structurally independent – and indeed structurally rather interesting, for the contrasting middle section in E minor makes no formal return later, despite the occurrence of the ensuing reprise of the opening theme less than half way through the movement. One can hear, though, one or two veiled echoes of its elements. Schubert's independence is shown further in the fact that the lilting rhythm he introduces into his third bar, not derived from Mozart, becomes an important source of subsidiary material and development. There is one further testimony to the young composer's indelible memory of the 'Prague' movement: just as Mozart alludes once to his first theme in the new key of E minor, but breaks new ground by changing the bass note at the third bar (Ex. 11(a)), so does Schubert, whose bass moves to the same note at the same moment (Ex. 11(b)). Also like Mozart, Schubert here has the top string line doubled an octave higher by the flute.

Ex. 11

The scoring of this simple, affecting movement extends the Mozartian tradition by its more marked dependence on the wind section, often in unsupported chorus. The emancipation of the wind choir was to reach its apogee in the Sixth Symphony. One imaginative episode has the cellos[10] high above middle C as bass to the woodwind choir, as though deputising for a bassoon. It is prophetic of poetic combinations in the last symphonies.

It is not surprising that Schubert's minuets in the early Symphonies are the most conservative of his symphonic

---

[10] Not the first violins, as stated by Mosco Carner in *ibid.*, p. 42.

types. The other 'types' inherited – outer movements and slow movements – although infected with traditions of their own almost offered the composer *carte blanche* in comparison with the minuet, which is laden with generic constraints and expectations. Schubert tests the genre here with a mixture of Haydnesque bonhomie and Beethovenian resolve, and the result is not particularly distinctive. He is content to remain in the tonic major for a Ländler-like trio which does nothing to threaten the eighteenth-century convention that the symphony should be at its most relaxed at this point. There is one moment where one of his boyhood favourites seems to seize his mind and direct his pen, a matter not of theme but of gesture. Before the internal reprise within the second section of the minuet, he circles round and settles upon an F sharp for some ten bars, inviting comparison with the distinctive episode at the corresponding point in the trio of Beethoven's Second Symphony.

It is likely that the composition of the finale followed that of the first movement by not many days. Even so, Schubert seems a degree more confident and subtle in his handling of symphonic sonata-form in this finale. The first theme trips along with carefree step and soon appears to be gathering itself for a *forte* restatement. The *forte* comes, but the restatement doesn't. Instead, a new theme is heard, though over the old accompaniment. This second theme behaves like any number of Beethoven's first themes, but the most apt analogy is with the opening *Allegro con brio* of his First Symphony. Ex. 12(a) gives a skeleton of parts of Beethoven's theme, transposed from C to D to facilitate comparison, above the equivalent segments of Schubert's in Ex. 12(b). The impression that Schubert had remembered the harmonic structure of Beethoven's theme is confirmed by his fairly precise retracing of its melodic path.

When Schubert repeats the whole cycle of *piano* first theme and *forte* second theme, he lets the second one lead

Ex. 12

(a)

(b)

off round new harmonic corners so that it serves as 'transition' to the dominant key ready for the arrival of the second subject. In this transition he recalls the little upbeat-figure, decorated by a grace-note which adorned the skipping steps of the first theme, and seems to make a point of keeping it in mind right up to the end of the exposition. Thus when the second subject (Ex. 7(c), p. 41) makes a feature of this very figure the continuity of the exposition is neatly sealed.

At the end of the exposition the listener is made to half-expect a repeat of the whole section, as in the Seventh Symphony. This expectation is effected by the cancellation of the second-subject key and signposting of a return to D, implicit in soft woodwind phrases (Ex. 13) which echo the basic cell of the second subject but end with a clear reminder of the first two notes of the *first* theme of the movement.

There could hardly be a more succinct preparation for the repeat of an exposition. But Schubert does not repeat. Did he have it in mind to do so? The autograph

Ex. 13

score gives no clue. What ultimately weighed with him was presumably that in this exposition (unlike that of the finale of the Seventh Symphony) a dual first-subject group has already been repeated, while the above-mentioned upbeat-figure has been worked throughout. At any rate, he obliterates the scent he has laid, and veers to F major to begin the development with new treatments of the second subject, including partial canon.

When he comes to prepare for the recapitulation, with a few bars of unaccompanied woodwind over a dominant pedal, does Schubert have in his mind the corresponding link in the first movement of his beloved Mozart Symphony No. 40? And if he does, the much longer passage at the same point in Schubert's first movement may be heard as a 'stretched' version of the same, with each constituent stage drawn out.

Having refrained from repeating his exposition, Schubert feels free to let the first two themes have two hearings apiece in the recapitulation, as before. But this time the first is repeated in the tonic minor key, and the second in B flat major. Thus the move away from home is brought forward, although only as a diversion which will ultimately lead back to D for the conventional re-statement of the second subject. Towards the end of the movement there are two further excursions, akin in spirit as in technique to those which impel the codas of Beethoven's Second Symphony. What could be more Beethovenian than the *fortissimo* bang which brings the second of these excursions to heel (that is, back to D)? And what more Mozartian than the figure, used intermittently earlier in the movement, in which all the strings unite shortly

afterwards, in the Symphony's final throes? It is indeed
the same figure, and in the same key, as Mozart used for
similar purpose (and likewise in octave-unisons in all the
strings near the end) in the Overture to *Don Giovanni*
(Ex. 14).

Ex. 14

Finis et fine, Schubert wrote at the end of his manuscript. This has been taken to point to the fact that he
had not only finished this symphony but in a few weeks
was to leave the *Stadtkonvikt*. Perhaps it was also a symbo-
lic farewell to a stage of symphonic apprenticeship. The
lessons of his great precursors had been openly learned;
in future they would be more thoroughly assimilated. As
if to underline the passing of this stage of development,
the key of his first two attempts at symphony writing, and
of all his overtures to date, would be abandoned and
another chosen for his Second Symphony.

The First Symphony is one of the essential measures of
Schubert's subsequent development as a symphonist. It
leans on the exploits of his precursors in a manner and to
an extent that has not previously been the subject of
detailed study. His dependence on others should be seen
in a critical light, but in the wider sense of criticism. Schubert was sixteen when he wrote this symphony. Research
has not yet revealed at what tender age other Classical
composers embarked on symphonic composition except
that the Symphony in D by Arriaga, who died in 1826 ten
days before his twentieth birthday, is a youthful miracle
in some way comparable to Schubert's. Beethoven was
about thirty when he showed the world his first. By that
relative or any absolute criterion Schubert's achievement
here was prodigious, and the promise for a symphonic

career immense.[11] Already he could compose, in a hal-
lowed genre and in the demanding medium of the late
Classical orchestra, with intrepid fluency, handling the
requirements of large-scale design with more than basic
competence. Although the standard of invention is not
that of which eternal masterpieces are made it is more
than serviceable for the largely self-instructive purpose of
the exercise. (One cannot imagine Salieri, his teacher at
the *Stadtkonvikt*, being able to teach him much about
large-scale instrumental composition: nor, for that matter,
Holzer, of the Liechtental Parish Church.) There is
hardly any place where his grasp of tonality or harmony
fails to satisfy, and there are hints, moreover, of a fecund
melodic imagination. The adolescent may be forgiven his
boyish garrulity, his way of working the orchestral *tutti*
too hard for the weight of the material, with the trumpets
deployed at a higher altitude and more persistently than
in any of his later symphonies.[12] In his orchestration he

[11] The following select list of the more prolific of Schubert's older contemporaries gives the number of surviving symphonies by each, and
(where known) the year in which his first published symphony
appeared. No details are known of any earlier symphonic activity by
any of these composers. The list does not aim to be complete. Symphonists who died before Schubert was born are excluded. The composers are listed chronologically by date of birth:
Cannabich (1731–98), c. 90; Dittersdorf (1739–99), c. 120 authenti-
cated of c. 210 attributed; Vanhal (1739–1813), c. 70; Boccherini
(1743–1805), 30; L. Koželuh (1747–1818), 4; Clementi (1752–1832), 8
(the first in 1786); Hoffmeister (1754–1812). c. 66; P. Wranitzky
(1756–1808), 51 (first 1786); Pleyel (1757–1831), 29; Krommer
(1759–1831), 9; Gyrowetz (1763–1850), c. 40; Ries (1784–1838), 8;
Onslow (1784–1853), 4; Spohr (1784–1859), 9; Berwald (1796–1868),
4 (first 1820).
   The following contemporaries wrote fewer than four symphonies
apiece; Tomášek, Weber, Hérold, Voříšek, Méhul, Cherubini, Toma-
sini, Rejcha.

[12] Similar treatment of the trumpets is found in the early overtures,
such as that to *Des Teufels Lustschloss*, D84 (1811).

tends to rely on established modes of scoring, but that is what best serves material which, for the time being, is to some considerable extent in an established mode. The doubling of a melodic line on the violins by the bassoon an octave lower is apt enough, for instance, if the material is Haydnesque in character and context. He had no manual of current orchestral practice to guide him. He learned from the music he played, heard and studied, and his instant proficiency in orchestral scoring in these early works, give or take a few miscalculations (such as the balance of chord-components in the second halves of the ninth and tenth bars of the First Symphony), suggests that he hardly had to learn at all: he could simply do it.

The make-up of the orchestra used in this symphony does, incidentally, reveal one omission which may seem odd to the student of early nineteenth-century orchestral music who has come to expect double woodwind as a standard resource: there is only one flute part. When Arthur Hutchings wrote[13] that 'there is no flute part' he clearly meant that there is no second flute part, and he suggests as the reason that the *Stadtkonvikt* orchestra could not 'muster two good flautists as well as oboists'. That is a plausible surmise – but an alternative reason bears consideration. Leaning on the experience of other composers Schubert may well have observed that none of Mozart's last three symphonies has more than one flute, and that several of Beethoven's orchestral works have only one flute, including the Fourth Symphony which Schubert admired sufficiently to make his own copy of the score. He would have asked himself why, and while Hutchings may offer one answer – that two flutes were not available – the more probable reason, especially in Beethoven's case, is that a second flute would have been superfluous to the composer's requirements. The composer who could add a third horn for a specific musical purpose, as in the *Eroica* Symphony, could equally

[13] *Schubert*, J. M. Dent, London, 1945, p. 190.

eliminate one instrument when the music did not require it. An understanding of the feasible role of two flutes, both of which have to be used for the most part 'above the stave', is one of the more sophisticated aspects of the early nineteenth-century orchestrator's art. An inexperienced composer may not appreciate, for example, that if one or two flutes have accompanimental matter above a leading violin line, perhaps doubling at a higher octave the oboes or clarinets which are below the violins, they will not necessarily usurp the status of the violin line as 'upper melody'. They may simply sound as insubstantial 'overtones' of the lower woodwind, outweighed by the tone of the (massed) violins. To understand when this effect may be safely tried required good judgement, which Schubert had developed in his mature symphonies. Mozart and Beethoven understood the principle, which was not only an obligatory part of the skill of the more conservative of later orchestrators (Mendelssohn, Schumann, Brahms) but also a *sine qua non* of the technique of the less orthodox orchestral writers, including Berlioz. In some kinds of late Classical orchestral texture the conventional presence of two flutes could be something of an embarrassment to a composer; certainly the absence of a second would have been no serious handicap. If it is true that the *Stadtkonvikt* could not muster a second flute, it apparently could fourteen months later, when Schubert began his Second Symphony, which was to be dedicated to the school's headmaster.[14] Henceforth he regularly required the second flute, except in the Fifth Symphony where its omission was part of a broader reduction in the size of the orchestra in any case.

[14] Hutchings' statement that 'the scoring, throughout the work, is for the same orchestra as in the First Symphony' is patently erroneous (*ibid.*, p. 91).

V

New Perspectives:
The Second Symphony

From 1813 onwards Schubert produced symphonies at an average rate of one a year, until 1818, the date of the Sixth Symphony. The second, in B flat major, was begun on 10 December 1814, and occupied him intermittently until 24 March 1815. The first movement was finished on 26 December. From what is known of Schubert's speed of composition in these early years, sixteen days was a long-ish time to spend on a first movement. Comparisons between the gestation periods of songs and symphonies are meaningless: the completion of *Gretchen am Spinnrade*, D118, within a single afternoon two months before he embarked on the Second Symphony, reflects not only an intensity of inspiration but also the compactness of the medium in all respects. More to the point is the fact that a month earlier still he had composed the first movement of his String Quartet in B flat, D112, in four-and-a-half hours, although how honest he was when writing 'In $4\frac{1}{2}$ Stunden verfertigt' after the final double bar is open to question: writing-time does not necessarily include think-ing-time, and moreover Schubert had first drafted this movement as a trio. In any case, he could evidently 'real-ise' a large and fairly complex structure, in its outline and details, in a short time. An orchestral score, in seventeen strands on eleven staves in the case of the Second Sym-phony, would take considerably longer to set down, and could not be so fully pre-composed in details of scoring prior to the physical act of writing. Not surprisingly, the first movement of the Quartet in B flat reveals a relaxed confidence in the way it blends lyrical and dramatic ingredients in an easy, natural continuity. Early in the summer, his first complete Mass, in F major, D105, which was to enjoy successful performances in both the Liechtental Parish Church and the Augustinerkirche in central Vienna before Schubert began the Second Symphony, had occupied him for nine-and-a-half weeks in its composition.

How long Schubert had spent writing his First Symphony is not known, but it is a well-documented fact that the entire Third Symphony was substantially complete in eight days, which was half the time spent on the first movement alone of the Second Symphony. The longer time for the Second was not taken to produce a work of enormous length: it normally requires a shorter time to perform than the First. A more likely explanation is that more reflection and self-questioning was required. Schubert, having successfully completed a symphony that was traditional and orthodox, and indebted to the existing symphonic repertory, took from that the confidence to attempt something more ambitious and less orthodox, reflecting a more personal attitude to symphonic construction. The Second Symphony displays more incident and drama than the First – and, it seems, more enigma. With its potentially disconcerting formal practices, it requires of its critics more care and understanding than any other of the first six Symphonies.

Schubert discovers a new sort of energy in the outer movements – but it is not simply a matter of short notes and fast tempi, of which the First Symphony had its share. Brilliance gives way to 'bite': well-placed accents make their contribution, and the composer becomes increasingly aware of the power of dissonance. Dissonance promotes energy, in a Classical symphony as in a Renaissance motet, by leading the ear forwards to its

resolution. No Classical symphonist harnessed this energy
more effectively than Beethoven, and its role in Mozart
and Schubert is the more easily overlooked. A notable
dissonance crowns the slow introduction of Mozart's Symphony No. 39 in E flat. Alfred Einstein[1] saw a 'free imitation' of this introduction in the slow introduction of
Schubert's Second Symphony. In the solid repeated
chords, with a dotted rhythm, followed by a long scurrying descent in the upper strings as upbeat to the second
chord, the connection is certainly audible – at least in the
first two or three bars. It is visible too, if one bar of Schubert's is read as two of Mozart's. In any case, there can be
little doubt that Schubert knew the Mozart work. There is
no counterpart in the Schubert, though, of what in
Mozart's introduction is the turning-point on which the
drama hinges, a powerful discord technically described as
a subdominant seventh in first inversion. It arrives in
Mozart's eighteenth bar, with a sudden *forte*. For Schubert to have adopted this as a high point in his own introduction would have been to lean overtly on Mozart. In
any case, he had already adopted it as the last 'crisis'
before the final harmonic homecoming in the first movement of his First Symphony. The two instances are shown
in Exx. 15 and 16, not to belabour any debt by one composer to another, but to allow further consideration of
Schubert's use of dissonance. In Mozart's chord (Ex. 15)
the most acutely dissonant interval between any two component notes is the minor second between the D flat and
the C. It is important, if this chord is to provide the maximum tension, that these two notes should be represented
in the same instrumental timbre. If Mozart had given the
D flat to a flute and the C to violins, and two octaves
lower replaced the pair of bassoons by one bassoon and
the violas, it would have been poor orchestration. Schubert learned this lesson quickly. Indeed, in his discord
(Ex. 16), which appears at bar 515 of the movement con-

[1]*Op. cit.*, p. 103.

cerned, the G and F sharp, the equivalent dissonant pair, are assigned not only to a pair of high trumpets and a pair of middle-register horns, but to pairs of clarinets and violins too. Schubert understood the value of dissonance, and how to use an orchestra to enhance it, from very early in his symphonic career.

Ex. 15

Ex. 16

In the first movement of the Second Symphony, as in the First Symphony, he reserves this resource for later, more critical stages in the discourse. Meanwhile the *Largo* introduction merely ambles its way through two short successive chord-circuits, to the second of which the trilling flute adds adornment high above an easy-going *pizzicato* bass which is perhaps the nearest Schubert comes in these early symphonies to justifying the epithet 'Biedermeyer'. The second circuit closes directly into the *Allegro vivace*, inviting one to ponder the function of a slow introduction if, like this one, it has no bearing on what follows once the *Allegro* has superseded it. (To be precise, it has no thematic connection. Moreover, it presents no persona comparable in any way with the first protagonist in the imminent faster tempo, nor even drops clues as to who or what that protagonist might be. Nonetheless, it can still serve a genuine and valid purpose if it merely establishes a setting, an atmosphere, a frame or a context; besides which, it widens the scope of the symphony by enabling its author to write a kind of music that would be neither apt nor possible in any other part of the standard symphonic design.) The resemblance of the opening of the *Allegro vivace* to its counterpart in Beethoven's *Prometheus* Overture has been observed by several writers, probably on account of the running quavers of the violins, their contour, their sequence a degree higher, and the general harmonic scheme. Moreover, while Beethoven introduces syncopations in his ninth bar, Schubert uses them as mainspring of the theme itself; and in both cases a *pianissimo* twelve-bar statement closes into a *fortissimo* varied restatement.

Schubert is soon settling on the threshold of a new key, with all the traditional means of emphasis, including big, wide-spaced chords answered by silence. But this is not a traditional symphony. What follows is not a second subject, although expectation has been aroused for a second subject and that is what follows the same two chords and silence in the *Prometheus* Overture. Instead there is a new treatment of the first subject, coupled with transitional harmony, all designed as preparation for the second subject. This preparatory passage is remarkable for its personal application of Beethoven's technique of 'foreshortening'.[2] The tail of the first theme is first lengthened to make a five-bar module, on unchanging harmony. The process continues, with a different single harmony underpinning each module, in the following pattern: 5-5-5-3-3-3-3-2-2. The second subject then follows. Where Beethoven used this 'tapering' device as a means of intensification, Schubert here is merely effecting a change of scene. He does so, too, with near-perfect craftsmanship, in that the two-bar span to which the first-subject

[2] I adopt Alfred Brendel's term, from *Musical Thoughts and Afterthoughts*, especially the appendix.

residue has been reduced lives on in the accompaniment to the second subject. Every two bars a cluster of quavers in the cellos and basses reminds the listener of the first subject. This degree of integration and continuity between first and second subjects is new to symphonic thinking. But Schubert has done nothing to sacrifice the contrast between the two subjects, which, rhythmically at least, is immense.

The second subject in turn leads to an energetic *tutti* in which, as in the sequel to the first subject, Schubert pits against continuous *staccato* quavers in the violins a distinctive and unanimous counter-rhythm in the rest of the orchestra. Such is the impact and importance of the counter-rhythm in these instances (the device appears with notable effect in the Fourth Symphony) that the listener who likes to sing through symphonic movements to himself, silently or aloud, will be uncertain at these points whether to pursue the relentless quick notes of the violins or merely grunt the counter-rhythm and 'hear' the violins. Soon harmonic tensions are added, and the rhythmic opposition intensified, heralding the most cataclysmic and Beethovenian of dissonances to be found in early Schubert (Ex. 17).

Ex. 17

col. 8

The dissonance is already present in the second bar of Ex. 17. It may be called a dominant of C over a C pedal. What is so Beethovenian, apart from the chord itself, is, after the removal of the lower pitches for a few tense moments, their sudden forceful re-addition (reaching down two octaves deeper than before) and, in particular,

the insertion of the pedal note (the most dissonant element) at an upper octave by the second trumpet, between
the neighbouring D and B natural. This passage recalls
moments in Beethoven's Fourth Symphony, or the very
last sounds heard in the scherzo of the Fifth as it resolves
into the finale. Yet Schubert's discord is the natural outcome of the growing tensions that precede it. It is also
something of a Schubertian record in another respect: its
five-and-a-half-octave spread exceeds anything found in
any of the other Symphonies, including the 'Great'.

When the resolution is made, with due emphasis, the
music is found to be poised on a dominant, not settled on
a tonic. And when that in turn resolves in a reprise of the
first subject in F major, Schubert is in gross breach of
convention and direct line of fire from his critics. What
are the bones of this contention, and what are their rami-
fications? By answering this question now the way may be
cleared for a proper consideration of the finale, as well as
the first movement.

The basic conventions of exposition-structure in Classical sonata-form, which a composer may observe or
ignore, are shown in Figure 1. The first subject or subject-group in the tonic key is followed by a second subject
or group in the dominant key. The dominant persists to
the end of the exposition, which may be terminated
thematically by short closing themes or by a codetta. The
term 'codetta' tends to imply an element of retrospect, of
referring back to the first subject, for that is a familiar
convention at this stage in sonata design. Schubert has
deviated from this scheme in two ways in this movement.
He has cast his second subject in the key of the subdominant, not the dominant (E flat, not F). And he has
then changed key to re-state his first theme in the dominant (Figure 2). There results a tripartite structure, on
three tonal planes. This 'three-key exposition' was to be a
feature of several later Schubert works (including the
Quartettsatz, D703, the *Grand Duo*, D812, and the Piano
Sonata in B flat, D960).

Figure 1

T	D	D
i	ii	(codetta)

Figure 2

T	SD	D
i	ii	i

Since some of Schubert's critics have found him inclined to adopt easy solutions and labour-saving policies in musical structure,[3] it is perhaps surprising that he has not been rebuked for choosing the subdominant key instead of the dominant for his second subject in this movement. One of the most demanding basic procedures any Classical composer had to master was that of modulating early in a piece direct from tonic to dominant. This move was, for technical reasons, against the tonal system's 'force of gravity'. The move to the subdominant was, on the contrary, assisted by that same force of gravity.[4] In

[3] *Cf.* pp. 56–57 and 105–7.

[4] A new key can be unambiguously established only by way of its dominant seventh chord. In the case of a move to the subdominant key, the composer has only to add a flattened seventh to his tonic chord and the dominant seventh of the new key is thereby created. To move to the dominant, he must first strain upwards to the sharpened fourth, an essential part of the new key's dominant. In practice, the composer

(continued on p. 62)

truth, Schubert probably chose the subdominant here because he was attracted by that particular key-relationship, or because his invention led him there and he saw no reason to raise objections. But once there he was faced with a dilemma. He could not remain in the subdominant until the end of the exposition, because of the difficulty of moving back from there to the tonic for a repeat of the exposition. He therefore had to proceed from the subdominant to the dominant, from where the return to the tonic would be unproblematic (for, to the dominant, a tonic stands as a subdominant and is therefore in the flow of gravity).

It is doubtful if Schubert saw this additional modulation as irksome or unwelcome. For one thing, it was not contrary to his musical nature. From much younger days he had been fascinated by the juxtaposition of keys and the ways of travelling between them. For another, Beethoven had long ago felt the urge to introduce a measure of tonal variety into the second group of an exposition, as some of the piano sonatas he wrote at the end of the previous century show (especially Op. 2, No. 2, and Op. 13). The three-key exposition was, then, both a potentially valuable innovation in sonata-form practice (Beethoven came closer to Schubert's conception in his *Waldstein* Sonata) and a scheme particularly congenial to Schubert. Yet to Maurice Brown the restatement of the first subject in F major as the third segment of the exposition in the Second Symphony was 'one of Schubert's miscalculations'. He finds that it 'prolongs the exposition section to an

---

usually feels obliged to go beyond the dominant and 'flirt' with *its* dominant key (what Tovey called 'enhancing the dominant'); he could then fall to the dominant in the same straightforward way by which he could have dropped from his original tonic to its subdominant. Modulation to the dominant requires such sophistication (one has only to study the first efforts of music students) that it is not flippant to suggest that some nineteenth-century composers' preference for other keys where the dominant was traditional may not be for wholly aesthetic reasons.

almost unendurable extent and seriously upsets the hitherto perfect balance of the movement'.[5] I must admit that I have always been intrigued by what Schubert was doing in this passage rather than worried by questions of structural balance. As one listened, one asked at the point where the first subject returned, 'Is this a repeat, real or illusory, of the exposition?' No, it couldn't be: it's in the wrong key. 'Is it the first return of the main theme in a rondo form, then?' Again, the key is wrong, or at least unconventional. But I began to sense after a mere twelve bars that there was an air of codetta about this passage, a sense of winding down. This, surely, is the way to an understanding of it. It represents Schubert's codetta, but instead of referring back to elements of his first theme or presenting it in a curtailed form, he restores it in its complete original twelve-bar form, although with some novel instrumental touches, and synchronises its beginning with the fulfilment of the modulation to the exposition's third key, all of which puts the listener off the scent. If the seventeen-year-old's experiment misfires, it is because only moments before this there was a shattering, dissonant, and well-prepared climax, after which any codetta would be expected to bring either a bigger climax or the merest residues of first-subject material. Schubert's sequel sits somewhat awkwardly between these alternative expectations. It is strange that Brown, who finds the result 'almost unendurable' on grounds of impaired structural balance or proportion, should find the finale of this symphony, which has exactly the same features in its exposition with the same proportions resulting, 'beautifully constructed'.[6]

Schubert's development section ignores the first subject. (The string quavers which run continuously through much of it are derived from it but become somewhat

[5] *Schubert Symphonies*, BBC, London, 1970, p. 13.

[6] *Ibid.*, p. 14.

neutral accompanimental matter.) It likewise ignores the second subject. Its topic is a three-note figure isolated from the final cadence formation of the exposition, and from this unpromising source a concise and highly evocative discourse is generated. Is it purely fortuitous that this figure, shown in Ex. 18(a), is the same as one appearing in the finale of Mozart's 'Jupiter' Symphony (Ex. 18(b)), where it is the 'answer-form' form of the first three notes of the second subject?

Ex. 18

(a)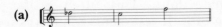

(b)

If so, is it also fortuitous that Mozart uses his figure (now in its 'subject-form') in overlapping imitations, or canon (Ex. 19), while Schubert does likewise (Ex. 20; strings omitted)?

Ex. 19

Ex. 20

Schubert did not think easily in terms of counterpoint, if by counterpoint is meant fugal or even merely imitative counterpoint. While he was second to none as the composer of a sublime countermelody to an already sublime principal melody, the close-knit argumentation of fugue – with the devices of invertible counterpoint, canon, stretto, augmentation and the like, which are common in fugal writing – came to him only with difficulty. At the age of 31, with an array of mature works to his name, he decided he should study counterpoint with the specialist teacher, Simon Sechter.[7] The nature and results of that study will be seen when the Tenth Symphony is discussed.[8] It would not be unnatural for one who had to work hard to acquire the art of counterpoint and who used intricate imitations only once in six youthful symphonies to base that one instance on a familiar and well-assimilated model. (It is not known how much of the 'Jupiter' Symphony Schubert copied out for study purposes, but the first eight bars of the minuet survive in his hand.[9])

At the recapitulation Schubert breaks with convention again. The convention is that 'recapitulation' entails a simultaneous tonal and thematic homecoming; at one and the same moment, the home key and the first theme return. But Schubert here brings back his first theme in E flat, not in B flat. He does observe the convention that the second subject in the recapitulation should be tonally resolved – that is, placed in the tonic key instead of the secondary key in which it had been heard in the exposition. It will be helpful here to consider Figure 1 (p. 62), the diagram of a conventional exposition, alongside that of Schubert's exposition-scheme in this movement; to

[7]*Cf.* note 4 on p. 259.

[8]*Cf.* pp. 259–50 and 269–64.

[9]Ernst Laaff, *Franz Schuberts Sinfonien*, H. Rauch, Wiesbaden, 1933, pp. 53 and 103.

which will now be added diagrams of the recapitulation in each case.

	Figure 3		
Conventional	T	D ·	D
Exposition	i	ii	(codetta)
Conventional	T	T	T
Recapitulation	i	ii	codetta/coda
Schubert Symphony No. 2(I)	T	SD	D
Exposition	i	ii	codetta
Schubert Symphony No. 2(I)	SD	T	T	T
Recapitulation	i	ii	codetta	coda

Much ink has been spilt over Schubert's motives for beginning a recapitulation in the subdominant. Mosco Carner voiced suspicions familiar enough when he wrote that this strategy 'allows him to repeat the exposition wholesale a fourth up without having to modify the modulation of the bridge passage between first and second subjects.'[10] In other words, it saves labour. Of the recapitulation in the first movement of the Second Symphony he says: '[it] is a literal repetition of the exposition except for its opening on the subdominant'. It is true that if Schubert had adopted the conventional keys in his exposition, the modulation required from tonic first subject to dominant second subject (up a fifth) could have been reproduced exactly, suitably transposed, to take him from the subdominant of his recapitulated first subject to the tonic of his recapitulated second subject (also up a

[10] *Loc. cit.*, p. 33.

fifth). But in defiance of convention he had set his second subject (in the exposition) in the subdominant. It was therefore necessary in the recapitulation to replace a modulation up a fourth with one up a fifth. How, then, could Schubert literally repeat music of the exposition at this point? He couldn't, and he didn't. Moreover, whereas in the full conventional scheme no further adjustment of key is necessary since in neither exposition nor recapitulation is there any further change of key, Schubert had modulated up a tone from his second subject to codetta in the exposition and therefore has to make a *second* adjustment in the recapitulation so that the codetta can remain in the same key as the second subject. He accordingly rewrites two portions of his exposition in the recapitulation, *pace* Carner. It is important to establish these facts, for this work is Schubert's first symphonic venture (or multi-movement venture of any kind – including sonata and quartet) entailing a subdominant recapitulation, and it demonstrates that the initial motive at least was not laziness.[11] In the case of a work like the 'Trout' Quintet, where the exposition of the finale is indeed literally transposed to make the recapitulation, there might have been an element of economy of time and labour. But the 'Trout' is an occasional piece written for the enjoyment of its participants and is in all respects more relaxed and less demanding of its composer's creative resources than a symphony. The Fifth Symphony is another special case, to be considered in due course.[12]

It remains to be said, of the first movement of the Second Symphony, that the reprise of the complete first theme in the codetta has a more specific value when it

[11] In his early quartets, Schubert broke with convention in other ways (not with subdominant recapitulations), but Jack Westrup felt compelled to note: 'It is obvious from these early examples that he abandoned orthodoxy not to make things easy for himself but in a spirit of adventure' (*loc. cit.*, pp. 90–91).

[12] *Cf.* pp. 115–117.

happens in the recapitulation, for it is the only tonal resolution (that is, statement in the tonic) of the theme, which
was previously recapitulated in E flat. Also Schubert's
coda of some two dozen bars is one of several places
which echo the spirit and sonority of Beethoven's Fourth
Symphony, which was performed in Vienna in 1807.
Schubert, after composing his first six symphonies,
appears to have made a special study of it, making his
own copy of the score.

Schubert was not as prolific or devoted a writer of sets
of variations as Beethoven, nor even as Haydn or Mozart.
His only symphonic use of the form is in the second
movement of the Second Symphony. Variation form may
be viewed cynically as a means of spinning out a long
movement on little material. If Schubert were as given to
prolixity yet as labour-shy as is sometimes claimed, he
would surely have used the variation form more often,
and would have made this particular example of it longer
than it is. There are only five variations, and a coda. The
whole is conceived as a modest, intimate interlude.
Although both the theme and the variations are somewhat Haydnesque, both bear Schubert's stamp. A distinguishing feature of the theme is that the last of its
entirely regular four-bar phrases is extended to five bars
by the insertion, as third bar, of a sequence to the second
bar. Classical variations being structurally identical to the
theme, whatever melodic or harmonic or rhythmic variation may occur, this feature is reproduced in every variation. The one departure from tradition is that the one
minor-key variation is not in the tonic minor. The movement is in E flat, but the fourth variation is in C minor,
the relative minor. The scoring abounds in delightful
detail, with some unusually gratifying flute writing.

With its air of dark resolve, the ensuing minuet would
not be out of place in the *Tragic* Symphony. Indeed, its
key is that of the *Tragic* Symphony, C minor. And what is
a C minor minuet doing in a B flat major symphony? For
that matter, what is the C minor *Tragic* Symphony doing

with a minuet in E flat major? These questions concern
one of the cardinal principles of Classical multi-movement tonal planning. The outer, framing movements of a
symphony (sonata, quartet, and so on) were traditionally
in the work's title key. The slow movement would normally be in a contrasting key, but the minuet or scherzo
was treated as part of the 'frame', and thus in the title
key. What gave Schubert the idea of deviating from this
practice? Was it simply part of his liberated outlook on
tonal planning? Was it the result of his acquaintance with
Beethoven's one departure from the convention, his
Seventh (1812)? Or was it part of a calculated plan for
this Second Symphony? Calculated or not, there is a plan,
in that the two central movements share a common two-
key focus, the C minor-E flat-C minor of the minuet-trio-
minuet being the converse of the second movement's E
flat-C minor-E flat. This is a far more characterful minuet
than that of the First Symphony, and in particular the
wholesale rhythmic counter-thrust of the wind body
against the choppy, purposeful activity of the massed
violins is fundamental to its effect. Even the tune of the
trio section, for all the freshness of the simple texture
that supports it, sets out (in the first two bars) as though it
were a fusion of those two counterpointed rhythmic
ingredients of the minuet.

After the minuet has closed in C minor, B flat is re-
instated by the four-bar preface to the finale (a seed, perhaps, of the Fifth Symphony's four-bar in-tempo introduction), whereupon one of Schubert's most infectious
finale tunes take over, as does the dactylic rhythm which
is its launch-pad. The first entry of the flute and oboe,
adding a fleeting gloss to the violins, is one of those felicitous details – perfectly crafted yet utterly natural – which
abound in early Schubert. That combination of qualities –
naturalness and craftsmanship – is so evident in the thematic treatment of the movement as a whole that a chart of
relationships is best suited to illuminate it. The chart

(Ex. 21) begins with the opening of the tune, x highlight-
ing the dactyl[13] which is also embodied in y.

After the first hushed statement of the theme comes
the not unexpected *forte* counterstatement. This counterstatement is largely a paraphrase of the first statement,
but it begins with its main deviation. The motive y, running from F to B flat within the first theme, is lifted so as
to run from B flat to E flat (z in Ex. 21). This development is an important one, on which later developments
will feed. Schubert concludes his counterstatement with
an emphatic unison version of z, extending its threefold
repetition of E flat to a forceful sevenfold one. There is a
pause, to which the surprise sequel is a second subject
taking that E flat as its key, the subdominant! Such a
pithy transition, taking a note by the scruff of the neck
and making a tonic of it without the ceremony of modulation, would have delighted the Beethoven who inspired it.

As in the first movement, then, the second subject is in
the subdominant, and this time the E flat sits beneath it in
the bass almost throughout, lingering on unaccompanied
when the residual echoes of the subject's final cadence
fade. Thus Schubert exposes the beams of his structure:
there is nothing else to listen to as the hushed E flat falls
away to darker regions, and to a sudden turbulent transition whose characteristic four hammer-blows are prophetic of the finale of the 'Great' C major Symphony. But a
transition to what? Again, as in the first movement, to a
codetta in the dominant encompassing a complete restatement of the first theme – and more: a further significant
new development of the first theme. If z is transposed
and augmented it becomes zz (*cf.* Ex. 21). Schubert's

[13] From the Greek for 'finger': bend all the joints of one finger and
measure the three sections; the second and third sections are each
about half the length of the first – hence 'dactyl' as a term in the analysis of poetic and musical rhythm. Other movements by Schubert which
take the dactyl rhythm as their starting point include one in the same
key as this finale, the last movement of the B flat Piano Trio.

Ex. 21

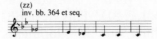

new ingredient in the codetta is a rhythmic variant of *zz*.

This chain of events is almost identical with that presented by the exposition of the first movement, and raises similar questions in the listening ear. There is less doubt about the effectiveness of the codetta *qua* codetta, because it incorporates an extensive 'bravura section' – an equivalent to that part of a concerto in the Classical period that concludes the exposition (and later the recapitulation) and is characterised by technically brilliant writing for the soloist supported by long drawn-out harmonies, usually with little thematic relevance. But Schubert never wrote a concerto and did not borrow this device from the concerto. It had already been borrowed by other composers, and had become an integral feature of many a sonata, string quartet and the like long before Schubert was old enough to hold a pen. It was especially Mozart, concerto writer *par excellence*, who transferred it to the small-scale instrumental medium, and Beethoven among others had made it common practice before the turn of the century.[14] Schubert invokes the tradition here not only in the vertiginous solo woodwind and first violin scales and the stretched cadence-harmonies. Even the long super-tonic trill which conventionally closes a concerto bravura section is echoed in the long supertonic which caps his final scale-ascent (Ex. 22).

Schubert has thus made a show of closing his exposition. Yet unlike the concerto composer, he has not totally banished thematic elements in doing so. He preserves his dactyls in Ex. 22, while between the short confirmatory *tutti* chords that follow they ring through in brass and woodwind like clarion calls (which they now are). This procedure is a key to the continuity of the movement, for the dactyls can now run without any break into the development section – and the development, which lasts 104 bars, consists of 104 dactyls. 'Iron rations', observes Brown, noting that this middle section is 'built entirely on a harmonic treatment of the opening four notes of the main theme.'[15] But Brown is taking a bar-for-bar view of the music; and the bars are grouped in eights, sometimes fours, but not singly. To return to Ex. 21, zz was the augmentation of z. If zz itself is augmented, the result is zzz. And it is zzz that the first violins play when next they enter: but zzz articulated in the dactyl rhythm of z. And what preceded the entry of the violins was an inversion of that, in the cellos and basses (bottom line of Ex. 21).

[14] Examples may be found in the first movements of Mozart's Piano Sonata in B flat, к570, Divertimento for string trio, к563, Clarinet Quintet, к581; in Haydn's String Quartet in C, Op. 50, No. 2; and in Beethoven's Piano Sonata in G, Op. 14, No. 2.

[15] *Op. cit.*, pp. 14–25.

Ex. 22

The entire development in this movement is occupied by a discourse on these derivative forms of *z*, the climax being generated by the addition of a further derivative, *zz* inverted (second extract in Ex. 21). The shaping of the section, towards, through, and away from that climax, is immaculate and imaginative – and all is impelled by the dactyls, which therefore act as a long preparation for the reprise of the source of the dactyls when the first bar of the recapitulation arrives. It is hard to think of any Classical development that operates more successfully as an integral part of the larger continuum.

As postscript to this commentary, three observations must be added. First, although the dactyl-inflected version of *zzz* is the first to be heard, the uninflected version in long notes does itself appear subsequently, as if to clarify the reference (first flute, bar 332). Second, the naked conflict of an F and adjacent G flat at the beginning of the development is an acute example of Schubert's current awareness of dissonance, and it signposts with deadly accuracy the atmosphere of taut energy and cogency which pervades this remarkable development. Third, the above thematic analysis should not necessarily be taken as a revelation of the workings of Schubert's conscious mind. Conscious or subconscious, the organisation – like that of the solar system – has inescapable effects on those who come under its influence.

Of the recapitulation all that remains to be said is that Schubert's liking for contrasts of key leads him to avoid the tonal plateau suggested by tradition – with first subject, second subject and codetta all in the tonic key – by placing his second subject in G minor. This instance may be the first when a composer working within a major home key chooses to adopt the minor for his recapitulated second subject. It is one more symptom of the enterprising nature of an outstanding finale of a symphony which probably promises more for the forthcoming symphonies of the composer's maturity than does any other of his first six.

VI

Serene Confidence:
The Third Symphony

Ostensibly, the Third Symphony marks a stage of re-
trenchment. The burgeoning spirit of adventure which
led to the expansion of the outer movements of the
Second Symphony, with their novel three-key exposition-
structure and enlarged codettas, yields in the Third to an
apparently easy acceptance of the older traditions. To be
sure, Schubert looks back further than his own First Symphony, although he again adopts its key of D major and
its tonal plan – the minuet and outside movements being
in D, with the slow movement in the subdominant key, G
major. In place of the prolixity of the First, he aspires to
a Classical economy. The scoring is more restrained, and
altogether there is a touch more Mozartian elegance and
polish. The emphasis is on geniality, suavity, finesse, even
in the racy finale, when Schubertian high spirits are at
their most insuppressible. The focus is on shades of light:
there are few, if any, dark corners in this Symphony. It is
not surprising that within a year of completing it Schubert undertook and finished his first symphony in a
minor key, the *Tragic* Symphony. The two works, like
companion pairs in Mozart's *œuvre* or in Brahms', represent sharply differing impulses of a single creative urge.

The Third was Schubert's shortest symphony so far.
That it was begun on 24 May 1815 and finished on 19 July
conceals the true speed of its composition, for Schubert

laid the work aside after writing the introduction and a few pages of the first movement proper, and returned to compose the remainder of the work within an eight-day period. The break between these two spurts of activity, during which he produced a large number of songs, a *Salve Regina* (in F, D223), the one-act operetta *Fernando*, and other works besides, would probably have been disastrous at a later stage in his career, almost certainly resulting in an unfinished symphony. But of that later period of crisis there is scarcely any hint at all in the early symphonies. Least of all is there any indication in the Third Symphony, so serenely confident and spontaneous in its gait and compact in its design, of any imminent problems of symphonic inconsummation.

As an aid to the appreciation of the first movement of the symphony, it will be useful to consider the value to Schubert of what may be called the 'afterstatement'. By 'afterstatement' is meant the immediate sequel to the first subject of a movement. This afterstatement, which usually coincides with a rise in dynamic level (often a sudden *forte*), has a variety of functions. Sometimes it amounts to a forceful repetition of a soft first subject, though it will soon lead to development of that subject or to the modulations necessary for transition to a second subject. But the 'afterstatement' may be developmental from the start, perhaps injecting new rhythmic life into the first subject, as in the String Quartet in D minor ('Death and the Maiden', D810) or the Piano Sonata in A minor, D784, or the String Quintet, D956. Whatever its function in those terms, it may have a more general value for a composer who is naturally lyrical by inclination, and for one who was a supreme melodist before he was a proven symphonist. Transition, codettas and development are the stuff symphonies are made of, as much as if not more than melodies. When Schubert wrote a first subject that was satisfying in its melodic contour and form but perhaps not obviously promising as symphonic material, the afterstatement could provide a sort of meeting-point, where the process of symphonic argumentation could be brought to bear on it. For such purposes it may be thought to have had more potential importance to the young Schubert up to, say, the year 1820 than to the mature Schubert of the 1820s, yet he continued to attach special significance and interest to the device throughout his career.

In the first movement of the Third Symphony the afterstatement is the very nub of the argument, and for reasons which go beyond those outlined above. The passage in question is shown in Ex. 23. It is not in any way a repetition of the first subject of the *Allegro con brio*. It is a new idea, approached from the quite independent first subject by way of a Beethovenian crescendo (which intensifies a Beethovenian dissonance) – new, at least, within the *Allegro con brio* itself. In truth, it owes its origin to the *Adagio maestoso* introduction. There the violins gradually build up, from the void of the opening unison and against the reiterated tonic chord in the woodwind, the scale which occupies the first half of its first bar. When the scale is fully formed, the violins add to it the fourfold repetition of its last note characteristic of its appearance in the afterstatement (Ex. 23). Thus Schubert forges a thematic link between the introduction and the main body of the movement, a link which bypasses the first subject altogether. The weight of cross-connection is carried, then, by the afterstatement, further enriching and strengthening its role in the cumulative practice of Schubert the instrumental composer. And it may be symptomatic of the relative certainty of purpose with which Schubert conceived this crucial afterstatement that he seems to have been *un*certain as to the detailed thematic formulation of the preceding first subject. Indications on the autograph score clearly suggest that the solo clarinet melody which now appears as the first 'theme', and which incidentally adumbrates the first theme of the first *Allegro* of the 'Great' C Major, was originally omitted,

leaving only its supporting string parts, so that what now
stands as 'string accompaniment' was once 'theme'.[1]

Another special function is implicit in this same after-
statement. It is the repository for an external influence.
This is self-evident when Exx. 23 and 24 are compared.
If Spaun had not revealed that Schubert's favourite
among Mozart symphonies was No. 40 in G minor, it
would have been possible to guess as much at this stage,
while the Fifth Symphony offers even stronger grounds
for such conjecture. It should be noted, moreover, that
the passage which Schubert could not shake from his
mind is the *afterstatement* of Mozart's first movement.

Ex. 23

Ex. 24

Nothing more has to be said about Schubert's slow
introduction, except that if the ear picks up the slow
descent of the bass through the semitones from the tonic
D to the dominant A and if this descent is recalled as
being the Mozartian foundation of the slow introduction
of Schubert's First Symphony, one may then expect Schubert's *Allegro* to begin at the tenth bar. But Schubert
deceives the ear; for he now plunges into F major, in the

[1]*Cf.* Eusebius Mandyczewski (ed.), *Revisionsbericht, Franz Schuberts
Werke: kritisch durchgesehene Gesamtausgabe*, Breitkopf und Härtel, Leipzig, 1897, p. 6.

Ex. 25

first dramatic example in the symphonies of a lifelong partiality for key-relationships based on the interval of a third. The relationship permits maximum colour while safeguarding a minimal coherence: one note has a pivotal presence in the two chords, which may otherwise be remotely related.

Schubert's afterstatement exerts further influence, in that it spawns the first ascent of the second subject (Ex. 25). The sequel, in this second subject, is the jaunty rhythm of the first subject, and with the help of this rhythmic common ground Schubert neatly sews the two subjects together towards the end of the recapitulation. In this manner, every personage in the drama is related to Adam, or at least to Amadeus. These considerations lead to what is perhaps the most important observation of all – that one can know this movement, and know it very well over many years, without ever pinpointing these thematic cross-references, and indeed without identifying any affinities with Mozart's G minor Symphony. Clearly Schubert has created a closely integrated discourse which is successful in its own terms and which makes its inheritance absolutely its own.

Two aspects of this first movement call for further comment. The development, as is usual in these early symphonies, is concerned with only one theme: by setting off one part of the second subject against another in a series of fragmentary exchanges, Schubert gives himself ideal material for the quickening repartee and tonal excursions proper to a development, yet preserves a clear focus and continuity. As the section draws to a close he thins out the action with admirable judgement: he had given careful attention to this point in his previous symphonies but had never forged the approach to the recapitulation as memorably as here. Secondly, there is an impressive coda which aptly uses the 'afterstatement' material, but punctuates it at every second bar with a falling third in the wind which originally adorned the first theme at each second bar. In turn, the first theme took it over from the slow introduction, where the clarinet had introduced it – and others immediately joined in exploring it – in the second of that introduction's two segments.

Finally, if all the unorthodoxies in Schubert's choice of key are to be chronicled, it should be noted that in the recapitulation he brings back the second subject in the subdominant key. What Einstein means when he says that this procedure is 'something that Beethoven would certainly have objected to as an unwarrantable convenience'[2] is not clear. It would have been more convenient to stay in the tonic than to travel to the subdominant, but Schubert was inclined to seek more key-colour than the traditional scheme for a recapitulation would admit.

None of Schubert's slow movements dallies less, or develops its material less, than the *Allegretto* which follows. There is no more lightweight movement to be found in any of the symphonies. A theme in binary form in G major is followed by a shorter contrasting theme in C major; the reprise of the first theme has the shortest of codas added to it. The delicacy of the scoring goes beyond that of the previous slow movements, for while the second flute is omitted (as in the First and Second Symphonies), more extensive use is made of the cellos as bass to the strings without the additional depth of the double-basses harnessed to them in parallel octaves below, and the horns have no part at all in the outer (G major) sections. Schubert reserves the horns for use in the middle section, where horns in C may be used, since they are more serviceable than horns in G,[3] as he had

[2] *Op. cit.*, p. 105.

[3] *Cf.* chapter III, pp. 33–34

reminded himself in the slow movement of the First Symphony.

As Carner observed, in the melody of the central C major section 'one finds within four bars four different rhythmic patterns'.[4] This variety is specially welcome in view of the rather pointed rhythmic consistency of the outer sections. The G major theme has two rhythmic motives, each a bar long (Ex. 26). The two rhythms, *a* and *b*, alternate regularly, although sometimes it is a part other than the leading melody that provides the *b* rhythm.

Ex. 26

This alternation continues for 22 bars,[5] until Schubert reaches something like a climax (for which he at last adds double-bass pitch, and a warming crescendo which however leads only to a *pianissimo*: there is but one short *forte*, in the coda, in this gentlest of movements). At this point, *a* is abandoned and *b* is heard circling for several bars and waning to near-stasis. The master-stroke is the sudden reinstatement of *b* in the woodwind as upbeat to the returning theme, with its restoration of the *ab* pattern. Such are the subtle delights of this charming intermezzo, whose last *forte* cadence is twice echoed, an octave lower each time, the final echo entailing a lower and thicker chordal texture on the strings than might

[4] *Loc. cit.*, p. 46.

[5] The movement is sixteen bars shorter than is indicated in all editions except that of the *Neue Schubert-Ausgabe*, which eliminates the corrupt repeat-dots at the end of the first section. That section already includes a written-out repeat – written-out, because the scoring is varied.

be expected before the era of *Der Freischütz* and early Berlioz.

Schubert not only returns to D major for his minuet but stays in that key for its trio. A striking feature of the minuet is its weighty, sonorous upbeats, which develop a trend to be discerned in the middle of the minuet of the Second Symphony and to have consequences in the minuet of the Fourth Symphony. And a striking feature of the Ländler-like trio is that having adopted the duo of oboe and bassoon as string-accompanied soloists for its first section, Schubert eschews contrast of timbre thereafter, preferring to work the oboe and bassoon – and no other wind voices – throughout. There was, indeed, no call to disturb a combination that was particularly apposite for the material in hand. Another factor was perhaps that the clarinet had been assigned three of the four major solo presentations of themes in the first movement, and the middle theme of the slow movement, and the balance of favours was now to be restored.

The finale hardly comes into this equation, for individual instrumental colours are not its concern. A spirited tarantella, with a fairly remote ancestor in the finale of Mozart's Symphony No. 34 in C, it is a marvel of ensemble scoring, using mixed colours to the almost total exclusion of solo timbres. There is something of the uninhibited, driving rhythmic energy of Beethoven's Seventh Symphony here, but little of its wildness. Rather, the spirit is that of Beethoven's Second, but only in a generalised sense. The thematic material is less sharply defined than in either of these symphonies by Beethoven, and it is the Beethovenian sense of gesture that has been most obviously assimilated. Schubert happily reconciles the explosive elements, though, with a prevailing urbanity typical of the Third Symphony as a whole, and the homogeneity of the scoring seems to contribute to this fusing of characteristics. The one miscalculation in the eighteen-year-old's superfine handling of the orchestra comes in the codetta, where a four-note motive assigned to the first flute doubled an octave below by first clarinet competes in the same pitch-area as the principal thematic idea being deployed at this point. An alert conductor can aid the balance without fully removing the listener's focal dilemma.

As was demonstrated in the previous chapter,[6] Schubert did not adopt the procedure of beginning a recapitulation in the subdominant key merely to save himself labour. It is in the finale of the Third Symphony that he first avoids the necessity of making a tonal adjustment between the first and second subjects in a recapitulation, and he does not do it by beginning in the subdominant. He does it, first, by placing the second subject in the subdominant in the exposition; and secondly, by beginning his recapitulation in the dominant (Figure 4). Thus on each occasion the second subject ensues a fifth below the first subject, and Schubert takes advantage of his correspondence to use the same music for both transitions. But does that advantage merely save composing effort? Or is it designed to enhance the driving continuity and homogeneity of the finale? (If the latter, it is possible to regard the lack of sharp differentiation between the first and second subjects as another facet of the homogeneity). As development sections require new (and un-reusable) thought on old material, one could as well blame Schubert

Figure 4			
Exposition	i	ii	codetta
	D	G	A
Recapitulation	i	ii	codetta/coda
	A	D	D

[6]*Cf.* pp. 66–67.

for his lethargy in writing a notably short development (it is actually shorter than his coda). If development provides some scope for conflict, and conflict is antithetical to homogeneity, this racy finale, a mini-marathon of perpetual exuberance as of perpetual motion, can do without a long development. Schubert treats it as an opportunity for a moment or two of relative relaxation, not conflict. The pause contained in it is taken up again at the end of the recapitulation, this time to gather wind for a long crescendo which, with its relentless one-bar rhythm, is perhaps the first anticipation in early Schubert of the inexhaustible impetus that was to energise the 'Great' C major Symphony some ten years later. But the harmonic model for this crescendo passage is most likely Beethoven – the far-reaching harmonic excursion, to be precise, in the coda of the first movement of Beethoven's Second. As Schubert turns the last corner on the outward leg of his excursion, to a climactic B flat chord with dissonances superimposed, how Beethovenian that the thematic references dry up and all that is left is harmony for a few thrilling moments!

Whatever finale problems were to tax Schubert later in his composing career, there is no hint of them in the Second or Third Symphonies. Both finales are intrinsically successful movements in their own right, and both complete their symphonic wholes with a fine judgement of character and proportion. Yet they owe little to each other. And neither became a prototype, although Schubert is found trying to make something new of the tarantella-finale in the unfinished last movement of D708A. It is already established, with Schubert in his nineteenth year, that so long as he is working for the most part within the parameters of pre-*Eroica* parlance and design he can conceive and execute a crowning movement which will be unlike any other from the same pen. Whatever reason may be held for averring that the big B minor Entr'acte from *Rosamunde* could not have been conceived as the finale of the 'Unfinished' Symphony,[7] it cannot be that it is unlike any other Schubert finale. Every finale, among the Schubert Symphonies, is unique.

With these Symphonies behind him, the third of them a consolidating rather than pioneering achievement, how would the teenage symphonist proceed next? He was not, at eighteen, ready for a leap forwards to compare to the heroic one of the 33-year-old Beethoven in *his* Third Symphony. Was there yet new ground to be tilled with the resources already at his command? He had not yet tried a symphony in a minor key.

[7] *Cf.* pp. 189–90 and 202–6.

VII

Sturm und Drang: The Fourth Symphony

Was there anything special in a symphony in a minor key? Indeed there was, although the fact may not be obvious. Early symphonic style, sometimes referred to as *galant*, had been quite distinct from the late Baroque style contemporary with it. Three elements of the 'mature Baroque' were largely alien to it: fugal counterpoint, chromaticism, and minor keys. The story of the dramatic re-entry of these ingredients into the thinking of symphonists in the late 1760s and early 1770s has been colourfully told by H. C. Robbins Landon.[1] Haydn had written about a quarter of his vast symphonic *œuvre* before he ventured a symphony in the minor. That known as No. 26 in D minor (1765) was his first. Entitled the *Lamentatione*, it makes use of a *cantus firmus* from a medieval Passion drama, and a Gregorian chant. Characteristic of these early minor-key symphonies (by Haydn and others such as C. P. E. Bach, J. C. Bach and Vanhal) was an emotional intensity which soon became a coveted foil to the inbred *galant* strain and absorbed *divertimento* spirit that were otherwise dominant. The new tendency was the counterpart in music of the literary *Sturm und Drang*, although the musical movement preceded the

---

[1] *Essays on the Viennese Classical Style*, Barrie and Rockliff, London, 1970, pp. 13–17.

literary one.[2] But one thing the musical *Sturm und Drang* did not do was to re-instate the minor key as an equally useful and available alternative to the major, as it had been for Baroque composers. Haydn wrote more than a hundred symphonies, but only eleven are in a minor key. Of Mozart's forty-odd symphonies, two are in the minor, in addition to an early A minor work catalogued by Köchel, which may correspond with an A minor Symphony newly discovered in the 1980s. Even the combined symphonic endeavours of Beethoven and Schubert – 22 attempts – reveal but four in minor keys.

This historical peculiarity is reflected also in the smaller musical media, if to a lesser degree. Even in the first thirty years of the nineteenth century a sonata or quartet in the minor was likely to bear some inscription, sometimes from publisher rather than composer, as testimony to its special emotional intent, such as *Appassionata*, *Serioso*, *Pathétique*, or *Lebensstürme* (*Life's Storms*). But still the minor-key symphony drew attention to itself by its comparative rarity. Of Schubert's songs, one third are in minor keys; of his piano sonatas and chamber works, a similar proportion in each case; but of the symphonies, the proportion is less than half that.

There are two facts here that seem to require explanation: the preference of the Classical period for major keys over minor keys, as framing tonalities for multi-movement or smaller works; and the still more marked avoidance of the minor for symphonies in particular. For the first of these circumstances there is probably no simple explanation, although it may be relevant to note that it is the experience of most twentieth-century teachers of

[2] The musical *Sturm und Drang* was at its height in the years 1766–72. The literary counterpart followed in the period 1773–8, its name being taken from a play by Friedrich Klinger (*Sturm und Drang*, 1776). Although both the literary and musical movements are characterised by a powerful intensity of expression, no evidence has been adduced to show a direct connection between the two.

tonal harmonic theory and practice that their students find the technical idiosyncrasies of the minor much harder to master. For the second, explanation may indeed be simple: it has to do with the limitations of the valveless horns and trumpets of the period.

The harmonic series (Ex. 3, p. 29), which determined what notes were available to brass instruments without valves, was a major-key phenomenon. The third it offered above its fundamental note was a major third (the fifth and tenth notes in Ex. 3): the minor third (E flat in the series built on C) simply was not available. Thus horns crooked in the key of a minor-key work could not play the all-important mediant of that key, the third of the tonic chord. A solution to this obstacle was soon found. In a symphony in G minor, one horn could be crooked in G, the other in B flat. This procedure had a double advantage. While obviating the problem of the missing minor third of G minor, since the second horn offered this B flat as a member of its harmonic series, it enabled the composer on modulating to B flat (the relative major, which tended to be used as a secondary key in the same way as the dominant was the usual secondary key in movements which began in the major) to have the full use of a horn crooked in that key. This advantage was not available in major-key works. On the other hand, there was a disadvantage. For some time when the music was in G minor, only one horn could be used; and for much of the time when the music was in B flat, only the one B flat horn was serviceable. Since, in the minds of Classical composers, horns naturally 'hunted in pairs' and their textural function depended largely on their being two of them at any one time, the arrangement described above was not entirely satisfactory. Nonetheless, Mozart used it in his Fortieth Symphony. This particular difficulty could be overcome by employing two horns in each of the two keys, making four in all, and this solution was the one adopted by Mozart in his earlier G minor symphony, No. 25. It worked well – so why did Mozart not

ask for four horns in No. 40 too? And why, of Haydn's
eleven minor-key symphonies, does only one – No. 39 in
G minor – use two pairs of horns? The likely reason is
that in demanding four horns the composer would have
been over-stretching the establishment of the orchestra
he was writing for, or the one which might play his symphony at some future date.

All in all, none of the possible ways of arranging the
horn section in a minor-key work wholly commended
itself; and this obstacle no doubt acted as a deterrent to
would-be minor-key symphonists. And what applied to
horns also applied to trumpets, of course. The only
minor-key symphony of Mozart or Haydn to use trumpets is Haydn's No. 95, in C minor, where the neat solution is to use trumpets in C, which cannot provide the
third of the tonic chord, and to crook *both* horns in the
relative major, E flat, to compensate for that deficiency.

By early 1816 Schubert had written more than fifty
songs in minor keys, but no minor-key symphony. He
took the plunge with his Fourth Symphony in C minor.
The temptation to do so must have been very strong for a
composer so committed to exploring a wide range of key-
relationships. The hierarchy of key-relationships dependent on a minor tonic is different from that dependent
on a major tonic, as the Fourth Symphony illustrates.
Moreover, the minor has arguably a wider expressive
function in the music of Schubert than in that of any
other composer of the period. Indeed, the expressive
range of both major and minor is so broadened and
diversified that he is sometimes found using one in a situation where it might be expected that he would use the
other.

Titles, for symphonies or any other kind of genre-
piece, are a blessing and a curse. A handy *cognomen* is a
marked convenience, but some titles focus on one aspect
of a work – often an ephemeral aspect – to the detriment
of other important ones, while others simply raise false
expectations. Schubert would have done better, it seems,

to have stuck to his original plan and given no title to his
Fourth Symphony. It was some time after its composition
that he appended the name *Tragic*, thus giving rise to
perennial misunderstanding. To expect echoes here of
the tragedies of Shakespeare or Goethe is to court disappointment. It is a mistake even to assume unremitting
melancholy. It is best to approach Schubert's Fourth in all
innocence, as one more in a line of youthful exercises in
non-programmatic, pure symphonic invention, like his
Second or Third. The true distinction between this and
the symphonies that preceded it will then be savoured.
Maurice Brown has argued that Schubert may have used
the title *Tragische* with humorous or ironic intent.[3]
Whether that is true or not, it is unwise to assume *Tragic*
to be a Beethovenian epithet. Schubert was still serving
his self-appointed apprenticeship to the great symphonists of the late eighteenth century, and his C minor Symphony is best approached as a *Sturm und Drang* work in
the eighteenth-century sense.

The possibility remains, even if Schubert's title for the
Symphony is not intended to indicate a programmatic
intent, that the impulse behind a programmatic minor-
key work written six months earlier had not been spent,
and the residual urge helped to create the *Tragic*. *Erlkönig*
is, after all, a tragedy of its own kind, and while program-
matically it has about as conclusive an end as one could
imagine, its demonic musical energy reverberates on, as
though the strange power of Goethe's text has unlocked a
seam of expression which Schubert has far from
exhausted. He never made the mistake of returning to
this seam at the exact point from which he had mined
that late-1815 masterpiece. When he next allowed his
minor-key impulses full rein in an instrumental medium,
in the Violin Sonata (also known as 'Sonatina') in A
minor, D385, a more tender, wistful kind of expression
emerged. The third of the three Sonatas of which D385

[3] *Op. cit.*, p. 18.

was the second (the first having been in D major, D384) was again to be in the minor; and, as in the A minor, any tempestuous inclinations in this G minor work (D408) are under tight rein, for these three consistently underrated works are above all beautifully wrought domestic pieces in the spirit of pure eighteenth-century chamber music. The Sonatas were written in March and April 1816. The Symphony followed later in April, and struck an express-ive stance somewhere between that of *Erlkönig* and the Sonatas, although there are poignant moments in the finale of the A minor Sonata that seem to adumbrate the restless yet essentially lyrical invention of the finale of the Symphony. C minor was, of course, a 'fateful' key for Beethoven. It was also the key in which, some twenty years before this *Tragic* Symphony, Haydn set about representing Chaos in the prelude to *The Creation*. It is not entirely beyond doubt that Schubert knew Haydn's great oratorio, although there were several performances in Vienna in Schubert's youth and it is hard to imagine so important and admired a work escaping his notice. To some readers, the juxtaposition of the openings of Haydn's 'Chaos' prelude and Schubert's *Tragic* Symphony in Exx. 27 and 28 will provide a clear enough indication that the astonishing first bars of the Haydn had not only been heard by Schubert but had also made an indelible impression on him. The relationship should be self-evi-dent, though the vertical alignment of the two extracts in Exx. 27 and 28 has been arranged to illuminate the simi-larities. Schubert's is, after all, a distant relative of its pro-posed model by virtue of the different metre – three beats to the bar instead of four. Perhaps it is because of this difference, and the fact that Schubert overlays the subconsciously recalled vestiges of the model with a more clearly defined melodic idea than Haydn's, that the resemblance has hitherto gone unnoticed. If modelling it be (in the sense in which I use the term, which is without any implication that the modeller is conscious that he is

Ex. 27

Ex. 28

working from a model) the result attests to a high degree
of assimilation and creativity on the modeller's part.

Although this is the longest, most searching and most
developed of Schubert's introductions so far, it retains
the succinctness proper to an introduction. Schubert
may have been under the influence of Haydn's depiction
of primeval chaos, but he was not evoking the cosmic
canvas of that vast oratorio-prelude. He does travel to
the furthest point in the tonal universe, G flat major, there
to pause as in the first bar and initiate a sort of counter-
exposition, but the outward and return journeys are
accomplished within a remarkably short span. Throughout, the first motive with its questing upward leap and
delayed resolution (the 'suspension' beloved of the eighteenth-century *Sturm und Drang*) yields every ounce of
expressivity to a composer with an acute ear for harmonic
colour and nuance. In one of his later symphonic introductions, to the 1818 fragment now referred to as D615,
Schubert was to explore new routes to and from the same
remote location – the key a tritone away from *terra firma*.

The first theme of the following *Allegro vivace* has been

seen by Einstein and others to betray the influence of
Beethoven, and especially of the String Quartet in C
minor, Op. 18, No. 4. Einstein adds *Coriolan*,[4] but the
Sonata *Pathétique*, Op. 13, invites comparison too. All that
should be added here is that both the Quartet and the
Sonata are eighteenth-century Beethoven, that both are
in C minor, that Schubert adopts what is patently string-
quartet texture for the first statement of his theme, and
that the all-important rhythm of Schubert's first bar is the
rhythm of the fifth bar of the Beethoven Quartet, a
rhythm which comes into its own in Beethoven's second
subject.

One notable feature of this *Allegro vivace*, as indeed of
the whole Symphony, is its heavy dependence on the
string section. This feature places the Fourth at an
opposite pole, among the early symphonies, to the Sixth,
in which the wind choir has unusual prominence and
independence. Not that the role of the wind instruments
is diminished: the wind group frequently functions as
purveyor, *en masse*, of a pointed rhythmic counterpoint to
the more athletic activity of the violins. This opposition is
illustrated, first, in the 'afterstatement' for full orchestra
which follows the first theme of the *Allegro vivace*: it is
equally a source of vitality at the equivalent place in the
finale. In both instances the violins pursue their energetic
quavers relentlessly; and in both movements the quavers
continue as accompaniment to the second subject and,
indeed, run on almost non-stop through the remainder
of the exposition.

The usual key for the second subject of a movement in
C minor is E flat, the 'relative major'. In his first movement, Schubert chooses A flat major. Having introduced
his second subject, an elegant lyrical melody in the violins
mirrored by an equally elegant bass line which matches its
rhythm and loosely inverts its contour, he continues with
the evident intention of closing the exposition in the same

[4]*Op. cit.*, p. 128.

key, A flat. It is, then, a conventional two-key exposition, although four bars are tacked on at the end to bring the music back to the threshold of C minor, in readiness for a repeat of the exposition or for the development. But within this A flat phase of the exposition Schubert ventures on an extraordinary cross-country excursion. Forsaking A flat, he moves downwards in three stages, by major thirds. Three major thirds add up to an octave, so that he ends where he began, in A flat. But meanwhile he has passed through F flat major (which he calls E major) and C major. For each stage he uses the same eight-bar module of music. It is a neat way of admitting remote key-colours within a short, broadly mono-tonal section of the movement, and it is of interest for two special reasons. First, the technique of cumulative modulation through a number of equal, identical stages is one that was to yield particularly fruitful applications in the 'Great' C major, and to some extent the 'Unfinished'. Secondly, the unlikely choice of E major and C major on a short round-trip from A flat major raises a question of causality. In both E major and C major and E naturals of the horns and trumpets in C may be used, whereas they cannot normally be used while the music remains in C minor, or in A flat. Did the already-elected presence of brass instruments in C suggest to Schubert the key-structure his music might follow, in order to make use of part of the meagre resource of these instruments that might otherwise go unused?

Mozart, in the finale of Schubert's favourite G minor symphony, the Fortieth, and Schubert in the first movement of his Fourth, are remarkably like-minded on how to begin their development section. They both take the 'head' of the first theme, announce it forcefully in octave-unisons involving all the strings and woodwind, follow the 'head' with sequences of it a fourth distant (a fourth down in Mozart's case, up in Schubert's), introduce rhetorical silences, and by way of a soft *legato* descent in oboes and bassoons lead to a fresh statement of the first theme in something like its original texture. The Mozart passage (Ex. 29) has arrested many a commentator, including Eric Blom[5] ('a strange, abrupt rhythmic distortion') and Gordon Jacob[6] ('as rough and unexpected as anything in Beethoven'). More than that, its volatile darting through remote pitches has engaged the interest of latter-day analysts looking for early 'twelve-note' tendencies, who have found Mozart here using up eleven of the twelve chromatic notes within the one short passage.[7] The Schubert passage (Ex. 30) also uses up eleven notes of twelve. If the Mozart has made such an impact on posterity, what must have been the effect – perhaps only twenty years after it was written – on the impressionable young Schubert, encountering it while playing in his school orchestra in his early teens? It would not be surprising if it embedded itself in the deepest recesses of his musical mind, along with the momentous opening of Haydn's *Creation*. And what could be more natural than for both products of minor-key thinking to surface when he was drafting his own first minor-key symphony?

The rest of Schubert's development is less Mozartian. First he is content to reproduce the whole of his first theme in B flat minor, scored as it was originally and with but one scarcely noticeable change of harmony. Then he repeats the theme, in the same key but now as a bass line, assigned to bassoon and cellos. It is as though, for the time being, he spurns the tonal instability and motivic

[5] 'Wolfgang Amadeus Mozart (1756–1791)', in Ralph Hill (ed.), *The Symphony*, Penguin Books, Harmondsworth, 1949, p. 81.

[6] In the Preface to his edition of Mozart's Symphony No. 40, Penguin Books, Harmondsworth, 1949, p.15.

[7] Heinrich Jalowetz, 'On the Spontaneity of Schoenberg's Music', *Musical Quarterly*, October, 1944, pp. 385–408; Hans Keller, 'Strict Serial Technique in Classical Music', *Tempo*, No. 37, 1955, pp. 12–24; and Luigi Dallapiccola, 'Notes on the Statue Scene in *Don Giovanni*', *Dallapiccola on Opera*, trans. and ed. Rudy Shackleford, Toccata Press, London, 1987, pp. 186–211.

Ex. 29

Ex. 30

cut-and-thrust characteristic of a development (and especially of the Mozart development referred to above), and prefers simply to re-activate the nervous little theme which, after all, once stated in a short space of time at the beginning of the exposition had little bearing on the subsequent course of that exposition, and to invest in it the responsibility for carrying the sonata-form drama forwards at this critical juncture. There are, of course, precedents for initiating a development with a complete thematic presentation on a tonal plateau. In the case of Mozart's 'Hunt' Quartet, к458, Hans Keller saw the F major theme which begins the development as a delayed second subject.[8] This instance in Schubert, judged in relation to his own habits in, say, the outer movements of the Second Symphony, where a whole first theme would return as part of a codetta, could almost be heard as a deferred codetta. But the disruptive outburst which precedes it, in the manner of Mozart's Fortieth Symphony, precludes that interpretation; and in any case that disruptive outburst itself justifies a relatively settled sequel. Whatever the immediate impression, there is a retrospective effect, for after Schubert has duly moved on from here with more obviously developmental processes, including imitative treatment of particles of the theme, and tonal meanderings, he veers to G minor and introduces yet another full statement, in that key, of the opening theme. Having already heard two full statements of the theme in the development (both in B flat minor), the ear accepts that there may be another, still within the development. But this G minor return is actually Schubert's recapitulation. Now, most well-seasoned listeners instinctively recognise a recapitulation, whether or not they can explain that response verbally – either aloud or in the imagination. But in this instance, it is not possible to know at the point of recapitulation that recapitulation

[8] 'The Chamber Music', in H. C. Robbins Landon and Donald Mitchell (eds.), *The Mozart Companion*, Faber, London, 1956, p. 120.

has begun. The fact is first suspected when the *forte* 'afterstatement' follows; and all else after that confirms the suspicion. Why is the G minor reprise of the theme not an explicit recapitulation? First, there is no sense – on any level of consciousness – of a tonal homecoming, as G minor is not the home key. Second, the advent of G minor is not preceded by prolonged dominant preparation or any other form of explicit signposting. Third, the woodwind's descent into G minor recalls that into B flat minor earlier, so appearing as a joint to a further limb of development. A statement which thus fails to declare its purport as recapitulation can be accepted as continuation of development if it extends the procedures of that development, as this one does.

As the recapitulation proceeds, Schubert reaches E flat major for his second subject. The move from G minor to E flat major being comparable to the move from C minor to A flat major, the keys of the two subjects in the exposition, it is not necessary now to make any adjustment in the transition to the second subject: Schubert simply transposes the exposition wholesale. This is the second time in his symphonic career that he has been able to do this: the first time was in the movement written immediately before this one, the finale of the Third Symphony. It should be noted that in neither case was it made possible by beginning the recapitulation in the subdominant, the alleged Schubert way of saving labour.

Since E flat major is no more the home tonic than G minor was, there remains the necessity of gravitating to C in order to conclude the movement. Schubert's solution is neat. In the exposition, the second subject in A flat had been followed by a complete tonal circuit from A flat back to A flat by drops of a major third (A flat-E-C-A flat). In the recapitulation, if the same circuit can be introduced, it can be arrested at C, the desired goal now. But how to enter the circuit from a starting-key of E flat? This Schubert does by shifting directly from E flat to E, which (as F flat) is the so-called Neapolitan key – a favourite relationship of Schubert's. At the point where he joins the circuit, he so arranges it that not a single new bar of music has to be invented. Up to that point, he has transposed his exposition down a fourth; from that point forwards, he re-runs the circuit described above, up to the arrival of C; and from there, he omits eight bars of exposition, transposing the remainder down a minor sixth. Finally, the addition of an eighteen-bar coda completes the movement.

The tonal manœuvres involved here have been examined in some detail, as they concern a controversial aspect of Schubert's attitude to musical structure in instrumental media. Undeniably, the recapitulation of the first movement of the Fourth Symphony displays an uncommon thrift with regard to material. Yet, had the purpose been to make the composer's task easier, it could have been better achieved by other means. The real issue here is not one of laziness, but one of aesthetic judgement. Did Schubert see aesthetic advantage in thrift, such as to offset the aesthetic disadvantages? And does posterity agree with his judgement? Much twentieth-century Schubert criticism has tended to assess Schubert's music by the yardstick of Beethoven's later style – a style, incidentally, which matured when Beethoven had more years behind him that Schubert was ever to enjoy. A salutary complementary view can be formulated by seeing Schubert as an heir to Haydn and Mozart, irrespective of the parallel exploits of Beethoven; and by taking into account the nature of Schubert's musical personality and its development. More will be said about this viewpoint in the concluding chapter of this study.[9] For the present, it should be borne in mind that Haydn and Mozart often made only small changes in a recapitulation; and Schubert abandoned in his symphonies one traditional repetition often observed by Haydn and Mozart, the repetition of the entire development-cum-recapitulation (indicated

[9]*Cf.* especially pp. 280 and 286.

by Mozart in the finales of all his last three symphonies);[10] and that Schubert's experience as a song composer sheds some light on his thrift, and his trust in repetitive processes. His attachment to the strophic principle in setting poems is well known. *Die Winterreise* earns applause for being more dependent on *modified* strophic form than *Die schöne Müllerin*. But while in many of the songs in *Die Winterreise* Schubert avoids the repetition of music from stanza to stanza, he often establishes in lieu his own musical strophe (which may comprise two stanzas of poetry) and repeats that with some or no variation. And sometimes, even in *Die Winterreise*, he does adopt pure strophic form with so minimal an amount of variation as to produce a very high degree of repetition, and he does so for poetic reasons. Instrumental works, as well as songs, have poetic schemes; indeed, it can be claimed that it is these schemes that distinguish one instrumental piece from another. The high incidence of repetition in the first movement of Beethoven's Sixth Symphony has to do with a poetic scheme, which is, at some remove, pastoral in its reference. In other symphonic works the reference may be less explicit, and less tangibly extra-musical. Repetitiveness, of various kinds and over various spans, was a strong element in many of Schubert's poetic schemes for instrumental works. It was, indeed, a central part of his musico-poetic make-up, and it was his way of providing space – an essential ingredient as 'context' for so many of his visions in pure abstract terms. It was an aspect of continuity and of unity, and in the association of psychological impulses that made up his creative personality it was a *bona fide* member.

Schubert ends his first movement in the major. It is arguably too facile a resolution. Had he been true to the Mozartian concept of a minor-key symphony, he would not have ended the first movement in the major, nor the

[10] Schubert abandons the first repetition (exposition) too in the first movement of his Seventh Symphony.

finale, for that matter. Mozart himself, whether he knew
it or not, was following the normal practice of Haydn's
true *Sturm und Drang* symphonies (No. 34, 39, 44, 45, 49
and 52) in leaving the supremacy of the minor unchallenged at the end of the first movement of his Fortieth
Symphony. (Haydn·did otherwise in his later minor-key
symphonies – Nos. 78, 80, 83 and 95). It is questionable
whether the concept of minor-major progression embodied in Beethoven's Fifth Symphony would have
entered Schubert's thinking. When writing in a minor key
he tended to regard the parallel major key (the tonic
major) as an extension of the resource of the minor, and
vice versa: the resources available once a tonic was established included the full harmonic vocabulary of both the
tonic major and the tonic minor, and the full range of
exit routes to other keys – which is effectively doubled if
minor and major are interchangeable. Moreover, a simplistic view of the relative emotional connotations of
major and minor will not explain Schubert's choice
between them. A study of the songs, where emotional
states are to some extent prescribed by the text, shows
him often using major where the simplistic choice would
have been minor, and the converse. The more sharply
defined distinction which permitted Beethoven to proceed
from the fateful persistence of the minor in his first and
third movements to the triumphant winning-through of
major in the finale was never part of Schubert's long-term
planning in multi-movement works. Even so, an audience
familiar with Beethoven's habits may fancy that a minor-
key ending to the first movement of Schubert's Fourth
Symphony would have made for a more taut, closely
integrated overall structure. Four years later he did adopt
this contrary procedure, in a string quartet in C minor.
After a recapitulation in C major he added a short
eleven-bar coda recalling the opening of the movement
and its key of C minor. Alas, the full four-movement
plan never materialised, as only the first movement –
the so-called *Quartettsatz* – was completed. Thematically,

as well as tonally, there could have been some benefit in opting for a minor-key coda in the Symphony, not necessarily longer than the major-key one actually composed. It could have included a valuable retrospect of the first theme; and it could have clarified, to the listener's subconscious if not conscious satisfaction, the source of the figure (Ex. 31) used in the strings in fine rising sequences at the end of the exposition and recapitulation, which is presumably a double-take of the upbeat to the first theme (Ex. 32).

Ex. 31

Ex. 32

The slow movement occupies a special place in the affections of Schubertians, despite a somewhat over-extended ending. A timeless grace is attractively suffused with the spirit of early Romanticism. The key is that same rare orchestral key, A flat major, that Mozart chose for the slow movement of his Symphony No. 39. Schubert, who must have responded to the serenity and perfect poise of Mozart's theme, recaptures something of its atmosphere; but there is no material debt, unless the easy dotted rhythms are a tangible link, or the sequences over a dominant pedal which follow the double statement of the first part of the theme in both movements. Schubert's theme as a whole displays a shade less restraint, admitting a hint of wistful yearning which perhaps overflows from other areas of his compositional activity. The general resemblance to the well-known *Impromptu* in A flat (D935) may not be significant, although there is a suggestion of a 'populist' bearing that would not have been out of place at a gathering of Schubert's friends.

Any such allusion is dismissed by the ensuing stab and pulsations of F minor, where *Sturm und Drang* tensions are given a sharp edge by a finely-chiselled thematic scrap which unmistakably echoes – although at this *Andante* tempo – the turmoil of the finale of Schubert's favourite Mozart symphony. Ex. 33(a) shows part of Mozart's theme, and Ex. 33(b) Schubert's idea. There is tonal turmoil too, comparatively speaking, until the music settles uneasily in C flat major and x alone (from Ex. 33(b)) holds the stage, its articulation now smoothed out. It is of interest, since there has already been cause to cite the slow movement of Mozart's No. 39, that the keys of F minor and C flat major are also of critical importance in that movement, although Mozart names C flat as B.

Ex. 33

What happens between here and the return of the opening theme merits study as the most remarkable and daring transition in symphonic Schubert so far. By now the semiquaver pulsations present throughout this section have developed a 'kink' (Ex. 34). While the woodwind treat x, present in every bar (but not shown in Ex. 34), the violins push the semiquaver figure progressively higher, bar by bar, and in contrary motion the bass descends in scale fashion, until the two strands have reached polar dominants (E flat) ready for the resumption of the A flat

theme. These purposeful lines are lightly filled in with
visionary harmonies, although a bare texture is risked, so
that the woodwind motive shows through. If the style of
the 'Unfinished' Symphony is prophesied anywhere in
these six early symphonies, it is perhaps here.

Ex. 34

As the first theme returns, the semiquaver figure
accompanies it for a short time. After a subsequent
reprise of the F minor episode, now beginning in B flat
minor, a further resumption of the first A flat theme is
accompanied throughout by the semiquaver figure – a
particularly felicitous way of unifying the contrasting lyrical and dramatic sections of the movement. At the close is
a coda based entirely on the first bar of the first theme,
supported by newly introduced triplets.

To follow this one can only expect, given the weight of
tradition, a minuet in C minor. Schubert does write
'Menuetto' at the head of his third movement, but proceeds to write what to our ears can only sound as a
scherzo. That he qualifies 'Menuetto' with 'Allegro vivace'
does not itself prove the point, for as far as Schubert is
concerned the difference between a minuet and a scherzo
does not reside in tempo alone. He called the third movements of all the first four symphonies 'Menuetto', *and*
marked them all either *Allegro* or *Vivace* or *Allegro vivace*.

Yet those in the first three symphonies sound like
minuets, however fast they are played, while that in the
Fourth comes out in performance as a scherzo. The
reason has to do with texture, harmonic rhythm, line,
and accentuation. Schubert did not use the term 'scherzo'
until the Sixth Symphony, but in the Fourth he has
already essayed the genre. As with Beethoven (for example, the Symphony No. 1 in C), the composer's heading
is not necessarily to be believed.

It is not, then, a minuet; and it is not in C minor, but
in E flat major. Here it is probable that Schubert was
breaking new ground, by including in a minor-key symphony a minuet or scherzo not in the tonic minor key.
(Already he had set a third movement in a key other than
the symphony's title key when that title key was a major
one, as Beethoven had in his major-key Seventh Symphony.) What is surprising in this E flat major scherzo is
that a measure of dark *Sturm und Drang* turbulence is
achieved although the mode is not minor. This effect is
achieved partly by the perverse slurring of the theme,
partly by its in-built chromaticism, and by the particular
placing of accents to underline these elements of instability. The theme is first given with Beethovenian vehe-
mence in unison, and repeated (Ex. 35) at once in fuller
texture.

Ex. 35

After a middle section that never loses sight of the peculiarities of the theme, the theme itself duly returns. But
is it 'theme' that is heard in the violins and upper

wood-wind? No; it is the bass of Ex. 35. And Schubert
has now relegated the theme to the bass. Thus the reprise
is itself a development, demonstrating the invertibility of
Ex. 35. By using 'double counterpoint' at all Schubert has
confounded those critics who have declared that such
contrapuntal devices are alien to his symphonic thinking.
By using it in this particular context and manner he has
anticipated Brahms in the scherzo of *his* Fourth Symphony. The character of the trio is ambivalent, a simple
(if not artless) dance tune giving way to more searching
thoughts which keep us in mind of its context in this
Sturm und Drang symphony.

A four-bar 'curtain' prefaces the finale, anticipating the
next symphonic movement to be written after this, the
first movement of the Fifth. A study of the composer's
autograph score reveals that the initial ascent in the bass,
in short notes, was an after-thought. It was possibly
added after Schubert had completed his exposition,
which ends in a conventional E flat major. He would have
asked himself at this point: 'Do I need a few first-time
bars to take me back to C minor for a repeat of the exposition?'. The answer was that he didn't, because the 'curtain' already added at the beginning of the movement
would act – the second time round – exactly as a 'first-
time bar'. It had been put there in the first place to ease
the shift from E flat major, the key of the third movement, to C minor, and that was precisely the purpose for
which it could serve again now. But, given the degree of
rhythmic activity firmly established by the end of the
exposition, there having been a run of virtually continuous quavers (in some part or other) from the beginning of the first theme, the long note which originally
began the 'curtain' would be an inappropriate shock and
a reduction to crotchet values would be relaxation
enough – hence the afterthought.

The first theme itself is expounded in a very broad
paragraph, whose consistency is aided by the fact that the

first violins are the melodists throughout. But it isn't monochrome: Schubert frequently varies the choice of woodwind instrument(s) to double the violin line, and takes obvious delight in doing so.

There are, in Schubert's sonata-form movements, two especially characteristic ways of leading into the second subject. One, found notably in the Seventh and Eighth Symphonies, is by way of a complete cæsura, or at least an arrest of motion. The other is by means of a continuous thread of short running notes, which are of primary importance in the transition itself but are continued, without respite, as an inner textural component once the second subject is under way. In the finale of the Fourth Symphony this continuity of quaver flow in second violins and violas enables Schubert to make expressive capital out of a fragmented leading second-subject melody, without the discontinuity that would otherwise result. The cell of this melody is a mere two notes, and although the key is a major one (A flat major, as in the first movement) the mode of articulation, coupled with the suppressed turbulence of the accompaniment, produces a hint of pathos reminiscent of the eighteenth-century *Empfindsamkeit*. At first the clarinet responds to the two notes of the violins with a true echo, but it is in the deviation from echo-like literalness in subsequent responses that much of the charm of this section lies. It is followed by a *tutti* in E flat, the orthodox end-of-exposition key, based on the rhythm of the first subject. This codetta abounds with wonderful tensions and releases, all most effectively scored.

Schubert, like Mozart, likes to carry forward into a development repercussions of the exposition's very last gestures. Here, these gestures are an exuberant paean in the woodwind, lifting the first-bar rhythm of the first theme through the notes of the tonic chord to the upper keynote; and a short silence. Preceded by a hushed oscillation in the strings, this 'package' is then developed by sequence and foreshortening, its final liquidation being

sealed by a plain hymn-like link, on the strings, into the
second phase of development. What follows is a delightful new theme-formation, a free paraphrase of parts of
the first long thematic paragraph of the finale. It lasts a
well-ordered eight bars, and is at once transposed down a
major third, from A to F; and again, down a further
third, to D flat. Now begins a sequential passage which, as
study of the autograph score reveals, was originally to
have been used as a transition from first to second subject
in the exposition. Schubert discarded it, probably because
it inhabited the wrong rhythmic climate for that context,
and led too quickly to the second-subject key (E flat, in
which key he had apparently planned to introduce *a*
second subject, but not the one eventually composed).[11]
But here it serves admirably, with suitable adjustments. A
brief resurgence of the tension of the codetta leads back
to the threshold of C, whereupon the four-bar 'curtain'
now opens on to C major for a major-key recapitulation
of the first theme.

Having prepared for and embarked on a major-key
recapitulation, however, Schubert moves aside to other
key regions. The first sixteen-bar strain of his first theme
would lend itself conveniently to transformation from
minor to major, so it is thus transformed. The remainder
would not; so Schubert falls the short distance required
to the relative minor, A minor, at the seventeenth bar,
there to restate the somewhat longer remaining portion
of the theme. The more cynical view would be that the
slip to A minor was a means of making it possible to write
the entire remainder of the recapitulation by reproducing a minor third lower the entire remainder of the exposition. That, undeniably, is one result of the move. The
key-scheme of the exposition (C minor-A flat major-E flat

[11] This discarded continuation is of some relevance to one's perception
of Schubert's symphonic sketching habits, a matter to be discussed in
chapter XIV, pp. 247–57.

major) becomes in the recapitulation, from the point designated, A minor-F major-C major.[12]

C major, then, is restored for the codetta; and to close the symphony Schubert adds but three bare Cs. Had he been writing six years later, he would have added more by way of coda than those three Cs – but then he would have written a different symphony in any case. A short coda would certainly have enhanced the Fourth Symphony. In his preference for a more compact ending Schubert seems to be anticipating the essential spirit of the Fifth Symphony, which he began only five months later.

[12] To date, new editions of the first three symphonies only have been issued by the *Neue Schubert-Ausgabe*. The revised editions of the later symphonies created by Stefano Mollo for a Deutsche Grammophon recording by Claudio Abbado and the Chamber Orchestra of Europe (DG 423 651-2GH5) raise more issues than they solve. Mollo's method of distinguishing Schubert's accent markings from his *diminuendo* hairpins is insupportable against the facts (*cf.* pp. 244–45). His claim that minor changes in the autograph of the Fourth Symphony were made by Brahms has not yet been substantiated. Similarly, more evidence is required to justify minor changes made by Mollo in the Sixth and Ninth Symphonies.

VIII

A Nostalgic Aside: The Fifth Symphony

Schubert waited only five months before beginning his Fifth Symphony, in September 1816. Is this quick renewal of appetite a sign that he was bursting to say something radically different from what he had so recently said in his Fourth? To be sure, among the first six symphonies there is no sharper contrast between immediate successors than between these two. Schubert follows his first minor-key symphony with an irrepressible celebration of the major. Shedding the two extra horns required for the *Tragic*, he dismisses also the trumpets and drums, the clarinets and the second flute, leaving a trim early-Classical ensemble. For this ensemble he writes music so eighteenth-century in scale and design that one could believe that it would not have been much different if Beethoven, who had already published eight nineteenth-century symphonies, had never lived.

Yet, for all Schubert's wholehearted acceptance of a concept of symphony-writing rendered outmoded by his fellow-resident in Vienna, his Symphony No. 5 in B flat has a genuine vitality of utterance that has made it the most popular of all his earlier symphonies with twentieth-century audiences. The reason is that he speaks his adopted language with absolute naturalness and conviction; and he enriches it with idioms of his own, but which for the time being require no fundamental transformation of the

110

language itself. In one sense, the Fifth Symphony could
have been composed a good quarter of a century earlier.
In another, it could not have been, because an essential
part of its appeal is a warm affection for the parlance of
musical works he grew up with – an affection emanating
from Schubert himself and coloured by his personality.
What one cannot say is that it is a wholly typical Schubert
symphony. It is his only 'chamber symphony', if that is
the term to denote the normal product of the years
1750–90. To know the Fifth alone is to know a work of
spontaneous charm, characterised by a near-Mozartian
formal clarity and melodic purity and by a special compactness and consistency. To know Schubert's symphonies, or even his early symphonies, is another matter.
Conclusions drawn from the Fifth are not necessarily
applicable to the entire *œuvre*.

To date, Schubert had never begun a symphony other
than with a slow introduction. It was his normal practice
in overtures too, and a few days before beginning his
Fifth Symphony he composed an Overture in B flat,
D470, which, while sharing the sunny *joie de vivre* and intimacy of the Fifth, employs the standard *Adagio-Allegro*
format. Days later the engrained habit was broken. Perhaps Schubert had conceived the *Allegro* theme and could
find no suitable way of prefacing it with material in a
slower tempo. Perhaps he wanted to sharpen the impact
of that theme by speeding it to the listener's fresh ear (he
must have realised it was his most winsome first-movement theme to date). Or perhaps he began with a poetic
image of the whole symphony and, planning an entity as
compact in structure as in instrumentation, decided that a
slow introduction – or, for that matter, a coda at the end
of the finale – would obscure that image. As an alternative he could have done as Mozart did in his only symphony after the 'Haffner' to lack a slow introduction,
No. 40, where he simply allows the accompaniment to
begin a moment or two before the theme. Schubert did
later adopt that plan in his String Quartet in A minor and

Fantasy in F minor for piano duet, where the theme is
delayed until the accompaniment pattern has shown itself
four times. For the Fifth Symphony he evolves a tiny preface almost as self-effacing: a mere four bars consisting of
a little circuit of chords in the woodwind as backdrop to a
pattering run of fourteen short notes in the violins, which
is in effect only an extended upbeat to the theme. It is
not long enough to steal the first theme's thunder,
or rather its sunshine; but it is a distinctive enough
pleasantry to offer potential for more use later in the
movement. The idea of a four-bar preface or 'curtain' to
a symphonic movement had originated only a few
months earlier in the finale of the Fourth Symphony. If
Schubert at that time had half a mind to use the strategy
again one day, here was the perfect context for it. The
curtain opens, with elegant despatch, on to one of Schubert's most lovable themes.[1]

The touch of dialogue imparted by the imitating cellos
and basses makes for a captivating texture, but it would
be a good theme without that – and its debt to Mozart
would be a shade more evident. Its basic outline, its
harmonic structure and its steady scale-descent in the
bass had clearly stayed in Schubert's mind since he first
encountered them as a much younger boy in Mozart's
Symphony No. 40. They belong to the 'afterstatement'
in Mozart's first movement. Schubert slows down the
pattern, taking two bars (Ex. 36(b)) to Mozart's one
(Ex. 36(a)), and at the same time enlivens the surface
rhythm. His paraphrase is as remarkable for its creativity
as for its closeness to the proposed model.

As if the similarities between the two composers'
thoughts are not telling enough, the identity of key drives
the point home. And the dissonances over an F pedal a

[1] Brown (*Schubert Symphonies*, p. 25) prefers to call this theme 'subsidiary', and the opening four bars the 'main theme', thus ignoring the
preludial, anacrusic character of the first four bars. He also ignores
the precedent in the finale of the Fourth Symphony.

Ex. 36

(a)

(b)

few bars later, in both Mozart and Schubert, sustain the connection (Ex. 37). There is, in these same opening bars, another reference to Mozart, observed by Arthur Hutchings, who hears in Schubert's principal figure (bar 1 of Ex. 36(b)) an echo of Mozart's in the first movement of his G minor String Quintet: 'a half-conscious or unconscious allusion?', he asks.[2] The allusion is more palpable if the fifth bar of Mozart's quintet theme is compared with the fifteenth of Schubert's (bar 1 of Ex. 37(b)). Neither Mozart nor Schubert made frequent use of inversion, but both invert their principal figures at these respective places.

Ex. 37

(a)

(b)

[2]*Op. cit.*, p. 93.

Schubert's transition, based on a joyous upward extension of his principal figure, duly prepares the way for a
second subject in the orthodox dominant key. If this subject (Ex. 38(a)) is set beside its counterpart in Mozart's
Fortieth Symphony (Ex 38(b)), what emerges, quite apart
from any melodic similarity, is a strong resemblance in
overall structure. Mozart's theme is in period form,

Ex. 38

(a)

(b)

comprising an antecedent and consequent. A consequent,
as defined by Schoenberg,[3] begins in the same way as the
antecedent, sometimes a degree higher, but leads to a different conclusion. It is normally the same length as the
antecedent. Schubert's theme obviously embodies this
pattern too, and where Mozart's consequent lacks the
subdivision in the middle of his antecedent and moves
more continuously towards a final note which arrives two
beats early, Schubert's behaves in just the same way. Perhaps Schubert had in mind, once more, a 'poetic image' –

[3] *Fundamentals of Musical Composition* (ed. Gerald Strang), Faber, London, 1967, pp. 25–31. Period form is common in shorter pieces, an
example being the opening piano strain of Schubert's song *Im Früh-
ling*, D882 (1826).

in this instance a particular second-subject structure much favoured by Mozart; the details were probably incidental to that structure. His procedure is symptomatic of the Fifth Symphony's loving embrace of early Classical practice. More details of this dependence on Classical practice will emerge as my commentary proceeds. Suffice it to draw attention here to the triadic basis of many of the themes, the clearly articulated cadences marking the termination of sections and of theme-groups, the relish with which Schubert employs phrase-overlap (first movement, bar 80; finale, bar 47), and the short-lived digression to the flat side of the key as soon as the second subject has been heard through twice (again, as at the equivalent point in Mozart's Symphony No. 40).

The remainder of the exposition is concise, yet dramatic enough, within the terms of reference. Schubert varies the degree of rhythmic activity to include slower, more emphatic motion, with no loss of momentum, appreciably quickening again towards the well-placed if traditional pedal-dissonance four bars before the end of the section. This dissonance, incidentally, should carry an accent, as at the equivalent point four bars from the end of the movement, and not the 'diminuendo' hairpin that appears in some editions.

The opening 'curtain' of the movement returns, not to herald the recapitulation as in the finale of the *Tragic*, but to lead into the development. Here its prefatory nature evaporates, for it becomes part of the development itself in two senses. It begins the process of thematic development by setting a late-exposition derivative of the initial figure of the first theme against the circuit of chords now transferred to the lower strings, and by means of three self-repetitions each a third lower it sets in motion the *Durchführung* or 'going through the keys' proper to a development. The development as a whole is eventful, but it is also succinct.

Two aspects of the recapitulation demand comment. Schubert begins it in the subdominant, 'in order',

according to Tovey's programme note on the work,[4] 'that
the second subject may come automatically into the tonic
without needing an altered transition-passage'. On the
contrary, Schubert does alter the transition, replacing
twelve bars of the original with sixteen bars of brand-new
invention which significantly develops the transition
material. Tovey's uncharacteristic *faux pas* is echoed by
Hutchings in his own unequivocal words,[5] and is
repeated by Hans Gál,[6] reviewing Schubert's attitude to
form in the middle-period works:

> Schubert's device is to follow a short development with
> the recapitulation starting on the subdominant, with the
> result that a transposed but *otherwise completely identical
> repetition* [my italics] of the exposition will lead without
> further trouble to the desired goal of ending in the tonic.
> He used this trick not only in the first movements of his
> Fifth Symphony [but also in the Piano Sonata in B major].

But the nineteen-year-old Schubert was not the idler this
kind of criticism implies. In the Fifth Symphony he did
vary his recapitulation, without having to do so. There is
no doubt that aesthetic considerations outweighed any
urge to get to the final double-bar with a minimum of
effort.

The other point worth noting here is that towards the
end of the movement Schubert again departs from 'completely identical repetition of the exposition'. He inserts a
sixteen-bar section of new music, in which a *tutti* octave-
unison scoring of the fourteen-note 'upbeat' first played
by the first violins in the Symphony's four-bar preface
leads to a spacious, soaring climax. Thus a satisfying symmetry is created, the *a tempo* introduction influencing the

[4]Published in *Essays in Musical Analysis*, Vol. 1, *Symphonies 1*, Oxford
University Press, London, 1935, p. 203.

[5]*Op. cit.*, p. 95.

[6]*Franz Schubert and the Essence of Melody*, S. Fischer Verlag, Frankfurt,
1970; transl. the author, Gollancz, London, 1974, p. 108.

beginning, middle and end of the movement. After this coda (if the term may be used here) the original eight-bar codetta makes a fine conclusion, taking the flute and first violins to their top B flat for the first and only time in the Symphony.

Tovey referred to the theme of the slow movement as 'Schubertized Mozart',[7] showing it to be reminiscent of a theme from Mozart's Violin Sonata in F, к377. Whatever its source, Schubert has made the theme his own by a variety of means. The leaps among the first five notes are his; so is the harmony. All is so low-pitched – especially the middle parts – that this strings-only first statement has a peculiarly rich eloquence. As the wind instruments are added, they tend to thicken the texture still further in the lower register, or double the melodic line in unison or at the octave. When later a middle part becomes more melodically active and imitative, that receives similar added colour from wind instruments. The whole of this first section is characterised by the luxuriant warmth imparted by these generous wind-and-string doublings.

The kind of contrast which follows is one which Schubert frequently aimed to achieve. One of his favourite textures was a simple patterned accompaniment above which melodic wisps in solo wind instruments and first violins could succeed one another and interwine. A development section often brought an opportunity for it, even the necessity of it. Contrasting middle sections in slow movements were another favoured location. In the movement under discussion, an open-textured passage of this kind succeeds the dark-hued density of the first section with particularly refreshing effect. Schubert sets up his new texture in C flat major after a short transition whose harmonic shifts reminded Mosco Carner[8] of the *Andante* of Mozart's Symphony No. 40. In due course the first

[7] *Op. cit.*, p. 204 (incl. Ex. 3).

[8] *Op. cit.*, p. 54.

theme returns, as does the second section thereafter, although both are interestingly modified; and a coda provides a subtle retrospect on the moods, and less obviously the materials, of both sections. One further aspect of the relationship between the alternating sections is worth noting. The prevailing impression in the first section, comprising the main theme, is of settled tonality. Any deviations from the E flat key are short-lived. The second section, on the contrary, makes a point of its tonal wanderlust, and whatever passing resolutions it may yield the only ultimate resolution is the return of E flat and the main theme. This contrast in tonal behaviour was another important kind of contrast to Schubert, and its presence here reflects a gradual change in his attitude to slow movements in his symphonies. After the Fifth Symphony, he invariably adopted sonata-form for his slow movements; up to the Fifth Symphony, he never did so. He preferred, in the early slow movements, a simple sectional form. In the Fourth Symphony, as in the Fifth, the alternating sections tend to be tonally footloose, offsetting the firm tonality of the main sections. Had Schubert modelled his slow movements structurally on those of, say, Mozart's last three symphonies or Beethoven's first two, he would have used sonata-form. He chose not to, at first; and it was perhaps because he aspired to the tonal discursiveness which Mozart in particular, in those last three symphonies, found attainable within a slow movement in sonata-form, that he sought scope for this discursiveness in the 'B' sections of his Fourth and Fifth Symphonies, then abandoned his simple sectional form altogether in favour of sonata-form. But in the Sixth Symphony he seemed too absorbed by Rossini's mannerisms to develop this discursive trait, which was to open up such rewarding new vistas in the sonata-form slow movements of the Seventh, Eighth and Ninth Symphonies.

Having given his preceding minor-key symphony a minuet in the major, Schubert gives his B flat major Symphony a minuet in G minor (he had first departed from long-standing tradition in this way in the Second Symphony). Commentators have drawn attention to general likenesses between Mozart's G minor minuet in his Symphony No. 40 and Schubert's G minor minuet here. There are, in addition, some more specific comparisons to be made.

First, Schubert's strong unharmonised opening contains echoes of Mozart's 'little G minor' (No. 25) as well as No. 40. Second, just as Mozart (in the Fortieth) eliminates shorter note-values at the approach of his main cadences and substitutes emphatic *staccato* crotchets with a chromatic descent in the top part (Ex. 39(a)), Schubert does likewise (Ex. 39(b)).

Ex. 39

(a)

(b)

Third, Schubert crooks both horns in G, as does Mozart, although in the other G minor movements of his symphony Mozart had asked for one in G and one in B flat for reasons explained in chapter VII.[9] Mozart uses two G horns in his minuet because the trio, which is to be in G major, will use the two horns as prominent soloists; the major third of G (B natural), not available on the B flat instrument, is here required from both players. Schubert, too, has a trio in G major, and the horns, both of which

[9]*Cf.* pp. 88–89.

need the major third, have parts which, if not so exposed as Mozart's, are calculated to shine clearly through the middle texture.

Schubert's tempo for his minuet, by the way, is *Allegro molto,* which brings it a step nearer the scherzo than Mozart's *Allegro* minuet, yet it is not more of a scherzo than the 'Menuetto' of the Fourth Symphony.

A *locus classicus* of early Schubertian dialogue is found at the beginning of the second section, where a major derivative of the minor theme is sung by the violins, to which the cellos and basses respond with the same, the oboe entering with a plaintive comment at the point where the cellos and basses deviate from the violins' version to lead towards a new key. A different sort of dialogue begins the second section of the trio, where upper woodwind answer the violins in exact canon. It is in order to allow the canonic reply to run its full course that Schubert here extends the four-bar phrase to six bars, thus departing from the trio's otherwise unvaried norm with delightful effect.

The finale displays a lightness of touch that seems to have spilled over from the finale of a Mozart string quartet – from к458 in B flat, for instance, or к465 in C. Its first theme shapes itself, with an internal repetition, more in the manner of a Haydn symphonic finale, begun in a whisper but soon bursting into an exuberant *forte.* The *fortissimo* sequel is an arresting contrast of long notes accompanied by bristling *tremolandi* (*cf.* к465), whose first three pitches, in B flat minor, are those of Mozart's Piano Concerto in C minor, к491, and Schubert's own later *Rosamunde* Overture. The second subject, preceded by a short silence as in early Classical practice, widens the focus to longer *cantabile* spans. This subject in turn has a short sequel in the minor, based on runs in parallel thirds in the entire woodwind section, which points forward to the finales of the Sixth and Seventh Symphonies, and through them to the 'Great' C major. And the triplets which then persist to the end of the exposition could almost have bubbled their way out of a carefree, intimate Mozart sonata for piano duet.

It is clear from the start that the development is to concern itself with the first bar of the first theme. More specifically it seems intent on divesting that bar of its downbeat quality and investing it with an upbeat quality. When first sounded at the beginning of the movement, it fell on the first and stronger bar of a two-bar grouping – a grouping which prevailed throughout the theme. Schubert now sets about the business of transforming it with a winsome wit that does not preclude depth of feeling, any more than it does in Mozart. The transformation is fully accomplished at the point shown in Ex. 40, by which time the figure has also taken on a chromatic contour. Here, once more, is a telling dialogue whose effect is achieved with a minimum of notes. That description, like the music itself, calls to mind Mozart – specifically the finale of the String Quartet in G, к387 (*cf.* Ex. 41).

Ex. 40

The resemblance to chamber music by Mozart is symptomatic of the lightness of touch Schubert aspires to in the finale of his 'chamber symphony', written for and performed at Otto Hatwig's music salon in the Schottenhof, where the performers were an ensemble formed around the nucleus of the Schubert family string quartet.

Ex. 41

Schubert soon reverses the process, restoring to the figure its downbeat function (with the help of a *forte-piano* stress). The recapitulation can then proceed, if in unorthodox fashion, running its course to the end of the Symphony as a transposition of the exposition, save for the necessary re-writing of the transition. In doing so, without a coda, it appears to illustrate the remarks of Hans Gál[10] on Schubert's attitude to form in the middle years, up to about 1818:

> As to the recapitulation [he] copies the exposition with as few changes as possible, and is also quite happy to leave it without a coda, a fuller, more circumstantial preparation for the conclusion. This is a definite weakness in formal design, since in a weighty, large-scale composition the conclusion is hardly convincing if one has already met with it before in exactly the same manner. In this respect the young Schubert reverted to a procedure which, though adequate for a slender, sonatina-like composition, would no longer do for the large type of form inaugurated by Beethoven.

Gál is obviously speaking of instrumental works in general, including symphonies. Yet the finale of the Fifth

[10] *Franz Schubert and the Essence of Melody*, p. 108.

Symphony is the only one, of more than twenty sonata-form movements in his Symphonies, in which he ends the movement in the same way as he ended its exposition. When the special nature of the Fifth is borne in mind, it will be appreciated why the finale of this symphony should be exceptional in this respect. No Schubert symphony aspires less to 'the large type of form inaugurated by Beethoven'. Scored for an orchestra of exactly the same size and constitution as that for which Mozart originally scored his Symphony No. 40, it is a re-incarnation of the spirit of the time when Haydn and Mozart were in their heyday as symphonists. In the 1780s, finales were, but for a handful of exceptions, more a means of sending an audience home in good spirits than a resolution of issues contained in the rest of the symphony. One Mozart symphony of that era known especially well to Schubert was the 'Prague' Symphony. Perhaps it is what Georges de Saint-Foix calls the 'rigorous symmetry'[11] of the sonata-form of the 'Prague' finale, in which the close of the movement differs from the close of the exposition merely by the insertion of two bars a little before the end, that finds an echo in the finale of Schubert's Fifth. The absence of a coda from the Ninth Symphony would clearly have amounted to a major flaw. But Einstein, for one, was able to say of the Fifth Symphony that 'from the point of view of form the finale is perhaps the purest, most polished and most balanced piece of instrumental music that Schubert had yet written'.[12]

[11] *The Symphonies of Mozart*, Dobson, London, 1947, p. 90.
[12] *Op. cit.*, p. 129.

IX

Crossroads:
The Sixth Symphony

Schubert must have realised that his Fifth was a little gem of a symphony. He probably knew also that it was to some extent an 'aside' from the main thrust of his symphonic career, with little bearing on the direction he would take thereafter. He waited a year before attempting another symphony, during which time he tried to make his way as a freelance composer, having abandoned his regular teaching post at his father's school in the autumn of 1816. But he soon had to return to teaching, evidently without much pleasure, and this worldly problem may explain why he took from October 1817 to February 1818 to produce a symphony which, according to Eduard von Bauernfeld,[1] he himself counted among his less success-ful works. But there were musical problems too. The Sixth Symphony highlights a double crisis of identity, a crisis he was doubtless alive to as he drew in the final double-bar a few days after his twenty-first birthday. The questions raised by this music are, intermittently, 'What is a symphony?' and rather more consistently, 'Is this really Schubert? Has the composer found himself?'

After pursuing his pleasures along a side track in the Fifth Symphony, Schubert now rejoins the main route,

---

[1] 'On Franz Schubert' (*Wiener Zeitschrift für Kunst*, 8, 9, 11, and 13 June 1829), in Deutsch (ed.), *Schubert – A Documentary Biography*, p. 888.

but immediately finds himself at a crossroads. He restores the instruments omitted from the Fifth, to the extent of including the trumpets and drums in his slow movement – a novelty which points forward to the regular inclusion of full brass and timpani in slow movements from the Eighth Symphony onwards. He eschews the idol whose memory warms every movement of the Fifth, Mozart, and now writes a symphony loaded with tacit homage to another idol, who had been banished from the pages of the Fifth. Bauernfeld, who will have had opportunity to hear the Sixth, as it was performed at least twice in Schubert's lifetime, found it 'written almost throughout in the manner of a master highly esteemed by the young composer'.[2] The more specific evocations of Beethoven have been listed by Roger Fiske,[3] and his observations are not over-fanciful. There are, besides, many more generalised echoes of the Beethoven manner. And as Fiske also points out, Schubert has adopted the broad tonal plan of Beethoven's First Symphony, as well as its key. At the same time, he cannot rid his reflexes of Rossini, whose operas were beginning to create a stir in Vienna. Schubert's partiality to the Rossini style affects overtures, symphonies, and other genres over a four-year period, resulting in pretty tunes, light, rhythmically pointed accompaniments, and sparkling orchestration. Another ingredient in the Sixth Symphony is likewise theatrical: Schubert's own overtures, which are less challenging and demanding on the listener than his symphonies usually are and were themselves becoming heavily impregnated with Italian elements, leave their mark here. And much of the music, in all movements except the

[2] *Ibid.*, p. 888.

[3] Preface, *Schubert's Symphony No. 6 in C, D589*, Eulenburg miniature score, London, 1974, p. iv. In Schubert's first movement, for example, Fiske finds echoes of Beethoven's Second Symphony (first movement, bb. 132–3, at Schubert's bb. 77–8) and of the overture *Leonora* No. 3 (bb. 606 *et seq.*, at Schubert's bb. 349 *et seq.*)

third, seems to have a balletic build and inspiration, in which it anticipates the ballet music Schubert assembled for *Rosamunde* in 1823. The overture in C now known as *Rosamunde* also comes to mind, although it was originally written for *Die Zauberharfe* in 1820. Additionally, Haydn re-enters the scene as Schubert's eighteenth-century mentor, replacing Mozart.

All these characteristics may seem to amount to a formula for a bad symphony. In truth, the Sixth is not a bad symphony; rather, it is an uncharacteristic one. It is uncharacteristic of the composer, and of the genre. To some, its unorthodoxies are failings; to others, they are virtues. (Maurice Brown conveniently summarises the division of opinion, quoting chapter and verse.[4]) What makes it more or less viable as a symphonic whole is the assured technique with which Schubert can now handle his chosen resources, especially the orchestra. What makes it fascinating for the historical observer, with the hindsight conferred by a knowledge of the composer's greater symphonic exploits to come, is the way in which it makes discoveries for further use, without for the present being able to harness their symphonic potential.

It may seem perverse that while Schubert's Vienna knew so little about his real symphonic achievements, just after his death the one of his symphonies that received a performance in the city – and another very soon after – should be the Sixth; but this accords with the Viennese taste of the day. The two overtures most closely akin to the Symphony, those 'In the Italian Style' in C major, D590, and D major, D591, also found popular favour in the city, probably for the same reason. Both works occasioned unusually warm eulogies from the press as soon as they were introduced in 1818, at a time when the Viennese enthusiasm for Rossini, whose operas had begun to reach the city in 1816, was well into the long crescendo that climaxed in the 1820s.

[4] *Schubert Symphonies*, p. 29.

The *Adagio* introduction begins grandly, with gestures derived from Beethoven's *Prometheus* Overture, but thereafter is rather lacking in character. When eventually the key of A flat is reached, Schubert duly adds an F sharp to the chord of A flat to assemble the 'augmented sixth' that will return him to C. It is an effective strategy which, although used by the earlier Classical composers, Schubert makes very much his own.[5] But there is a tendency to resort to the process – the move to A flat and the return by augmented sixth – too frequently in this symphony.

The *Allegro* opens with a theme which would remind the listener of Haydn's 'Military' Symphony (No. 100) even if it were not scored in the same way for unaccompanied high woodwind. Its treatment, here and in the immediate sequel, is crisp and incisive, but based on rather square gestures from which there is welcome relief in the transition, and in the second subject with its recurring syncopations. Schubert then seizes on the two-bar tail of this second subject (Ex. 42(a)) as a basis for antiphonal exchanges which restore the modular manner of progress. A derivative of this figure soon appears in the woodwind in quasi-canon over a tonic pedal. The third and fourth notes of Ex. 42(a), a downward step, are replaced in Ex. 42(b) by two identical notes, and these two notes become – by stages which a study of the intervening music in the score makes perfectly clear – the launching pad for a closing theme, Ex. 42(c), which is thus distinguished from Ex. 42(d), which begins the second subject in Beethoven's First Symphony.

The two-note upbeat is soon isolated in the wind, through and beyond the big cadences at the end of the exposition, and into the development, which is first concerned with the closing theme, until the first theme

[5] A well-known example appears in the song *Ständchen*, D889 (1826), where Schubert twice returns from A flat major to C major by this route.

Ex. 42

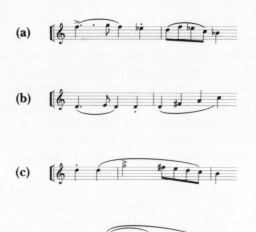

returns in E flat. By now the recapitulation is imminent. The modulation from E flat to C which is Schubert's route to the recapitulation is so audacious, and so prophetic (Ex. 43(a)), that it must be seen alongside an extract from the String Quintet of 1828 (Ex. 43(b)).

Ex. 43

The recapitulation requires no comment, but the coda brings a witty new tonic reply to the dominant third and fourth bars of the first theme, first from the solo clarinet, then – after a quickening of tempo which occasions dissonances perhaps remembered from Beethoven's Overture *Leonora* No. 3 – from the string body in insistent response to the wind choir. The whole movement is as easy to digest as a Rossini overture, which is not to say that Rossini could have written its development section or would have ventured the dissonances of its coda. Another aspect of its digestibility is the scoring, with its frequent dependence on the clear-cut opposition of wind and string groupings. Indeed, the emancipation of the wind choir in the Sixth Symphony as a whole is in striking contrast to the relatively string-based orchestration of the Fourth Symphony.

If Rossini had shared the composition of a slow movement theme with Haydn, the result might have been something like that of Schubert's *Andante*. Only when the oboe belatedly appears, to imitate an intense little utterance from the strings, is the parlance unmistakably that of Schubert. The contrasting episode (one hesitates to say 'second theme' for what is more a hubbub of triplets) demands attention when it turns to the minor and generates a *fortissimo* cry of throbbing minor-ninth chords. When the first theme returns it is enlivened by this triplet rhythm, and when after that the alternating episode returns, Schubert omits the first part of it and plunges straight into the minor sequel, with fine effect.

The most successful movement of the Symphony is the scherzo. Schubert marks it *Presto* and gives the title 'scherzo' for the first time in his symphonic career. It is cast in the traditional binary form, but the first section is longer than any counterpart in a Beethoven symphony before his Ninth. Indeed, the clear sonata-form structure of Beethoven's last symphonic scherzo is anticipated by Schubert here. There is a 'second group' so explicit that not only is it first announced and later recapitulated in

the opposite keys typical of sonata-form, but elements
from it are separately developed in the development.
Moreover, the development is nearly one-and-a-half
times the length of either the exposition or the
recapitulation.

The dynamic contrasts in this scherzo, and especially
the off-beat accents, naturally enough remind one of
Beethoven, as do some of the modulations. To be precise,
they call to mind the scherzo (called minuet) of Beethoven's First Symphony. Was that movement, from Beethoven's Symphony in C, a particular influence as Schubert
set about the scherzo of his own Symphony in C? Given
the distinctive rhythmic character of that movement,
Schubert may have found he couldn't shake the rhythm
of its first theme (Ex. 44) out of his head.

Ex. 44

At any rate, he seems to have accepted it as the natural
basis of the theme of his own first symphonic scherzo.
But in accepting its rhythm, he would have to devise a
new melodic contour. Perhaps the perky finale tune of
Mozart's K459 Piano Concerto in F major (shown transposed to C in Ex. 45) would lend itself to adaptation as a
scherzo theme in triple time (Ex. 46x). There is no evidence to suggest that Schubert realised he was marrying
Mozart's line to Beethoven's rhythm, unless the evidence
is that he found it hard to choose between Mozart's intervening rests and Beethoven's long minims, so first
adopted the one (Ex. 46x) and then, eight bars later, the
other (Ex. 46x[1]). His 'appropriation' of models was probably quite as unthinking as his imitation of his own
scherzo rhythm from the 'Trout' Quintet in the scherzo
of his B flat Trio.

Ex. 45

Ex. 46

Such allegiances in no way reduce the brilliant success of the scherzo, by any standard. The development is not only brilliant, but original – and prophetic. After a linking passage the violins lead off with Ex. 47.

Ex. 47

On to the end of a new idea (y in Ex. 47) Schubert tacks x^2, which is none other than the first theme (Ex. 46) with the gaps filled by note-repetition. The first theme having thus served to lend the new one its company and make it 'belong', Schubert gives y a life of its own, in the form of y^1, which is to y what x^1 is to x^2. For some 40 bars this y^1 takes the stage, a newcomer ingeniously integrated into the argument. As for the prophetic nature of what is happening here, the regular appearance of this theme in parallel thirds, doubled by as many woodwind pairs as Schubert sees fit, looks forward seven years to the 'Great' C major, where parallel thirds in the wind section become a *modus operandi* which is almost thematic in itself. The linking work between the two Symphonies in this respect is the Seventh.

The only weakness of the movement is its trio. In choosing a slower tempo (*Più lento*) Schubert may have had the Fourth and Seventh Symphonies of Beethoven in mind, just as he may have aspired to the more drawn-out rhythm Beethoven favours in those trios. But Beethoven's trios have more character, melodically and harmonically. Schubert successfully leaves behind the *tout simple* tunefulness of his earlier trios, but cannot yet find – in the rotating harmonies and meagre scraps of melody – any convincing substitute. But at least the seeds are sown from which will germinate a distinctive new growth in the trios of the Seventh and Ninth Symphonies. This is one symptom of the crossroads at which Schubert now finds himself. Another is the plan, well-conceived but not too happily executed, of repeating not the whole of the second section of the trio but only the last two-thirds of it. For the first time, too, he considers the integration of trio with scherzo to the extent of writing a special connecting passage to lead back from the trio to the reprise of the scherzo.

More than any other movement, the finale epitomises the composer's stance at this time. Once the pretty first tune has run its course – a tune none the worse for a touch of the hedonism that must have commended Rossini to the Viennese – Schubert overthrows the finale traditions of his own and of others, and replaces them with a patchwork of episodes so loosely related and so under-nourished in terms of symphonic thrust and causality that one could not honestly say that it adds up to more than the sum of its parts. Early in one's acquaintance with it, this finale appears to be structurally akin to a Schubert slow movement. Perhaps for that reason, after episode has succeeded episode and it is sensed that the movement has proceeded beyond its first half and well into its second, an unmistakable sense of relaxation has been induced (the tempo being a gentle *Allegro moderato*). Then, suddenly, Schubert is heard thinking aloud: 'This won't do. I am coming to the end of a symphony. I must stir up some excitement, set in motion an irresistible drive to the conclusion, prepare for a suitably imposing end'. The last pages are indeed both exciting and colourful, but they are not an inevitable nor even a particularly likely fulfilment of what has gone before; and the problem lies, of course, with what has gone before.

On closer study, one can detect clear vestiges of another genre with its own formal idiosyncrasies: the overture. The standard pattern for an overture, subscribed to by Schubert as by Rossini, was sonata-form without development. The exposition would end in the dominant, whereupon a short direct link back to the tonic would follow, and the recapitulation would begin without further ado. The theory was either that one must not keep a theatre audience waiting too long before curtain-rise, or that a 'development' would tax the musical understanding of a theatre clientele, or both. Taking this overture scheme as the model, the form of the finale of the Sixth Symphony can be represented as in Figure 5.

Figure 5

Exposition						Recapitulation					
I	tr	II(i)	(ii)	(iii)	link	I tr	II(i)	(ii)	(iii)	coda
C	A	C	A	E	CG	CE	C	D	A	CC	C
	flat			flat			flat			flat	

Roman numerals are subject-groups: tr = transition: square brackets indicate the same material stated in two keys in immediate succession

---

The main grounds for identifying the overture background in this moment are; that section II(iii) is a long
one, implanting the dominant key for as long as the first
subject implants the tonic, and ends with the rounding-
off gestures typical of the close of an exposition; that the
following link simply adds a seventh to the chord of G,
reminding the listener of many a Rossini overture; and
that the keys in which II(i) and II(ii) return in the recapitulation have a rough logic in their relation to the keys in
which this material appeared in the exposition. Against
this interpretation it must be said that the discursive tonality coupled with the discursiveness of the material so as
to produce a marked sectional effect does not leave the
listener with much impression of sonata-form. Moreover,
if Schubert conceived the movement along these lines, he
was clearly extending the concept of a three-key exposition (as found in the Second Symphony) to a new
extreme: this one would have to be called at least a five-
key exposition. It is nevertheless possible that a diversified sonata-form was the intention, in view of Schubert's
unorthodox, not to say libertarian, attitude to the form.

Whatever the oddities of this movement as a finale, critical hindsight suggests that it was useful to its composer
as a medium in which to try out textures and procedures
that would come to fruition in the 'Great' C major Symphony. The repetition of small rhythmic motives from
bar to bar over fairly long periods is one such procedure.
Another is the frequent use of a pair of woodwind instruments in parallel thirds, other pairs being added to
double the first pair, usually at the distance of an octave.
Both these devices are seen at work in Ex. 48, the finale's
'second subject' referred to as II(i) in Figure 5. The
doubled parallel thirds of the theme itself, in flutes and
oboes, are underpinned by a persistent one-bar rhythm
in the lower strings, creating the kind of sound-image to
be met again in the second subject of the finale of the
'Great'. The dotted rhythms form another connection

Ex. 48

here, and the sequential path followed by the themes of both movements is also analogous. There is a striking harmonic anticipation of the 'Great' in the last pages of the Sixth, when a B major triad and dominant seventh of C are juxtaposed (Ex. 49(a)). The juxtaposition has a similar purpose, and enjoys the same prominence through long rhythmic values, in the introduction to the Ninth (Ex. 49(b)).[6]

The Sixth Symphony, then, at the same time as it moves beyond past accomplishments, points the way somewhat tentatively to future possibilities. If Schubert was unsure which way to turn after the Fifth Symphony, the Sixth brought no answer. It represents a faintly detached examination of some of the options. The temporary influence of Rossini is incidental to the broader issues now to be faced. Schubert had served an apprenticeship with

[6]Schubert apparently remembered this striking succession of chords in the quasi-symphonic climax of his 1822 song *Aus Heliopolis*, II, D754, at the words 'lass die Leidenschaften sausen im metallenen Akkord' – 'Let the passions swell in brassy harmony' (transl. Norma Deane and Celia Larner, in John Reed, *The Schubert Song Companion*, Manchester University Press, Manchester, 1985).

Ex. 49

Haydn and Mozart, *in absentia,* as it were. He had learned from Beethoven, but realised he must not allow that indelible musical personality to swamp his own. He evidently felt the necessity of a change in his symphonic outlook. In which direction should he go? And could he attain maturity as a symphonist and write impressive symphonies that were unmistakably of his time without simply following the trail already blazed by Beethoven's post-*Eroica* Symphonies?

It may reasonably be assumed that Schubert played in the private performance of the Sixth Symphony given in the year of its composition by Otto Hatwig's orchestra. Did he receive any helpful criticism from his fellow-players? Most of them will have played in the Fifth Symphony earlier in the year, but it is possible that only a few of them, if any, knew his earlier symphonies. The composer may have been the only musician with a total view of his achievement as a symphonist so far. One wonders if he reflected, at this juncture, on his compositional strengths and how far the latest symphony had made use of them. Certainly the virtues of some of his earlier symphonies were not all in strong evidence in the Sixth. The intensity that runs through parts of the Second, Fourth and Fifth had to be rekindled. The budding teenage master of the long lyrical melodic line had not given himself a fair hearing in the Sixth. And there was surely scope for the development of his flair for the daring harmonic excursion within a secure tonal framework, in which respect the finale of the Third remained unsurpassed. In the Sixth, only the scherzo rediscovers the sheer momentum and assurance of the earlier works. Certainly, if Schubert could now move forward on the basis of what was best in these six youthful symphonies, his future endeavours would bear rich fruit. It was a question not so much of technique as of self-knowledge, inspiration, and judgement.

X

The Way Ahead

Schubert moved ahead too fast. Only a few months after the Sixth Symphony he was at work on its successor. His efforts came to nothing, for he lost heart after sketching two fragments in piano score. Now known as D615, and dated May 1818 in Schubert's hand, these fragments were intended to form the basis of another symphony in D major. The first movement begins with a slow introduction in D minor, and the following *Allegro moderato* is sketched up to the end of the exposition. The second fragment begins on the next line of paper but one, and is evidently a sketch of a movement in rondo form, breaking off during the first reprise of its rondo-theme.

The *Adagio* introduction is very promising indeed. It has a visionary quality far removed from that of the Sixth Symphony, and shows Schubert setting out on a path which was to raise the status of the slow introduction from mere curtain-raiser to first act of the drama. That transformation was to be pursued and completed in the Seventh and Ninth Symphonies. The prime cell is simply a firm unison tonic-to-dominant, which may remind the listener of another D minor slow introduction, that to Haydn's 'London' Symphony (No. 104). The soft sequel, probably intended for the woodwind, does not go far beyond Haydn's world (Ex. 50). But when the opening figure is resumed, the move from D to A being replaced by A to E flat, the wonderful woodwind continuation gradually creates a harmonic context in which the long-

Ex. 50

sustained E flat can be heard as a dominant in its own
right, and with perfect timing Schubert prepares and
accomplishes a cadence to the remote key of A flat major,
a tritone distant from the key in which the symphony
began thirteen bars previously. He had made a comparable move in the introduction to the *Tragic* Symphony,
prompted perhaps by the strange harmonic probings of
Haydn's 'Chaos' Prelude to *The Creation*; here he continues with further swift moves towards the flat side,
touching successively on D flat major, G flat major, C flat
minor (which he calls, for convenience, B minor), G
minor, and by this route homes in on D again, postpon-
ing the cadential advent of D to coincide with the onset of
the *Allegro moderato*. The whole of this excursion is
encompassed within a rather short space of time, and, the
tempo being *Adagio*, within a remarkably small number of
notes. It is only just the longest introduction Schubert
had so far planned for a symphony, despite the illusion
created by the distance it travels. It is a model of how
richness and compactness can be reconciled, and that
makes one all the more disappointed when the *Allegro
moderato* fails to sustain its degree of imagination.

But disappointment should not blind anyone to what
Schubert is trying to achieve in this movement. The initial
contour of the first theme of the *Allegro moderato* (Ex. 51)
is carefully prepared in the last few bars of *Adagio*, and

Ex. 51

the theme begins with the upbeat in dotted rhythm which
has been the most persistent motivic feature of the introduction.[1] Later, the second subject forms itself from
another idea developed in the course of the introduction
(Ex. 52).

Ex. 52

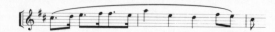

Moreover, the transition between these two subjects is
shot through with references to the three-note figure
which began the introduction – now heard at the faster
speed, of course. By these procedures Schubert attempts
to integrate the introduction and first movement proper
on various levels. Such a concept of first-movement unity
is Schubert's own, quite different from Beethoven's ways
of integrating an introduction, and it is a pity that his
plan for the entire first movement was unfulfilled. It is
possible that there was no such plan in any case, for the
impression given by that much of the movement that *is*
sketched is one of declining impetus, compatible with the
view that Schubert improvised his plan as he composed.
This way of operating had worked well enough in the
first six symphonies, if, as I believe, those symphonies
were composed directly into orchestral score and there
are no lost piano sketches.[2] In the present movement,
where the composer was conceiving also a new pattern of
inter-relationships as he worked, it was less certain of success. He probably composed the introduction with no

[1] The incipit given in the 1978 updating of Deutsch's catalogue omits
this important feature.

[2] A hypothesis concerning the role of sketches in relation to the composition of all the Symphonies is advanced at the end of chapter XIV,
pp. 249–57.

preconception of the *Allegro,* until he reached the final dominant pedal. Having set the *Allegro* in motion, he then seems to have set his sights on a second subject based on introduction material, by way of a rhythmically germane transition, letting other considerations look after themselves. What went wrong was that the unification was too consciously applied and the muse would bestow on Schubert only rather poor supporting material.

His own awareness of these deficiencies is suggested by the fact that, having ended the exposition, he left no room for the completion of the movement. He left only one blank stave before beginning the next movement (p. 143). In other symphonic sketches he normally left plenty of space – at least the remainder of the page – before continuing with another movement. Because the movement Schubert sketches next follows that closely, one's first instinct is to suppose that it is a slow movement. To Maurice Brown it was a slow movement, 'unmistakably'.[3] I believe it is unmistakably a finale. The material strongly suggests this conclusion, unless one has a fixed idea that a finale must be very fast. Its tempo (which is unmarked, although *Allegretto* seems appropriate) would place it closer to the finale of the Sixth Symphony than any other. A second factor is that its key is D major, and Schubert would not cast a slow movement in the same key as his outer movements. The fact that it follows immediately after the end of the first-movement sketch should not deter one from accepting this conclusion. Either way, Schubert had not left sufficient room between the two sketched movements, whether for the second half of the first movement or for that and two further whole middle movements. As for the composer setting about a finale before the middle movements (a procedure sometimes adopted by Beethoven), and so composing out of sequence, the most likely time for him to address the

'finale problem' head-on in this way was a few months
after completing his least satisfactory symphonic finale, to
the Sixth Symphony.

The tune which begins the D615 finale (Schubert did
not indicate what sort of accompaniment it was to have)
has a feline grace typical of middle-period Schubert at its
best (Ex. 53).

Ex. 53

A short interlude-like section follows, suggesting a return
to the episodic, balletic construction of the finale of the
Sixth Symphony. When the first forceful gesture of the
movement ensues – essentially the rhythm of the first five
notes of the movement on a monotone (although fully
harmonised) – it is heard as the start of a further episode.
But the response, in short notes, is destined to challenge
the episodic manner of progress, for soon these short
notes become established, running continuously through
to the end of the first theme-group and into a second
subject, as its accompaniment. This procedure has its origins in the outer movements of the *Tragic* Symphony.
Meanwhile, both the transition and second subject are
based on the five-note rhythm, used in effective close
imitation.

At length the forceful gesture returns, after the second
subject, as if to summarise the discourse on its rhythm
that has just been enjoyed. This time, it is followed by a
flutter of soft repeated chords (Ex. 54), which itself becomes the subject of antiphonal exchanges (between

*The third page of the piano sketch for a symphony in D major, D615
(1818), shows Schubert abandoning the first movement at the end of the
exposition (top) and commencing the finale (Wiener Stadt- und
Landesbibliothek, Vienna).*

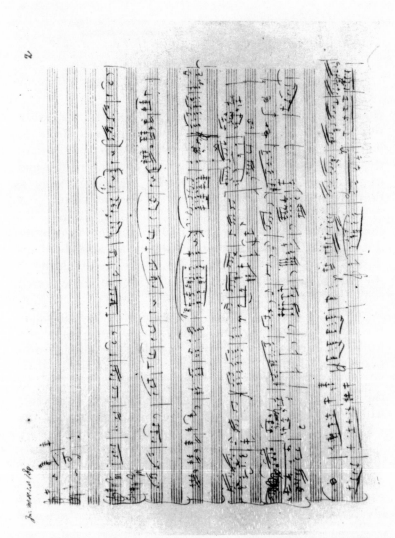

Ex. 54

woodwind and strings, presumably). This effects a transition back to D major, where the exchanges continue as
backdrop to the returning first theme. After four bars of
this, the sketch ends abruptly, some way before the end
of a page. That is all there is of D615. There is no suggestion that Schubert ever went back to the sketch and
attempted to extend or orchestrate it. There are no other
sources, no references to it in any nineteenth-century
documents. One senses that Schubert had already abandoned this symphony when he broke off in the middle of
the first movement, and continued with the finale sketch
only because he had an idea he wanted to work out.
When he laid down his pen in the finale, it was probably
not on account of the finale itself but because there was
no point in completing a finale to what was already destined to be an unfinished symphony. Indeed, the finale is
attractive as far as it goes, and particularly felicitous at
the point where it stops. Of all the Schubert fragments
which break off in mid-flow, one wonders if there is any
where silence intervenes quite so painfully as here.

The D615 finale is thus a bonus which, it may be tentatively suggested, almost did not get begun. The first
movement contained flaws which spelt the demise of this
particular symphony, added to which the composer possibly felt that the work was not going to be sufficiently

---

*Opposite: Schubert ceases sketching the scherzo of his symphony in D
major, D708A (1820–21), at the point where the cellos lead to a
reprise, and jumps ahead to sketch a trio, which he relinquishes (at
the end of the page) a few bars before its completion (Wiener
Stadt-und Landesbibliothek, Vienna)*

distinct in style and outlook from its precursors. When it
was abandoned, a long silence followed. It appears that
Schubert did not venture another symphony for nearly
three years. Then, early in 1821, he again chose to sketch
in D major, and again in piano score.

This sketch, called D708A, from early in 1821, is more
ambitious. In the first place, Schubert sketched something of all four movements. Although he had completed
only the exposition of the first movement, he began and
wrote perhaps a third of a slow movement, then outlined
so much of the third movement that relatively little effort
would have been required to finish it, and had two
attempts at a finale, taking the second attempt to the
point where the first theme returns in the dominant
either as 'recapitulation' in an unorthodox key or as first
rondo return in an equally unorthodox key. Secondly,
this symphony breaks important new ground, at least in
its first three movements, and it was to have been a symphony on a larger scale than any of the first six.

In all, the sketch amounts to 685 bars of music.
Through all this, Schubert gives indications of instrumentation in only six places. He had been a little more generous in D615, with instrumental indications in four places
over 259 bars. The reader of the D708A sketch[4] gains
the distinct impression that the composer is working in a
hurry, setting down the essentials of his thought and not
much more. There are extended passages where only one
or two lines of music are given – music of an evidently
fuller intended texture. Details of orchestration could be
left out almost entirely, as scoring was largely a matter of
the selection of options and applying of technique (which
Schubert now had in good measure) to the material
composed. Of course, the purpose of sketching in piano
score was to enable the composer to work fast, losing as
little time as possible in notational exertion. Where a

---

[4] Available in facsimile, with D615 and D936A: *Franz Schubert, Drei
Symphonie-Fragmente*, Bärenreiter, Kassel, 1978.

contrapuntal texture is intended, as in parts of the second and third movements, this is naturally sketched in more detail.

Schubert dispenses with a slow introduction. He had done this once before, in the Fifth Symphony. But D708A is to be no slender, lightweight symphony in the eighteenth-century manner, and Schubert seems here to be compensating for the absence of an introduction by building something of the atmosphere associated with a slow introduction (mystery, grandeur, expectation) into the first movement proper. He does it too, one supposes, without trombones: for although there is no indication of the constitution of the orchestra used, it appears from the character of the music – even at its grander moments – that Schubert still has the sonority of his customary symphony orchestra in mind. In a few months, he would be bringing in three trombones as a permanent addition. He had almost reached that point where his symphonic thinking demanded them, but not quite.

Schubert's substitute for an introduction, in his instrumental works, is often a re-introduction: that is to say, he announces his first subject directly, but rather than giving it any sense of completion he turns aside, perhaps in an atmosphere of drama, mystery, or suspense, in order to re-approach the first subject, which is then restated with fresh vigour. This is the scheme adopted in D708A. The first subject comprises a strong unison and a soft scurrying figure, followed by two sequences, a degree higher each time (Ex. 55). The grandiloquent sequel culminates in a dramatic held chord followed by silence. The chord is one that is almost unique to Schubert among Classical composers, and was to become a special feature of his later style, notably in the 'Great' C major Symphony.[5] A hushed chordal passage seeks a way back to the tonic chord for the restatement. This time Schubert diverges at the fifth bar, and the scurrying quavers soon establish

[5] Technically, the chord is a German sixth on the subdominant.

Ex. 55

themselves in *moto perpetuo* fashion (as in the Fourth Symphony and D615) running right through the transition and, without let-up, into the second subject, where the sketch clearly implies that they should form a continuing inner textural thread. Before the second subject is examined, it should be noted that the first subject is a promising one for a first movement without introduction. It has already generated two different continuations, and could easily have led to several further ones in the recapitulation and coda, if only Schubert had kept going that far.

The second subject is laid out in quasi-canonic manner (Ex. 56), the melody being imitated in rough approximation one bar later in the bass.

Ex. 56

But the most remarkable aspect of it is its key. It is in A flat major, a tritone away from the tonic D. This choice of key for a second subject was unprecedented. Even Beethoven, who often departed from orthodoxy at this point, would not have risked it. When Schubert chose such a remote key in which to begin a second subject, he would as a matter of course veer back to the orthodox key (the dominant), to play out the last portion of the exposition there. As a rule, the more remote the initial key of the second subject, the sooner the composer would veer to the dominant, so that orthodoxy could have a longer innings through which to offset that remoteness. In this movement, A flat major has a very short reign indeed. It prevails only for the eight-bar antecedent of the second subject and the beginning of the consequent,[6] which is extended to thirteen bars to incorporate the modulation to the dominant, A major. The modulation is something of a wrench, and although Schubert may have derived some passing satisfaction from the experiment, he may have felt in retrospect that it misfired. In later years he was able to cope more successfully with this kind of situation, as can be seen in the *Allegro* in A minor for piano duet (*'Lebensstürme'*) of 1828, where the second subject begins in the major key on the leading note. The resulting tonal balance of the three-key exposition in D708A, incidentally, is, in terms of bar numbers (transitional sections omitted): 50 in D, 14 in A flat, and 79 in A.

The third section of the exposition, in A major, is exclusively concerned with developing the second subject already stated. Schubert builds a fine sustained climax in this way, one which lends itself well to orchestration although he left not a single clue as to the instrumentation in the entire movement. Tovey, to whom this symphony was unknown, took Schubert to task in other instances where, having begun the second subject in a deviant key, he used the third section in the traditional key to 'develop' the second subject. He notes that:

Schubert, feeling that the rest of his exposition must not be less spacious than its enormous opening, fills up most

[6] These terms are defined on p. 141.

of what he guesses to be the required interval with a
vigorous discussion of the matter already in hand. Even if
the discussion does not lead him too far afield, it inevitably tends to obliterate the vital distinction between exposition and development.

And he continues later:

Development is, of course, already at an almost hopeless
disadvantage in Schubert because his Exposition will have
already digressed into developments of its own.[7]

There is, in all this, a certain ambiguity in Tovey's use of
the term 'development'. In a development section proper
the two usual ingredients are a fluidity of key and a pre-
occupation with radical reshaping of the material already
presented. Theorists in the Classical period attached
more importance to the first than the second of these.[8]
Even where a composer chooses a 'free fantasia' type of
development not based on thematic material from the
exposition, or decides to introduce new themes, the state
of tonal flux still prevails. What Schubert does in the last
stage of an exposition is quite different. The purpose of
this section is to stabilise the tonality, for the time being:
the 'deviant' tonality of the second subject is to be superseded by the expected dominant, which must be unequi-
vocally enthroned. When Schubert 'develops' his second
subject at this point, in this fixed tonal framework, he
does so only in those limited ways open to a composer
whose purpose is to confirm a key rather than promote
tonal instability. A different range of options awaits him
in the 'development' section – different enough to give
old and well-worked material a distinctly fresh complexion. In any case, the development section may totally
ignore the second subject, as many do. There is no rule,
based on aesthetics rather than dogma, which forbids

[7]'Franz Schubert', in Hubert J. Foss (ed.), *The Heritage of Music*,
Oxford University Press, London, 1927, pp. 106 and 110.

[8]*Cf.* L. Ratner, 'Harmonic Aspects of Classic Form', *Journal of the Amer-
ican Musicological Society*, Vol. 2., No. 3, 1949.

development in this Schubertian sense outside a development section. When Beethoven does the same thing, as
he often does, he is applauded (by Tovey among others)
for bending sonata-form to make it the servant of his ideas.

The second movement of D708A is, as expected, a slow
movement. The key is A major, and the opening theme
(Ex. 57) is more characterful than it would have been had
Schubert not changed the second note, B, to G sharp,
and the fifth note, D, to B sharp.

Ex. 57

A section in the minor follows, and after the first theme
has then been recalled in F major Schubert introduces a
passage in double counterpoint – a device so far rare in
his symphonic writing. Perhaps it was the elegant beauty
of this passage, in which instruments in the treble and
tenor registers sustain a shapely dialogue over a steady
bass line (Ex. 58), the two conversing voices later changing places, that persuaded Schubert to take more interest
in contrapuntal device in his later instrumental works –
including the third movement of this very symphony.

Ex. 58

A few bars further on, after an evocative digression, a
hastily implied cadence in F is the last thing penned in
this promisingly lovely movement.

The character of the following scherzo, in D major,
suggests a new determination to investigate counterpoint
as a symphonic force. To some extent it goes against
Schubert's nature, for he had made little use of counterpoint of the formal sort in his earlier symphonies. But
this exercise in fugal writing, double counterpoint and
canon succeeds well, even brilliantly, and should have
gone some way towards allaying any fears he may have
had that contrapuntal device was not compatible with his
natural lyricism. Unfinished works can be as significant
for aspects of a composer's development as finished ones.
Anyway, he took the trouble to leave the movement in a
much more advanced stage of completion than any other
movement of this symphony.

The first theme (Ex. 59) is represented in a four-part
fugal exposition obviously conceived for strings, although
Schubert does not specify this instrumentation. The four
entries are all marked *pianissimo*, and lead directly to a
fortissimo restatement of the theme, now with a distinctive
counter-theme added in the bass (Ex. 60).

Ex. 59

Ex. 60

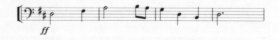

There is a quick modulation to the dominant, where the
counter-theme immediately appears over the original
theme, thus exploiting the invertibility of the counterpoint.

But what sets the seal on Schubert's contrapuntal
ingenuity is that he then recalls the original countersubject (begun in the lower part in the fifth bar of
Ex. 59), combining it with a new derivative in parallel
thirds of the first theme (Ex. 61).

Ex. 61

These two newly combined elements constitute invertible
counterpoint, although Schubert does not exploit this
invertibility; but it seems safe to assume that if he had
gone on to compose the reprise within the second section
of the scherzo, he would almost certainly have used the
inversion there. Meanwhile, the new derivative (Ex. 61)
has another value: after the further developments that
take place in the long first section, it can act most effectively as a 'closing theme'.

It also begins the second section – a development, since
this is a miniature sonata-form; but it is now prefaced by
three crotchets of scale-ascent, and in this new form it becomes the subject of a forceful two-part canon which is
the apt climax of the development. Thereafter the tension is unwound, and the way paved for a recapitulation.
Schubert composes right up to this recapitulation, but
saves himself the trouble of writing even the first note of
the recapitulation itself.[9] Instead, he proceeds directly
to the trio, the first theme of which is marked for the
clarinet, and gives a texturally full sketch of the whole
trio but for its last seven bars, which can be deduced without difficulty. Even at the point where the second section

[9] There are sketches for 115 bars of scherzo. The revised Deutsch catalogue gives the total as 113, presumably because the compiler has
overlooked the repeat-signs enclosing bars 34–35. The same catalogue
gives the theme of the second movement with two misprints.

of the trio breaks off Schubert is in the process of inverting some counterpoint introduced in its first section.

As far as the composer was concerned, it is possible that this sketch was virtually complete. He had left only two spare staves between the unfinished scherzo and the trio. This gap was not enough room for the scherzo's recapitulation, which he would not have sketched but would have composed when making his orchestral score.

There remains one feature of the movement which must not pass without comment. Although Schubert abandoned the scherzo, along with the rest of the symphony, he salvaged its first bar and – some four years later – used it to begin the scherzo of his 'Great' C major Symphony. The later scherzo is a more heavyweight affair, largely lacking the counterpoint, sometimes delicate, sometimes incisive, of the earlier scherzo. But again he introduces a slower-moving second theme, initially triadic as in Ex. 60, as a foil to the first.

More than half-way through this D708A symphony, Schubert still cared enough about it to see that its third movement was virtually complete. The fact that he then sketched twenty bars of finale but crossed them through and began again with completely different material suggests that the will to make a viable complete symphony was with him into the finale. The discarded opening was rejected probably because it began in B minor and hovered uneasily between that key and D major, just as it hovered uneasily between $\frac{2}{4}$ and $\frac{6}{8}$ time. Schubert was later to master the out-of-key opening to a finale, in such instances as the last B flat Piano Sonata, D960. In this instance he seems to have found his opening too indecisive, and the material not promising enough for symphonic use. His second attempt at the finale was again in $\frac{2}{4}$ with triplets present, but the triplets are so pervasive that the aural impression is of $\frac{6}{8}$ time with an occasional $\frac{2}{4}$ overlay.

Schubert indicates clearly that the first theme is for solo flute, with a light string accompaniment. It is a gently rejoicing *moto perpetuo*. The *tutti* after-statement, long delayed and preceded by a short crescendo, is impelled by a variant in the bass, and leads to a second subject in F major (Ex. 62). Before long Schubert makes a further transition to A major where, according to a familiar Schubertian three-key plan, the second subject is restated. Soon a further transition leads to F sharp minor, where the second subject appears in an approximate inversion (Ex. 63).

Ex. 62

Ex. 63

The rate of travel to other keys increases until a climactic chord of A flat major is reached, followed by one of C sharp major. This evidently occurs in mid-development, and after a rather protracted period of relaxation Schubert swerves to A major, begins a reprise of the first theme in that key, and sets down his pen.

Through all this section Schubert either indicates or implies that a pretty consistent thread of triplet quavers runs, as a bass or an inner accompaniment. Indeed, it would seem that it is absent for only six bars of the 227-bar fragment. The piece thus acquires a regular *moto perpetuo* character which, given the $\frac{6}{8}$ metre, is reminiscent of the tarantella-like finale of the Third Symphony. Perhaps Schubert was aware of the likeness; perhaps he was deliberately casting an eye back to what he may have regarded as his most recent totally successful symphonic finale, in the hope that he might will himself to achieve another sure-fire success. At any rate, if the last thing he put on paper in D708A, the reprise of the first theme in A major, is taken as the beginning of a recapitulation in a movement in sonata-form, the key (A major, the dominant) is exactly the same as that used for the recapitulation in the Third Symphony (both symphonies are in D). These are the only two movements in Schubert's symphonic *œuvre* which have dominant recapitulations.

Why did Schubert leave this symphony, and others, not to mention numerous non-symphonic works, unfinished? There are several possible reasons for incompletion, and in every case except that which is discussed in chapter XV of this study[10] it is possible that two or more of them were contributing factors:

(a) compositional obstacles to continuation;
(b) dissatisfaction with the material sketched;
(c) problems of orchestration, in the case of a piano sketch;
(d) in the period 1818–22, problems caused by fast stylistic development;
(e) distraction from the task in hand, caused by
   (i) enormous appetite for composition in a wide variety of media;
   (ii) rival motivation for song-composition, related more directly to his circle of friends, and involving personal friendships and loyalties;
   (iii) other more urgent tasks (such as operatic ventures);
   (iv) illness;
(f) poor prospects of performance;
(g) demoralisation in the face of Beethoven's instrumental genius.

Factors (f) and (g) could have affected any work from 1818 on, when Otto Hatwig had abandoned his music salons, and Beethoven had become almost a legend in his

---

[10] *Cf.* especially pp. 259 and 268.

lifetime. Factor (a) would not have hindered the completion of D708A, but factor (c) may have done: could it be,
for example, that the inability of the valveless horns and
trumpets, and of the kettledrums, to provide for Schubert any notes at all in the climactic chords of A flat major
and C sharp major in the finale was a deterrent? It is not
clear whether factor (e) affected D708A, but the outcome
may well have turned on a combination of factors (b) and
(d), particularly (d). It was only in six months or so that
Schubert was to begin the Seventh Symphony, which
marks a considerable stylistic advance on D708A. Impatient
to find a new, more distinctive symphonic style, perhaps
to correspond with the astonishing advance in chamber-
music style already made with the *Quartettsatz* in C minor
of 1820, he could have found that even a few days after
sketching D708A he saw in it grounds for dissatisfaction
with the symphonic outlook it represented as measured
against the vision he had for the future (realised partly in
the Seventh, and more fully in the Eighth and Ninth).

Lacking a full chronicle of the day-to-day pressures,
compositional or otherwise, which governed Schubert's
pattern of work at any time in his career, his biographers
and critics can do no more than conjecture on these
matters. The range of possibilities obliges them to keep a
fairly open mind. In particular, it should never be too
readily assumed that any work abandoned by Schubert
was necessarily an inferior product: the quality of the
Quartettsatz could surely have no bearing on the incompletion of the 1820 Quartet in C minor. To see the position
in a more relative setting, it is worth reflecting that in a
sense an artist's *finished* works are merely sketches, but
their creators feel impelled to go on and produce new
works rather than go back and revise (or 'realise') these
earlier efforts. To some extent an artist may move on to
create further new works in order to re-embody older
experiences (those already embodied in works finished
earlier) in new ways or with the keener vision and technique of maturity. He does not normally suppress the

sketches (that is, the earlier finished works). For Schubert in 1828, his First Symphony of 1813 and an unfinished symphony of 1821 may have been of equal importance. For posterity, though, there is the problem of relative accessibility. The musical world today, or in Schubert's time for that matter, has no mechanism for 'marketing' unfinished works, while by virtue of its finished state a complete work is at once eligible for entry into a repertory, as soon as composed or at any time thereafter. In terms of market value, an unfinished musical work is worth almost nothing, except as a collectors' item.[11] It is patently not that to its composer. Since Schubert may possibly have heard as few as two of his symphonies performed, it is easy to realise that for him the object of finishing a symphony on paper rather than finishing it only in his head would have been merely to secure some small chance of having it played.

It is not out of the question, moreover, that for him the urge to compose was stronger than the desire to secure performances, and that the act of composing today and the prospect of composing tomorrow were more important than the fate of what he had composed yesterday, whether or not yesterday's work was finished. His mental completion of the work would probably have brought him some fulfilment. It seems unlikely that D708A was finished in Schubert's head, but it remains possible that it was, and that work on a new project was more inviting than the mechanical chore of committing to paper, perhaps to no purpose at all, the residue of the symphony still existing only in his thoughts. With his next unfinished symphony, the Seventh, that possibility is less hard to accept.

[11] An obvious exception is Schubert's Symphony No. 8, which is not so much an unfinished work as a finished half-work.

XI

Glimpse of Transition:
The Seventh Symphony

Only a few months passed before Schubert began his E
major Symphony, now known as the Seventh,[1] in
August 1821. His renewed appetite for symphonic writing at this time may be attributable in part to the pattern
of his other composing work in the years 1820–21. He
had begun the oratorio *Lazarus* and abandoned it towards
the end of the second act. With his opera *Sakuntala* he
had got only as far as sketching two acts. He did complete
the commissioned *Die Zauberharfe*, a spectacular magic
play demanding little of the composer that he could not
supply by studying current popular taste and applying his
professionalism to meeting it. And he began a Mass
which he evidently took more seriously, setting it aside
and returning to finish it after a two-year gestation, in
1822 (the Mass in A flat, D678). Although he was failing,
in one obvious sense, as a composer of large-scale projects, it was here that his present ambitions lay, and he
was not to be deflected: for month after month, few or no
songs appeared. If he suffered bouts of despair, he
would not be helped by reflecting on the abortive symphonic efforts of D615 and D708A. But he could only
have taken heart if he recalled what he must have

[1] A note on the numeration of the symphonies is given in Appendix 2
(pp. 291–93).

recognised as the signal success of the *Quartettsatz* in
C minor in December 1820. Here was a piece which,
alone in this period, satisfied two pressing requirements:
it was completed down to the last note, and it displayed
new powers of expression and technique in both the
detail and wholeness of its structure. Schubert's work
on *Lazarus* and *Sakuntala* perhaps left him ready for
a change of outlet. *Lazarus*, in particular, shows no arrest
in the development of the composer's expressive powers
or appetite for sustained invention. A symphony would
offer respite from working to a text or dramatic scheme,
and allow him to liberate in a different (but favourite)
context the powers recently consolidated in those other
areas. Although, as it turned out, Schubert was destined
to be back at the operatic drawing-board in little over
a month's time, with another unfinished symphony
in his drawer, the Seventh was to be a valuable and possibly indispensable step on the path to later symphonic
success.

The sketch, which after Schubert's death was passed by
his brother Ferdinand to Mendelssohn, and eventually
found its way into the possession of George Grove, who
bequeathed it to the Royal College of Music in London,[2]
is unique among Schubert manuscripts. It is entirely in
orchestral score. Schubert completed a slow introduction
and 110 bars of the first movement proper; this much is
fully composed and scored. Thereafter he evidently
decided that the burden of filling fourteen staves of score
was checking the pace of his thought to an adverse
degree, and so from this point on he proceeded to write
only a leading melodic line; it is usually assigned to the
violins, but sometimes to a woodwind instrument. On
occasions a fragment of bass line is given too, and at

[2] The sketch remains at the RCM to this day (not at the British
Museum, as stated by Brown in *Schubert: A Critical Biography*, Macmillan, London, 1958, p. 112, and *Schubert Symphonies*, p. 39).

points where a change of texture is required some clue of that is also given. At its fullest point the sketch has seven of the fourteen staves filled.

Schubert completed not only the first movement but also the remaining three movements in this way. At the beginning of each · fresh movement the names of the instruments are newly written in, and for every page orchestral paper is used although most of the staves remain empty. On the last page of the symphony a bold double-bar is drawn in, and the word *Fine* is written across the middle of the page with a flourish. The work was indeed finished in a structural sense, for every bar is present, and there is at least a note – or a rest – in each one. Yet more than two-thirds of the symphony consists of a single line of music only – that is, about 950 of a total of 1,340 bars. But Schubert knew what he was doing. He left space for the missing instrumental parts, throughout the score, because he was seeing to it at every juncture that the sketch was of the minimal fullness to enable him to complete the symphony at a later date. Readers of the sketch today may at first be inclined to doubt whether it is full enough for that purpose. The more one reflects on Schubert's way of composing symphonies and considers the scraps of evidence on this matter,[3] the more these doubts will be dispelled.

If, when he had penned his *Fine* to indicate complete-ness in the mind if not on paper, there was no immediate prospect of a performance of the work, he could reason-ably have decided to put it to one side for a short period. (Hatwig's music salons had ceased in 1818, and although the players continued to meet at the apartment of Anton von Pettenkoffer they seem to have been concerned there with oratorios above all; in any case, the circle abandoned its activities, according to Leopold von Sonnleithner,[4]

[3] *Cf.* chapter XIV, pp. 247–57.

[4] In Deutsch, *Schubert: Memoirs by his Friends,* pp. 340–41.

when Pettenkoffer left Vienna in 1820.) Schubert had, in
any event, planned to leave Vienna in September 1821 to
spend a few weeks at St Pölten in order to work with
Schober[5] on an opera. The opera was *Alfonso und
Estrella*, and the two men duly arrived at St Pölten to
begin work. The first act is dated 20 September 1821.
The opera occupied Schubert for most of the remainder
of 1821, and early in 1822 he was busy seeing to the publication of various works. If the symphony was obliged to
lie unattended for so long, it may well have fallen victim
to the composer's impatient ambition to find a new symphonic voice. A few months before he found that voice in
the Eighth Symphony (dated September 1822) he may
well have found that his current aspirations in symphonic
style had moved on since the previous year's symphony,
leaving him less inclined to finish it (and perhaps less able
to without stylistic incongruity) than to contemplate a new
symphony.

To the reader of Schubert's sketch, the first pages of
the Seventh Symphony are impressive in a number of
ways. First, there is the atmosphere of the introduction,
which is a solemn and dignified but also moving *Adagio* in
the minor leading to a particularly bright and spirited
Allegro in the major. The contrast is starker than Schubert
had achieved in earlier symphonies, yet it is achieved
without the remote harmonic and tonal colouring which
suffused his previous slow introduction, in D615, or that
of the *Tragic* Symphony. And it is achieved despite the
risk Schubert takes in anticipating the advent of the
major key by including a nine-bar passage in E major in
the introduction. Only once before had he prefaced his
first movement, in a major-key symphony, with an introduction in the minor – in D615 three years earlier (1818).

---

[5] Franz von Schober, poet and dilettante, provided Schubert with texts
for several of his songs, including *An die Musik*. A man of private
means, he several times offered accommodation to Schubert at his
own premises (in 1816, 1822–23, 1826, and 1827–28).

'Fine' writes Schubert at the end of his orchestral sketch of
the Symphony No. 7 in E, D729. The first violins appear at the
top, the remainder of the page lying empty, as is the case for
two-thirds of the forty-minute work (Royal College of
Music, London)

Between these two symphonies, in 1819, he had done two
things that may have a bearing on this aspect of the
Seventh. He had composed an Overture in E minor/
major which anticipates the symphony's progress from E
minor to E major in its first movement. And he had
begun to make his own copy of the score of Beethoven's
Fourth Symphony, which is the only symphony by Beethoven to preface a major-key first movement with a slow
introduction in the minor. If Schubert had taken that
work as a demonstration of the potential for extreme

contrast between an introduction and an *Allegro*, he could
hardly have done better.

The second impressive feature is Schubert's inclusion
of three trombones in the score. The third is a new depth
and grandeur of sonority, announcing a new sound-
world in the context of a Schubert symphony. The two
circumstances are doubtless related, as chicken and egg.
Did Schubert conceive a sonority, and decide that it
called for trombones? Or did he decide that now was
the time to add these instruments to his symphonic resource, and devise an orchestral texture that
exploited their presence? Whatever the answers may be,
the weight of the *tutti* sections marvellously sets off such
moments as the hushed close of the introduction. The
Adagio had begun with a two-note motive in the clarinets
(supported by bassoons) in rising sequences above a
steady marching bass from the strings plucked in unison
(Ex. 64).[6]

Ex. 64

At the close, after a pause on a dominant seventh
which ends the E major section, the first bar returns
exactly as it was (Ex. 65). A half-bar silence delays the
sequence, which is chromatically modified, and transferred to bowed strings, with the plucked bass now
transformed as a whispered descant in the flutes. The
remote harmonic region touched on here has a

[6] In the incipit given in the revised Deutsch catalogue there are two
errors in the transposition of the clarinets.

Ex. 65

further half-bar in which to resound before the two-note motive is brought back to the home dominant in readiness for the *Allegro*. These final bars of introduction exert the magic of Schubert at his best – a magic to be explained, as far as explanation is possible, by the radical re-interpretation of the motive by three means: metrical displacement (which itself gives it a new meaning), a profound change of orchestral colour, and a daring harmonic dislocation.

In the *Allegro* theme that follows (Ex. 66) there is already a trace of the Rossini influence, noted also in connection with the Sixth Symphony. Whatever its provenance[7] it is an exhilarating tune, whose five-bar phrase-structure makes it Schubert rather than Rossini.

Ex. 66

It is extended to considerable lengths, though for not a bar too long, before the full orchestra enters *fortissimo* with the after-statement. This after-statement gradually assumes a transitional role, and it is shortly before the last formal cadences heralding the second subject that Schubert gives up the attempt to maintain a full score. The

[7]It is also reminiscent of the second subject (first movement) of Beethoven's Second Symphony (bars 74–6 of that movement).

second subject is preceded by a two-bar silence. The silence seems long, perhaps too long, yet it is certain that Schubert intended it. If he had wanted something to happen in those bars, he would have given a hint of it. He had taken a similar risk two years earlier in the Overture in E minor (D648). At the equivalent point, before a second subject in the same key as in the symphony, the note B is held for four whole bars by flute and oboe in octaves (*pianissimo*), while nothing else happens. Moreover, in the song 'Der Wegweiser' ('The Signpost') in *Die Winterreise* (1827) Schubert separates the third stanza from the second with a similarly arresting cæsura. The silence looks short on paper but sounds long in performance: if one sees through the written notation, taking differences in tempo and time-signature into account, and judges the length of the silence in proportion to the real (heard) pulse of the music, the two examples (that in 'Der Wegweiser' and that in the Seventh Symphony) are almost identical.

The second subject, whose short phrases tend to be too restricted in pitch, treading the same ground repetitiously like a caged beast, is in G major, the flat mediant. Its final strain finds itself surprisingly, and refreshingly, in B flat major, from where a short transitional passage, which looks forward in its atmosphere to the Eighth Symphony, leads to B major for the third phase of Schubert's typical three-key exposition. This can be conveniently called a codetta, although it is based on the second rather than the first subject. It forms a fine climax to the exposition, but at the same time moves irrevocably forward to the next stage of the movement, for Schubert avoids the expected clear-cut cadential ending in B major which will lead easily to a repeat of the exposition. Instead, he turns abruptly at the last minute and closes the exposition on the threshold of C major, in which key the first theme returns after a short link. Thus he has ruled out any possibility of the exposition being repeated, which is not short-sighted in that this first movement has already

Schubert's room at the house in Wipplingerstrasse 15 where the Symphony No. 7 in E, D729, was sketched. Etching by Leo Diet from an ink drawing by von Schwind (1821). (Historisches Museum, Vienna).

committed itself to a scale of design so large that it will outlast any of his previous symphonic first movements, even if their repeats are observed.[8] This subtle bonding of exposition to development is the first of several structural

[8] The lack of exposition repeat is a feature of overtures, common to all of Schubert's overtures and Rossini's too.

procedures which appear in the Seventh for the first time in Schubert's symphonies.

The development has two main concerns. The first is to allow the first and second subjects to confront each other, fragments of the second punctuating (in the woodwind) the various segments of the first in the strings. The second is to generate a steady build-up over a gradually rising bass, which will both encompass a rich succession of harmonic vistas and lead to the restoration of E major for the recapitulation.

At the point of recapitulation comes the second new structural device. Schubert omits the first subject, which has enjoyed considerable exposure in the development, and goes straight into the after-statement. Thus the recapitulation can begin as a *fortissimo* climax and resolution of the development, and again two sections have been firmly bonded together. The transition is adapted so that the second subject can return in the conventional tonic key, and further adjustments bring the so-called codetta back in that key too. As the codetta was a particularly successful part of the exposition, it would be unreasonable to complain that Schubert now makes full use of it again, suitably transposed down a fifth. If he had done the usual thing and repeated the exposition it would then have been heard twice in any case. Where it originally veered at the last minute from B major to the threshold of C major for the development, it now veers from E major to the threshold of F major, where the coda begins rather as the development did. Schubert had not had the opportunity to write a symphonic coda for three years, since he had not progressed that far in any movement undertaken since the Sixth Symphony. He had the resource now to construct a bigger and more imposing coda than any in the earlier symphonies, and one appropriate to the scale and bearing of the movement it concludes.

Schubert obviously admired the formal clarity of Haydn and Mozart, and on the whole accepted it as a cornerstone of his own endeavours in instrumental composition.

That he so frankly aligned himself with that tradition in his Fifth Symphony suggests that he felt a deep-rooted affiliation to Classical ideals. There was an element of caution too. His experience in other spheres of composition was all the time inclining him towards a richer expression that must at some point threaten the relatively conventional propriety of his symphonic thought. In the Seventh Symphony he was ready to meet this challenge. In the first place, he was content to let the flow of ideas take precedence over formalism. If it can be said of his earlier symphonic *allegri* that the ear could never mistake his double-bars, this view is far less tenable in the case of the first movement of the Seventh, which is his most seamless sonata-form structure to date. The sheer thrust of invention seems to take over, leaving the listener to ask himself at any point 'Where has Schubert reached in the sonata-form scheme now?' – at any point, that is, after the arrival of the second subject, for Schubert does make a ceremony of that, and the cæsura is a welcome one even if its length is misconceived. In the second place, Schubert is more inclined in this symphony to enjoy the passing moment, to find scope for Romantic colour, to sketch in an ear-tickling texture (like that of the second subject of the finale). This inclination is especially evident in transitional passages: Schubert increases their number, and treats them as opportunities for heart-easing modulations which are quite up-to-date in the chronicle of his developing style and which point ahead into and beyond this new-born Romantic decade of *Der Freischütz*. Since Schubert is merely sketching his intentions, his manuscript does not always show the method of modulation fully mapped out; but several of the transitions do have their harmony fairly clearly indicated, and in less fully-formed instances the imagination (if fed on a knowledge of his habits at this time) can deduce what he probably had in mind.

The growing obsession with the concept of transition affects the slow movement no less than the first movement.

Indeed, this gentle A major *Andante* in $\frac{6}{8}$ time might almost be subtitled 'Themes and Transitions': Schubert articulates his concise sonata-form-without-development as if with that effect in mind. The first theme, for which the harmony is not supplied, has a simple lyric grace, although some chromatic colouring would surely have warmed the harmony of its fourth bar (Ex. 67).[9]

Ex. 67

It is stated first by the strings, then by the wind, whereupon a short transition melts into D major for a second theme, which begins in the bass (Ex. 68).

Ex. 68

The next transition lights up several key-areas in succession but eventually settles for F sharp minor, where clarinets in thirds introduce a poignant third theme rhythmically related to the first (Ex. 69).

Ex. 69

The rest of the story is briefly told. The shortest transition of all links the end of this third theme to the recapitulation of the first, and all three themes are duly heard

---

[9] I am indebted to Todd Crow for pointing out that the first four notes of this theme are a retrograde of the first four notes of the slow movement of Beethoven's Second Symphony, in the same key of A major. One can only guess by what subconscious process, if any, Schubert derived his idea from Beethoven's.

again with modified transitions between (how Schubert enjoys modifying them!), a short coda based on the first theme laying the movement to rest.

The terms 'first subject' and 'second subject' have been avoided in this outline account of a movement in sonata-form, and not without reason. Is the third theme really a 'second theme within the second group'? Or is the second theme a second theme of the first group? Or has Schubert invented a three-subject exposition in some way analogous with his familiar three-*key* exposition? The reader will have to make up his or her own mind. The keys of the three themes when recapitulated (A major, F major, and A minor) do not provide an unassailable answer. And it is not appropriate to fall back on the usual convenience of calling the third theme a codetta, for it is so obviously a theme and not a codetta. Anyway, this haunting little movement has a build, as well as an eloquence, of its own, and it could only have been written at this time in Schubert's life. It clearly stands closer in spirit, style and technique to the Eighth Symphony than to the youthful works that preceded it. At the same time, while the slow movements of the 'Unfinished' and the 'Great' C major chart territory left uncharted by this movement, there is something special and wondrous here that those later slow movements did not recapture, nor tried to.

For the second time in his career, Schubert uses the title 'Scherzo' for the third movement of a symphony. For the second time, he chooses the key of C major (although the symphony is in E).[10] And for the second time, he follows the C major scherzo with a trio in A major. These parallels could be a coincidence, but that he does all these

---

[10] Brahms is known to have seen the sketch of this symphony and to have been impressed and touched by it (letter to Joachim, December 1868, referred to by Hans Gál in *Franz Schubert and the Essence of Melody*, p. 160). Could it be that the memory of a symphony which began in E minor and had a scherzo in C major stayed with him until the time he planned his own Fourth Symphony, which adopts the same scheme?

things again four years later in the 'Great' makes it a significant coincidence. Schubert had found himself as a composer of symphonic scherzos in the Sixth, having moved gingerly towards the genre in his previous symphonies. Perhaps having won this confidence in C major he found that the ideas for the present scherzo involuntarily came to him in that key. There would be no reason to reject the key. He had cast his third movement in a key other than the title-key in the Second, Fourth and Fifth Symphonies, and C major was as close to hand now as were the keys chosen then.

This scherzo is an altogether weightier affair than that of the Sixth. For one thing, it is conceived for an orchestra including trombones. For another, it begins with a noisy presentation of its theme (Ex. 70) followed by a soft presentation, rather than vice versa; and at its opposite end, a steady growth in sonority (obvious from the sketch even where only a melodic line is given) leads to a prolonged, resounding peroration.

Ex. 70

Not only in its weighty bearing but in other points of style too, this scherzo is the natural precursor of the scherzo in the Ninth Symphony. This prophetic aspect is underlined when, at its close, a sustained and unaccompanied E swings the music from C major (whose third it is) to A major (where it acts as fifth) for the trio. The repeated (rather than sustained) Es at the same place in the 'Great' act as a pivot between the same two keys in exactly the same way.

Parts of the trio sketch have fairly full indications of scoring. The violas are used more prominently than Schubert had dared before: *divisi*, they present the theme, doubled by the bassoons. A new, rich vein of lyricism is attempted here, and it is closer to chamber music than to the massive swinging dance found at this point in the 'Great' C major. Schubert composes a few special linking bars to lead back from the trio to the scherzo, as he did in the Sixth Symphony.

No clue to the stature of the finale is given by its opening. It begins, like Mozart's Symphony No. 40, with an accompaniment which is little more than an activated tonic chord. To it the first violins add a tune (Ex. 71). But neither Schubert's tune nor his accompaniment have anything to do with the pathos of the Mozart example. They are as bright and bouncy as Rossini, although there are inflections – especially towards the end of the first long paragraph Schubert makes of them – which could only have come from their author.

Ex. 71

As the after-statement duly follows, with a blaze of orchestral *tutti*, there is still no hint that this is to be the most innovative and forward-looking movement of the symphony. A Schubert after-statement usually takes some aspect of the first theme as its starting-point. This one begins with held notes and scale-flourishes that are entirely new, and only at the end of the phrase is it thematically cemented into context by an eleventh-hour reference to the initial motive of the first theme (*x* in Ex. 72).

Ex. 72

In this instance the after-statement does not show itself, at some point in its course, to be a transition. It clings to the tonic key – in spite of some sideways pulls – and closes affirmatively therein. Only then comes the transition, soft, mysterious, and relatively short. It is impelled by the figure *y* in Ex. 72, and when this turns out to be but an anticipation of the imminent second subject (Ex. 73), it is clear that the tail of the after-statement (Ex. 72) has neatly sewn together the first and second subjects, in what is presumably a sublime artistic accident.

Ex. 73

The second subject is in G major, reflecting the practice of the first movement, but the texture Schubert sets up in his sketch at this point is remarkable. It offers the kind of variegated interest found in Schubert's writing for the large chamber ensembles – in the slow movement of the String Quintet, D956, for example, or the first movement of the 'Trout' Quintet, D667, bars 75–84. Against new repeated triplets in the middle strings, the cellos pluck a rising scale-figure, while the first violins repeat the head of the first theme. But all this is only an 'accompaniment': the flute enters shortly with the second subject itself, and the accompanying texture is clearly intended to continue, and develop, beneath it. Thus the combining of first and second subject elements, already seen in the after-statement, is more overtly a feature of the second subject itself. The ear has to focus on two leading melodic lines, in the flute and first violins, undistracted by comments from the cellos which are hardly self-effacing. It is a daring and imaginative textural scheme, and a novel one. (The presence of traces of first-subject rhythm below the second subject of the first movement of Beethoven's Fifth Symphony, for example, poses no such problems of aural focus.)

Schubert has at this point reached the second span of a three-key exposition, the third part of which is to be in the dominant, B major. But he imparts a new expansiveness to this scheme. After the long second subject and its appendages have closed, still in G major, he introduces a transition of some two dozen bars to link it to the third section in B major (which is based on existing material, mainly from the second subject, and so would be called 'codetta'). This transition is highly developmental. Schubert enlarges his vision still more by inserting into the B major section a colourful digression to C major. With B major restored, he then writes two alternative endings to the exposition. The first, comprising the 'first-time bars', is designed to lead back to the beginning for a repeat of the exposition. Schubert took care to finalise every detail of these bars, a clear enough indication that he wished the repeat to be observed and was not absent-mindedly or half-heartedly adopting an outworn convention.

The second-time bars lead likewise to a resumption of the first subject, now within the development. This development is noteworthy for its stripping down of the texture, hand-in-hand with the avoidance of any action-packed drama such as is often generated in a development by contrapuntal cut-and-thrust. The two characteristics coincide in extreme manner at the point where the first horn softly repeats the first four notes of the first

theme, joined shortly by the second horn. Harmonic
action is here suspended: only the maintained rhythmic
activity averts total disintegration. The result is a kind of
'animated stasis' that prophesies Bruckner. When
Bruckner achieves this state, again the stasis is harmonic – and melodic in that thematic scraps are liqui-
dated or repeatedly self-effacingly – while the animation
often takes the form of string tremoli. Examples may be
found in the Ninth Symphony (first movement, bars
153–66), the Seventh (first movement, bars 311–20), and
the Fourth (finale, bars 221–48).

A delayed accretion of texture and dynamics indicates
that the recapitulation is approaching. The final gestures
heralding the recapitulation are rhetorical, almost vulgar;
but they serve to prepare the way for the recapitulation
to begin not with the first theme, nor with the after-statement (as in the first movement), but with the tail of the
after-statement's first phrase (from *y* in Ex. 72). Following
this imaginative elision, the spirit of development spills
over into the ensuing continuation of the after-statement,
which instead of clinging to its initial key as before roves
from E major to G major and to B major. A revised transition then opens the way to C major for the second subject, the key of the flattened submediant acting as
Beethovenian resolution – or at least counterpoise – to
the flattened mediant in which the second subject first
appeared.

As Schubert lets the second subject run its entire course
in this key, it is natural enough that the codetta (in E,
bringing the awaited tonal resolution) is extended into a
big coda. This coda not only consolidates the tonal resolution, but also casts fascinating new light on all the thematic ingredients of the movement. Such a comprehensive
coda, to a rich and spaciously planned finale, merits a
special highpoint. When the highpoint comes – and Schubert reserves his triple *forte* for it – it is a clamorous turn
to the subdominant that unmistakably echoes the thun-
derous climactic subdominant turn for which Beethoven

reserves *his* triple *forte* at the end of his Seventh Symphony.[11]

A work written down in such a way that the composer can make fast progress in delineating its structure will perhaps have a stronger inherent unity than one which is the result of a more laboured approach. The unity is likely to be more spontaneous and less contrived. Large-scale works of Mozart and Schubert, two 'speedy' composers whose relationship in the matter of conceiving and writing down music is discussed further in chapter XIV,[12] often display a subtle, almost casual unity that one fancies could only be accidental. The principal unifying features in the Seventh Symphony are of this type. The themes of the slow introduction and first *Allegro* share a common initial contour (compare *x* in Ex. 64 with *y* in Ex. 66) although no show is made of the connection, and of course the immense contrast in tempo helps to conceal it. Still more interesting is the common underlying phrase-structure shared by the opening themes of this first *Allegro*, the second movement, and the third movement. All are based on a five-bar phrase-length. (In the second movement it is five half-bars, and in the third five pairs of bars, but these are merely notational differences.) In each case the phrase is essentially a four-bar one expanded from within: the second bar (or half-bar, or pair of bars) is followed by an immediate repetition or near-repetition of itself. This construction, quite distinct from the five-bar phrase which opens the B flat Trio, D898 (a clear 4+1), is not unknown elsewhere in Schubert[13] but in no other work does it have a such an obsessive (yet unobtrusive) influence. These three themes also share a remarkably similar contour, as far as their first

[11] Indeed, Beethoven's *fff* at this point represents his first use of this marking in any symphony. He was evidently well aware of the cataclysmic nature of this climax, as was Schubert.

[12] *Cf.* pp. 247–57.

[13] *Cf.*, for example, the finale of the A minor String Quartet.

phrases are concerned, although again the resemblance is barely explicit, let alone ostentatious.[14]

If Schubert had died at the end of 1821 his sketched Seventh Symphony would then have been seen in the same way as his sketched Tenth is now seen. It would have signalled, tantalisingly, a dramatic leap forward in style destined to have unknown and unimaginable consequences. What new kind of symphony might he have written thereafter? With the knowledge of the 'Unfinished' and the 'Great', today's listener knows the answer to this hypothetical question. But generations of Schubert-lovers have begun with the 'Unfinished' and 'Great', and not known the Seventh. The inverted question, raised by the 'Unfinished' and 'Great', and to be answered by the Seventh, is thus: how did Schubert accomplish the vast stylistic step that marks off the Eighth Symphony from the Sixth of four years earlier? The Seventh provides a fascinating link, reflecting the familiar middle-period Schubert, assimilating (especially in its themes) his current interest in Rossini, and anticipating – in its transitions rather than its themes, but not exclusively so – several facets of the sound-worlds to come in the imminent masterpieces of the fully mature symphonist.

[14] This kinship is diagrammatically elucidated in Brian Newbould, 'La Symphonie No. 7 en mi majeur et sa réalisation', in *La Revue musicale*, triple numéro 355-356-357 (*Franz Schubert et la symphonie*), Paris, 1982.

XII

Immortality without End:
The Eighth Symphony

The work in which Schubert truly came to symphonic manhood followed little more than a year after the Seventh. It must have been in September or October 1822 that he began to compose his Eighth Symphony in B minor. After a few weeks' work, and with ostensibly only two movements absolutely complete, he shelved the symphony. The resultant torso has come down to us as the 'Unfinished', a name applied since the second half of the nineteenth century. As the enigma of its incompletion has been amply discussed elsewhere,[1] it is necessary here only to outline the facts of the work's history and summarise the main strands of speculation.

Schubert began writing his full score on 30 October 1822. With two movements completed, he began the orchestration of the third but broke off after two pages. Earlier, he had made preliminary piano sketches of at least three movements. Of these sketches all but the first part of the opening movement have survived. A possible

---

[1] Chiefly in Gerald Abraham (ed.), *Schubert: A Symposium*, pp. 63–4; Maurice J. E. Brown, *Schubert: A Critical Biography*, pp. 119–21; articles by Otto Erich Deutsch and Martin Chusid, in Martin Chusid (ed.), *Schubert: Symphony in B minor ('Unfinished')*, Norton Critical Score, Norton, New York/Chappell, London, 1968, pp. 91–110; and Hans Gál, *Franz Schubert and the Essence of Melody*, pp. 152–77.

clue to the date on which this sketch was begun is thus
lost, for Schubert would probably have dated the first
page. In September 1823 Schubert received an honorary
diploma from the Styrian Music Society in Graz. He
wrote an acknowledgement to the Society on 20 September, adding: 'So as to express my sincere gratitude in
music too, I shall soon be taking the liberty of presenting
to your honourable Society one of my symphonies in full
score'. He duly gave the score of the B minor Symphony
to Anselm Hüttenbrenner, as representative of the Graz
Society, some time later that year. Anselm kept the score
until the conductor Johann Herbeck, who had heard of
the existence of it from Anselm's brother Josef in 1860,
succeeded in persuading him to hand over the manuscript in 1865. Herbeck then gave the first performance
of the two-movement symphony on 17 December 1865,
adding as finale the last movement of Schubert's Third
Symphony. Schubert had retained the piano sketches of
the 'Unfinished' Symphony, which passed to his brother
Ferdinand after his death.

So much for the facts; the rest is speculation. Why did
Schubert not complete the third movement, which was
nearly finished in piano score? Did he compose a finale,
and if so what happened to it? Would he have presented
a half-finished symphony to the Styrian Society? Why did
Hüttenbrenner hoard the score for more than forty
years? To take the last and least important question first,
it appears that Anselm thought highly of himself as a
composer and may have resented his friend Schubert's
success in the years up to his death in 1828. In that case,
his brother Josef was perhaps making excuses for him
when he wrote, around 1868: 'The B minor, which my
brother and I place on a par with Beethoven, could not
find an orchestra to accept it anywhere'.[2]

As to the other questions, one view – held by Hans

---

[2] Deutsch, *Schubert: Memoirs by his Friends*, p. 193.

Gál[3] among others – is that Schubert realised his scherzo was not on the same artistic plane as the other two movements, and so abandoned the symphony. Another, put forward by Martin Chusid,[4] is that Schubert was embarrassed by the strong thematic kinship of his trio with the trio of Beethoven's Second Symphony. The hypothesis advanced by some that the work was conceived as a two-movement entity in the first place should not detain us. While there are specific arguments to be advanced for regarding the Tenth Symphony as a three-movement work by intention, there are no such arguments in the case of the Eighth; besides, Schubert did begin a scherzo, The possibility that the score given to Anselm by Schubert was a complete one, and that Anselm subsequently lost part of it, has long since been disproved. When in 1968 Christa Landon discovered a second page of the full score of the scherzo (up to then it was thought only the first page existed) it was established that Schubert had cut this page out of the score before sending it to Hüttenbrenner, and that this was definitely the last page to be scored by Schubert, as blank pages follow it.[5] The first page of the scherzo could not be removed, as it backed on to the last page of the slow movement.

Hans Gál suggests[6] that Schubert, haunted by the failure of the project, was desperate:

> he tore the work from his heart and gave the manuscript away, in order not to have it before his eyes any longer. It would never have crossed his mind that half a symphony could be performed. So it was immaterial to him who

[3] *Franz Schubert and the Essence of Melody*, pp. 152–177.

[4] *Op. cit.*, pp. 98–110.

[5] *Cf. Österreichische Musikzeitschrift*, XXIV/5–6, May–June 1969, pp. 299–323; also Christa Landon, 'New Schubert Finds', *The Music Review*, XXXI/3, August 1970, pp. 225–6, 230.

[6] *Franz Schubert and the Essence of Melody*, p. 174.

finally kept the manuscript. He never asked about it. He deliberately banished the work from his consciousness.

Gál is of the opinion that by this time Schubert had given up any hope of finishing the work: he 'deliberately let his masterpiece disappear from sight because he despaired of completing it'. If this is true, is it not strange that Schubert held on to the piano sketches throughout his life (along with the severed second page of the scherzo score)? Neither Tovey[7] nor Hutchings[8] found the material of the scherzo inadequate, and Mosco Carner was convinced that Schubert would have 'found an adequate conclusion had he gone back to it in later years'.[9] It is not impossible that Schubert retained the piano sketches with that possibility in mind, and that meanwhile he forwarded the first two movements to the Hüttenbrenners knowing that he could not finish the work for the time being, but anxious not to delay the fulfilment of his promise to the Styrian Society. The score was handed over in person to Anselm Hüttenbrenner; there is therefore no letter recording the terms of the gift. Schubert may have explained the situation verbally to Anselm, perhaps adding that the remainder of the symphony would follow when he had time to finish it. It would be an unusual circumstance, but not unthinkable. Moreover, the possibility of the work being performed in its half-finished state should not have been ruled out. Individual movements of symphonies were often performed separately at concerts in Schubert's Vienna. Twentieth-century audiences value the 'Unfinished' torso enough to want to hear it performed in its incomplete state, to the extent that they tolerate or ignore the absurdity of a Classical symphony thus beginning in one key and ending in another; and Schubert surely knew he had created

---

[7] *Essays in Musical Analysis*, Vol. 1, p. 215.

[8] *Op. cit.*, p. 98.

[9] *Loc. cit.*, p. 73.

something very special, and therefore probably wanted it to be heard by the contemporary world. As he had no opportunity to have new symphonies performed in Vienna at this time, he may have positively hoped for a performance of these two movements in Graz.

A performance might even have helped him to finish the work, an access of public acclaim restoring the self-confidence which had been undermined by a chain of abortive projects over the preceding four years. Realising that he had taken an enormous step forward with this symphony, it is unlikely that he would have wished to present to the Styrian Music Society one of his much earlier symphonies, written four years or more before this one, as that would not have been representative of the mature composer newly honoured. Equally, to have deferred fulfilment of his promise to the Society until such time as he completed a further symphony might have threatened to impose on his creative faculties too inhibiting an obligation, at this critical and difficult stage in his development.

If, then, the incompletion of the symphony was a temporary state of affairs, as Schubert saw it at the time, the explanation for it may lie among the reasons given in connection with the symphonic fragments.[10] In particular it has to be borne in mind that the longer completion was postponed the harder it was to achieve. So fleetly and eagerly did Schubert's inventive fancy roam from one arena to another – and operatic endeavours had a strong claim on his attention in the early 1820s – that once he had put a score to one side its completion may well have seemed less attractive than the beckoning tasks of a new day, especially at a time when yesterday's abandoned work represented a superseded phase of his style. (Even with the 'Unfinished', Schubert's new-found maturity did not project him into a promised land which offered a balmy plateau of undifferentiated masterpieces: as the

[10] *Cf.* chapter X, pp. 156–58.

'Unfinished' differs from its precursors, so the 'Great' is different again). One of the beckoning tasks which could have caused a temporary arrest of progress on the 'Unfinished' was, as Charles Osborne suggests,[11] the 'Wanderer' Fantasy, D760. Osborne's other suggestion apparently seeks to explain a more permanent state of impasse on Schubert's part. Referring to Schubert's syphilis, he proposes that it 'may be that the sexual act which caused the disease occurred when Schubert was working on the symphony, and that he subsequently associated the unfinished work with events he preferred to forget, and thus chose not to return it'. But there is no evidence that the contraction of syphilis dates from 1822, the year given by Osborne. Early 1823 is the preferred date,[12] by which time what was written of the symphony was written and already set aside.

It has been said that, in the 'Unfinished', song enters the world of symphony. The impression is one that cannot be escaped, although 'song' should be qualified as 'idealised song' – song moulded to the context and requirements of the particular symphony which Schubert was in the act of creating. The use of a specific, pre-existent song in an instrumental work is one thing; the adoption of the spirit of song, of the generalised musical characteristics shorn of the allusive specifics of a text, is quite another. When Schubert used one of his songs within an instrumental work, which he did in chamber music rather than symphony, he was acknowledging that the musical ideas concerned offered more mileage, in terms of expressive potential, than could be explored in the song; he was releasing the ideas from their partnership with a text, the text having come first. When idealised song enters textless music, the music is first-born,

[11] *Schubert and his Vienna*, Weidenfeld & Nicolson, London, 1985, pp. 94–5.

[12] Eric Sams, 'Schubert's Illness Re-examined', *The Musical Times*, cxxi, 1980, pp. 15–22, esp. pp. 15–16.

and supports its own meanings. In the 'Unfinished' Symphony, sonata-form drama provides a framework for and influence on meaning in all strata of design, from local detail to overall shape and direction. But the lyrical impulse appears so strong – within the constraints of symphonic propriety – that drama and lyricism meet and merge as never before: they are facets of the one mode of utterance, which is Schubert's new-found own. These elements have here found their first perfect fusion in a symphonic context.

Beethoven, in his Op. 101 Piano Sonata in A major (1816), had attained a new extreme of lyricism within first-movement form, although this had entailed minimising the dynamic aspect of sonata-form. He never attempted in the symphony what Schubert achieved in the 'Unfinished', where drama always flows from lyricism and brings its own lyrical aftermath. Schubert's sonata-form here ventures nothing outrageous or dangerous, preferring neat and simple solutions, and inclining to an economy and succinctness which might be called Mozartian although any more tangible sign of Schubert being visited by Mozart, as in the earlier symphonies, is missing. Schubert is even conventional enough to ask for a repeat of the exposition, which may be viewed as not so much an error of judgement as a loss of opportunity, for, as Maurice Brown has observed, the exposition displays an 'inexorable progress to the development section'.[13] Schubert could have effected an eloquent compression by welding the development to the exposition without the interruption of first-time bars and formal repeat, if he had remembered the example of his own Seventh Symphony. Beethoven in his Op. 101 Sonata had abandoned the exposition-repeat and been almost as evasive (as Schubert in his Seventh Symphony) about signalling the end of the exposition.

Another salient quality of this symphony is the way in

[13] *Schubert Symphonies*, p. 43.

which it uses the orchestra, which is exemplary by two distinct criteria. First of all, the orchestration is entirely effective as functional orchestration, serving to present the themes, accompaniments and manifold textures with clarity, provided that the conductor helps the low-placed upper woodwind to show through with their germane figure at bar 63 in 'the first movement, as they must and can. Second, much of the music is tailored to its instrumental medium with something above functionality. Whether in the matching of melodic and rhythmic contour to a particular woodwind timbre, or in the pitching and density of a trombone chord, or in the idiosyncratic mixing of string and wind colours, the score reflects a sharp response to the 'genius' of instruments at every turn. With this acute aural imagination, which is as prophetic of Romanticism as is the rich harmonic colouring, goes a heightened sensitivity to the vertical spacing of sonorities, resulting in evocative textures which again invite the epithet 'Romantic' rather than 'Classical'. It is in such miracles of creative inner hearing, among other things, that the bewitching poetry of the 'Unfinished' Symphony resides.

At the same time a new spaciousness enters the symphonic vocabulary. The 'Unfinished' and the 'Great', separated by three years, are spacious in different ways. The 'Unfinished' implies space in its leisurely tempi, the *Allegro moderato* in the first movement being notoriously close to the *Andante con moto* of the second; in its wide-spaced and sometimes spare textures, as at the beginning of the development in the first movement; in its traversal of vast tonal distances within the length of a phrase (*cf.* the second subject of the second movement); and in the immediate juxtaposition of starkly different rates of activity. This last point is exemplified near the end of the second movement, in the last *fortissimo* section, where a hyperactive *tutti* with demisemiquavers in the bass suddenly yields to a solo oboe singing – above a soft wind chord – in its own remote time-world. And it is illustrated just before the arrival of the second subject in the first movement, where a busy *tutti* gives way to a long-held D in horns and bassoons which eventually splays into the *Einschleife*[14] that leads into the second subject. It is interesting that the long D, although it lasts two seconds longer than the silence which occurs in the Seventh Symphony at the equivalent place, is less disruptive and troubling – either because of the continuity of sound, or because the D poses a question of key which is only resolved when the following cadence is reached.

Schubert chose for this symphony a key very rare in the Classical symphonic repertory. Mosco Carner therefore supposed that a special kind of poetic idea was guiding him, and drew attention to the fact that Schubert's songs in B minor (of which there are 21) share with this symphony a broadly 'depressive' character.[15] He also observed an important musical relationship between the song *Suleika* I and the 'Unfinished'. The opposite question to that considered by Carner might fruitfully be asked – 'Why should Schubert *not* write a symphony in B minor?' A simple answer to that question might be: 'Because neither Haydn nor Mozart nor Beethoven did'. It may be that Schubert's is actually the first B minor symphony of all time. Why did other composers avoid the key? They avoided it most conspicuously in their orchestral writing. Haydn did cast one symphony in B major (No. 46), but wrote no other orchestral work with B as its keynote – out of more than a hundred symphonies, innumerable divertimenti, cassations, concertos, marches, and other pieces. But he used the keynote B for 22 non-orchestral works, ranging from ensemble pieces to folksong

---

[14] In a waltz, the *Einschleife* is the anacrusic sliding-in bar, usually a rising scale-figure leading into the waltz tune itself. Schubert's evocation of the device is not inappropriate if his second subject is derived from another form of popular music, the Viennese street song (*cf.* Martin Chusid, *op. cit.*, p. 81).

[15] *Loc. cit.*, p. 65.

arrangements and including two string quartets, three piano trios, and a piano sonata. To explain this fact, and Mozart's and Beethoven's total abstinence from B minor and B major in orchestral works of any kind,[16] it is necessary to explore a little further the problems besetting composers using valveless brass instruments in Classical times.

The crooks which would have enabled horns and trumpets to play their limited repertoire of notes in B as in other keys did not exist, except as workshop curiosities. There were no B natural crooks, *alto* or *basso*, in use.[17] There is one apparent exception to this categorical view. Haydn chose B major as the key of his Symphony No. 46, and asked for two horns crooked in that key. H. C. Robbins Landon explains[18] that Haydn got his horn players in Vienna to construct a crook that lowered the pitch of the instrument by one semitone, and supports the view of Paul Bryan[19] that this crook was built to commission for use in both Nos. 45 and 46. No. 45 is in F sharp minor, and for the last two movements, which are in the major, Haydn specifies horns in F sharp. By using a G crook with the added semitone crook Haydn was able to set his horns in F sharp major. The semitone crook, added to a C *alto* horn, produced a horn in B *alto* for the Symphony No. 46. A surviving bill from the horn-maker Joseph Stärzer, dated Eisenstadt, October 1772, refers to 'What I did in the way of work for the hunting-horn player', and cites 'Two crooks for lowering a half-note [. . .] 1 Fl.'[20]

[16] The slow movement (in B major) of Beethoven's Fifth Piano Concerto is an exception.

[17] Forsyth, *op. cit.*, p. 78. In the slow movement of the Fifth Piano Concerto Beethoven uses horns in D, and reserves them for use in an important episode in Ð major.

[18] *Haydn: Chronicle and Works*, Vol. II, *Haydn at Esterháza, 1766–1790*, Thames and Hudson, London, 1978, p. 180.

[19] *Haydn-Studien*, III/I, 1973, pp. 52 *et seq.*

[20] *Ibid.*, p. 180.

Since no such crook was required in the music of the following half-century, it is clear that the item from Stärzer's workshop was a one-off product which set no pattern for future practice. The late Alan Civil, a leading orchestral horn-player, shared this view, adding[21] that out of the two hundred or so horn-players at a meeting of the British Horn Society in March 1986 'no one had any knowledge that the [B] crook was in normal use in Schubert's time'.

In the first movement of the 'Unfinished' Schubert uses trumpets in E, a strategy which allows them to play in 100 of 368 bars, although there are places where they are required but cannot contribute. His two horns are in D, which means that they can provide the mediant note of B minor, and can contribute usefully in the second subject keys of G and D. The horns and trumpets are again in D and E respectively in the first pages of score of the scherzo, where Schubert returns to B minor after a slow movement in E major.

Against this background it is worth considering alternative theories concerning the finale of the Symphony. These are either that the big B minor Entr'acte from *Rosamunde* was originally the Symphony's finale; or that Schubert wrote a different finale which is now lost; or that he did not get as far as beginning a finale. One of the arguments supporting the thesis that the Entr'acte from *Rosamunde* was the finale (a question to be discussed more fully later in this chapter[22]) is that the orchestra required for it is the same as that required for the Symphony. The Entr'acte uses horns in D and trumpets in E, like the other B minor movements of the Symphony. But if Schubert wrote no finale, he may have failed to embark on one because an anxiety about the role of the brass in it unnerved him. He might have expected, after all, that the

[21] Letter to the author, dated 1 April 1986.

[22] *Cf.* pp. 202–6.

finale, if not in B major from the start, would turn to the
major at some point and contain substantial portions in
that key, perhaps ending in it. Horns in D could not supply the mediant of B major; and horns in B were not
available to him. This obstacle may indeed account for
peculiarities of the B minor Entr'acte, whether it was
once the finale of the Symphony or not: B major is used
only for a short, soft intermediate theme which demands
no participation by the brass, and for the last seven bars
of the coda. In Schubert's previous minor-key symphony,
the *Tragic* in C minor, sizable portions of both the first
and last movement were in C major. In that work there
was no comparable obstacle, as crooks in C as well as E
flat were available. If it is true that unease about the
progress of the scherzo caused Schubert to abandon the
'Unfinished', fears about the prospects for the finale on
these grounds could have intensified his unease.

   The first movement lacks a slow introduction, but
begins spaciously enough to admit an introductory theme
before the first theme proper. Strictly speaking, this
introductory theme may be referred to as the first theme
of the first subject group, in which case the theme which
follows it is the second theme of that group. Its meaning,
and its role later in the movement, are ambivalent, but
the long note on which it rests before the next theme
ensues seems to confirm its introductory character, and
for my purposes it will be called the introductory theme.
Spaciousness is suggested by other means too, for with
this theme (Ex. 74) Schubert begins to chart the vast

Ex. 74

orchestral pitch-space of his incipient symphony by at
once focusing on one extreme of it. Even although the
first move of the cellos and basses is upwards, the heart of
the theme lies in its subsequent expressive descent to the
lowest point of an inverted arch. That arch is completed
in the first note of the first theme, or rather in the first
bass note of its accompaniment, for Schubert takes time
to spread out a leisurely accompaniment pattern, hushed
and eloquent, and allow the pattern to be heard twice (as
in the A minor String Quartet, D804), before sounding
the theme itself. The theme is given to an oboe and clarinet in unison, a doubling on which Gordon Jacob advised
caution to student readers of his orchestration manual:[23]
'the resulting sound is quite agreeable in small quantities'.
In Schubert's hands it is a doubling of poignant strength,
revealing its richness especially in the little crescendo at
the sixth bar. How right Schubert was to avoid any of his
favourite octave-doublings at this point, and concentrate
the line at a single pitch.

As the theme proceeds, other timbres are skilfully
added, aiding a *crescendo* which culminates in a tonic
cadence in which the full sonority of the orchestra, and
something like its full pitch-compass, is set before the ear.
It is on the rebound after this cadence, as it were, that the
long D is struck, which will lead into the second subject.
And four bars later a cadence in G sets the scene for the
second subject in that key. From the structural point of
view, what has happened so far is straightforward, but in
relation to tradition – tradition in Schubert's own music
as in the Classical period – it is extraordinary. Schubert
has abandoned the typical 'after-statement' of his youth.
Where the old after-statement would lead to or itself
assume the role of a transition, in this first paragraph of
the 'Unfinished' he does not follow up the implied deflect-
ions towards other keys but instead ends the paragraph

[23] *Orchestral Technique*, Oxford University Press, London, 1931, p. 37.

with a strong cadential resolution to the tonic.[24] The transition is thus compressed into the tiny space of the held D and the *Einschleife*. While Beethoven occasionally makes his transition in as short a time as this (Piano Sonata in F, Op. 10, No. 2, and Symphony No. 9), he follows it either with something that is key-confirmation material above all, or with a second subject which first has to work hard to establish that it *is* a second subject and that a second-subject key has indeed taken root. Schubert here requires no such gestures of re-assurance: his famous cello tune sails in on the calmest G major waters. But it is preceded by some bars of accompaniment-without-theme, as was the first theme. This syncopated accompaniment later appears as an important element in its own right, without the theme. The keys used for the second subject, by the way, G in the exposition and D in the recapitulation, are bound by the same relationship as their counterparts in the first movement of the Fourth Symphony.

Most students of music are 'educated' into the view that a first modulation in a piece takes time to accomplish, and that therefore a span of some length known as a transition connects a first-subject group to a second group. To be exact, they are 'educated' as much by their experience of the way Classical movements behave as by 'educators'. This tradition is naturally adopted as a premise in textbooks on musical form. It comes as a shock, therefore, to find Schubert compressing his transition in the first movement of the 'Unfinished', as was noted above, into a mere four bars. It is still more shocking that in the 'Great' C major Schubert makes a transition in one bar. What will be made clear in the next chapter, on the C major Symphony, is that transition in that work has to be understood in the light of this four-bar transition in the

---

[24] A precedent, the only one in all the symphonies, was noted in the finale of the sketched Seventh.

'Unfinished'.[25] In turn, the transition in the 'Unfinished' is better understood in the light of Schubert's practice in smaller forms.

The song *Der Musensohn*, D764, written three months after the 'Unfinished', comprises three stanzas of which the first and third are set in G major and the second in B major. The keys are a third apart, as are those of the first and second subjects in the Symphony (B minor and G major). Schubert accepts the presence of a common note between the tonic chords of the keys of successive stanzas (G major – B major, then B major – G major) as justification for making no modulation at all in the strict sense: the first stanza ends with a tonic chord in G major, and the second moves off at once with a tonic chord in B major. The result is wholly convincing and delightful and does not invite any more recondite explanation than I have given. Schubert adopts a similar strategy in the larger context of the 'Unfinished', and shows that where keys a third apart are involved there is no necessity for the time-consuming preparatory manœuvres of a conventional transition.

As the movement unfolds, drama and contrast come to the fore. The contrast is coherent, the drama born of the lyricism. As the second subject fades, space intervenes (Ex. 75), a full bar of it.

Ex. 75

Sound is resumed after the silence – although the easy lyrical flow of the second subject is not – in a resolute and weighty downward plunge of a fifth. The dramatic contrast is immense. But the falling fifth is a drawn-out

[25] *Cf.* pp. 227 *et seq.*

sequence of the bar which preceded the silence (*x* in Ex. 75). The lyrical has spawned the dramatic, giving coherence to the contrast. The drama continues, for something close in bearing to a development has begun, casting existing thematic elements (from the second subject) into new tonal contexts. But G major is restored for an epilogue in which answering voices share the opening strain of the second subject, and the exposition ends. The sudden restoration of the note B by the full orchestra implies a homeward move from G major to B minor (for the exposition-repeat) as sudden as the outward move from B minor to G for the second subject.[26]

If Beethoven had been writing a symphonic movement on Schubert's introductory theme, he would probably have ended the movement with a 'thematic resolution' of it. That is to say, where the theme at its first appearance descends to a point one degree short of the lower keynote and turns up to the dominant (*cf*. Ex. 74), he would have arranged for a final statement of it to 'go home' to the lower keynote, probably with some emphasis. Schubert himself provides this resolution in the middle of his development section, with the whole weight of the orchestra behind the theme for the first time. In the light of this observation one can better appreciate what he does in the beginning of the development, which could claim to be the most imaginative passage in the entire symphony if such distinctions were possible or necessary. This theme re-appears here in E minor and descends not only to the low tonic E (third bar of Ex. 76) but through E to D, and beyond to C. The tread has been slowed to one note a bar, and each step sounds a daring adventure. The *tremolando* on the bottom note intensifies the mystery of this

[26] Most editions of the score deviate from the autograph score in the bar before the reprise, where an internal pedal B (first horn and second bassoon) is indicated. The Norton Critical Score follows the autograph. *Cf.* Adam Carse, 'Editing Schubert's Unfinished Symphony', *The Musical Times*, xcv, 1954, pp. 143–45.

Ex. 76

new remote region, and Schubert introduces the violins
in their 'normal' register as though to underline the distance travelled by the descending bass. But for an imitation of the violins by bassoons and violas in the intervening pitch-space, a vast textural hollow is maintained
(the score looks more like Shostakovich than Schubert in
its exploitation of space) and the tension is screwed up, by
means of a simple *crescendo*, to such a degree that some
filling-in support must be given. As instruments are
added, with the trombones prominent, Schubert applies
the Beethovenian technique of foreshortening, progressively reducing a repeated two-bar idea until each repetition occupies only one bar. This quickening of activity
intensifies the dominant ninth of B minor which underpins it, until the demand for a resolution can be resisted
no longer. But the resolution is a shock, for it lights up
the threshold of C sharp minor. Further shocks follow:
any prospect of crossing the threshold of C sharp minor
is removed as D minor and E minor supervene, and when
in that last key the 'thematic resolution' referred to above
arrives, the atmosphere remains highly charged.

At this point, the two large paragraphs which make
up the development intersect. Brahms, a later master of
the art of integrating lyrical and dramatic elements,
who was himself inclined to construct a development in
two large paragraphs, probably learned no less from
Schubert's paragraph here than from any other composer; at least, the equivalent passages in the Piano
Quintet in F minor and the Clarinet Quintet suggest as
much. Schubert's subtle variety in the timing of incidents,

of harmonic change, and of modulation in the first
paragraph implies a truly fecund imagination and a
mature control on the part of its 25-year-old composer.

A more orderly, even orthodox manner of development ensues. The first three notes of the introductory
theme are treated imitatively; then its next six notes similarly. Meanwhile new forms of rhythmic animation are
added: continuous short notes, then a galloping dotted
rhythm. This all culminates in another texture which is
remarkable *as* texture. It can be reduced to its essentials
as in Ex. 77, but as he spreads it over about five octaves
Schubert allots special weight to the strongly moving
inside part (an inversion of the first three notes of the
introductory theme). When the C natural is present, the
chord has the formation of an inverted C major triad.
This chord appears and sounds remote from B minor,
Schubert's destination key, yet as an inverted Neapolitan
Sixth it can be treated as a chromatic chord in B minor.
In effect, Schubert is playing on its ambiguity: C major,
or B minor? When the C natural is changed to a C sharp,
the issue would seem to be settled in favour of B minor
(Ex. 77). But a new ambiguity arises, for the destination

Ex. 77

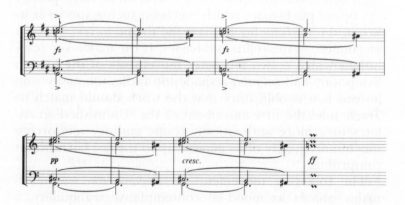

could now be B minor or – D major. The remainder of the development makes capital out of this latest ambiguity, a noisy, stamping cadential gesture in D giving way, twice, to a quiet and relatively inactive swing to B minor. As B minor prevails, the atmosphere is becalmed, ready for the recapitulation.

The recapitulation begins with the first theme, not the introductory theme. The introductory theme has dominated the development, and in any case at the end of the development the function of preparing for the first theme (fulfilled by the introductory theme at the beginning of the symphony) is now fulfilled by the long becalmed dominant of B minor. Schubert adjusts the continuation of the first theme so that the second subject arrives in D major, and adjusts the second subject so that the 'epilogue' appears in B major. But B major is short-lived. The minor is re-instated in a coda which in its final form considerably expands the coda originally drafted in the piano sketch. At first it seems to offer a subdued, resigned recollection of the long-built climax which began the development. This time the spaciously scored climax takes the first violins to the high B for the first and only time. In its wake, the introductory theme has the energy to reiterate only its first three notes, in a sixfold statement which, in moving through the registers from middle to high and finally low, presents a microcosmic retrospect of the broad pitch-space which has been such a special feature of the movement, and lays the theme to rest where it originated, in the cellos and basses. If the major-key resolutions which crown the outer movements of the Fourth Symphony had seemed a shade too facile, too easily won indeed if it is obligatory that the work should match its *Tragic* title, the first movement of the 'Unfinished' gravitates to a more authentically tragic ending, reinforcing the 'minor' quality of its genesis up to the last bar without compromise.

The following movement, an *Andante con moto* in E major, shares its mood of contemplative tranquillity, a

simply lyrical beauty almost pastoral in association, with
several of Schubert's songs in that key. Yet it is an unexpected key for a slow movement of a B minor symphony.
Did Schubert avoid the obvious and more likely related
major keys, G and D, because these had been used for the
second subject in the first movement and he wanted to
maximise the tonal range of his symphony? Equally
plausible is Martin Chusid's proposed reason for the
choice.[27] The opening bars, a short 'refrain' prefacing
the first theme, consist of the first three notes of the
ascending scale harmonised over a *pizzicato* bass which
falls through an octave from tonic to tonic (Ex. 78). The
pizzicato line is assigned to the double-basses. The note
which completes this line, the low E, is the bottom note
available on the double-bass Schubert had at his disposal.
Thus Schubert could complete the descent, unbroken, as
long as the keynote was E rather than D, and at the same
time could exploit the depth of the double-bass range to
its limit.

Ex. 78

The passage derives a large degree of its effectiveness
from the scoring, writes Chusid;[28] and it should be
added that the *pizzicato* line, which is marked *pizzicato* in
the preliminary piano sketch (from which Ex. 78 is
taken), could not have been assigned to the cellos (bottom
note: C) because they were required for the bowed bass
line to the first theme, whose first note coincides with the

[27] *Op. cit.*, pp. 83–84.

[28] *Ibid.*, p. 83.

last note of *pizzicato* by an overlap of phrases. Another point has to do with the similarity of tempo between the two movements. *Allegro moderato* ($^3_4$) and *Andante con moto* ($^3_8$) are very close, as Schubert may or may not have realised at the time. There is a danger of the slow movement following on at the speed of the first movement, and it is no doubt in trying to avoid this danger that conductors sometimes pace it too slow. For the listener, the similarity of tempo is offset by the unexpectedness of key.

The 'refrain' that both precedes and follows the first phrase of the theme refers to the last three notes of that theme (*cf.* the end of Ex. 78). These elements alternate, irregularly throughout the first section of the movement. But this is the kind of Schubert slow movement that embraces strong contrasts, thus requiring (unlike the slow movement of the Seventh) the full orchestral complement; and in the middle of this section there is a variant of the theme sung in full-throated chorus by the wind above a tread of quavers behind which the entire string section puts its weight. The refrain returns in its original form to close the first section, which is nothing other than the first subject-group of a sonata-form exposition. But this first subject has ended, as did that of the first movement, with a perfect cadence in the key in which it began. And the following transition is as short as that in the first movement, and even simpler: the first violins gently rise an octave, then fall by thirds until the chord of the new tonic is reached (C sharp minor), whereupon a softly quivering syncopated accompaniment lays a foundation for the second subject. The two movements of the 'Unfinished' are astonishingly like-minded, then, in their concept of transition to second subject, and in their subsequent activating of an accompaniment before the second subject itself enters.

Schubert now unfurls on the solo clarinet one of his most remarkable themes. A sequential section based on a rising third ascends to a long high note, after which falling sequences and repetitions on a second figure close in another long high note. Looking at the melody alone in Ex. 79 one would not suspect that the two long notes are the twin hinges on which the theme's structure and emotional complexion turn.

Ex. 79

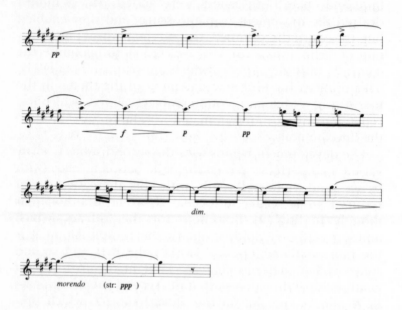

This is because the crucial events are harmonic ones. Under the high A the syncopated strings make a highly charged modulation to D major and a serene one to F major (both distant keys), while below the high G sharp they play through to their cadence, tapering to a rapt *ppp* just at the moment where a C sharp *major* resolution is attained. This is the first time Schubert has used the triple *piano* marking in a symphony, and it is a symptom of the new poetry to which the 'Unfinished' aspires. That this poetry is founded on a heightened harmonic imagination and intensified sensitivity to instrumental nuance, no less than melodic inspiration, is especially evident at this juncture.

The oboe takes up the theme in the major, the cellos adding a new response in the 'weak' bars which Schubert has already reinforced with accents (*cf.* Ex. 79). This time there is no modulation, and the apex of the melody falls away in a nonchalant new figure which is twice echoed, by flute and oboe. Both echoes were added after Schubert drafted the movement in piano score, and they enabled him to reduce the volume – true to the natural phenomenon of 'echo' – to a further triple *piano* to maximise the contrasts with the *fortissimo* which interrupts immediately. This brings a forceful new statement of the theme in the bass, with a dynamic countersubject above, which on repetition with a more animated middle texture leads to the development.

The development begins with the second subject, softly varied, in a perfectly poised dialogue between cellos (with basses) and violins. It ends with this thematic variant reduced to a recurrent octave drop in the horn, as though 'finding' its first note for the 'refrain' which announces the recapitulation. In the recapitulation it is the more dynamic episodes within the first and second subjects that undergo change. That in the first subject changes tonal direction so that the second subject appears in A minor; and that in the second subject, which presented a new countersubject above the theme in the bass, now inverts the counterpoint, setting the countersubject as bass to the theme.

The first concern of the coda is to present a thematic resolution of the 'refrain'. This is perhaps the most significant afterthought conceived by Schubert between first sketching the movement and finally writing up his score. The ascending scale is extended upwards, then arched to end where it began. Thus, a fragment finds ultimate fulfilment by blossoming into a theme, which is at once repeated in richer orchestral colouring. Recollections of other elements follow, including a statement of part of the first theme in distant A flat major in which Schubert makes a virtue of a necessity by using the bass trombone as bass to the clarinets and bassoons. In this remote key the horns, a more obvious choice for the purpose, could provide none of the notes required.

What Schubert planned next was a scherzo in B minor. It is a fine, promising movement in its sketched form, with a theme of well-defined character which is worked more extensively and adventurously than any of his earlier scherzo themes. If one reads the sketch with imagination (for it is rather bare in its later stages and several important dynamic markings are omitted), one perceives a number of impressive things in it, like the strong two-part canon, which begins the second section, the more relaxed episode in the 'Neapolitan' key of C major, and the well-managed build-up to the imposing finish. Of the trio in G major Schubert sketched only the first section, and only the melodic line of that. The accompaniment would presumably have been a simple though not colourless one in the trio tradition, and the second section would have been based on the first, whose theme contains material enough for the kind of development and varied reprise that is appropriate.

The *da capo* of Schubert's scherzo was to have brought the whole movement to an end with a final cadence in B minor underpinned by an upward scale-run from the dominant to the tonic. If the finale had then announced itself with the same scale-run, the continuity of thought would have been sealed. Or so the critic may observe, with the benefit of hindsight. There is, among Schubert's later works, a movement which begins in this way. And that movement presents several internal reasons, as well as some external ones, for considering the possibility that it could originally have been conceived as the finale of the 'Unfinished' and was pressed into service in its later context as a time-saving expedient. Indeed, the movement in question, the Entr'acte in B minor from the incidental music to *Rosamunde* (1823), was played as finale at the very first English performance of the 'Unfinished' Symphony on 6 April 1867, and it has been so used on numerous occasions since.

The internal reasons are, in short, that the Entr'acte is in the same (rare) key as the Symphony and requires the same orchestral forces, is cast in Schubert's usual finale form (sonata-form), is planned on a big enough scale to complement the design of the symphony as it stands, and inhabits a similar emotional world. The external reasons are that it is disproportionately big for the function assigned to it within *Rosamunde*, and that Schubert evidently assembled his *Rosamunde* music in considerable haste.[29] As overture he used the one he had already composed, or was already working on, for *Alfonso und Estrella*.[30] For an interlude in one of the entr'actes he orchestrated one of his own songs (*Der Leidende*, D432, 1816). In two instances within *Rosamunde* itself the music of one piece is re-used in another piece. Given this degree of thrifty re-cycling, by which Schubert doubtless sought to save time, it seems probable that rather than writing an over-long new entr'acte from scratch he would take a pre-existent movement which had been drafted but never used. If this is what he did, he may have wished to conceal the fact from the commissioner of the incidental music: the scale and bearing of the Entr'acte in B minor might arouse suspicion. One of the other entr'actes (also in B minor) makes use of some of the same material as this big B minor Entr'acte. Could it be that Schubert based a smaller entr'acte on the same material in order to reduce the risk of the bigger entr'acte calling attention to itself as a gatecrasher and a misfit?

[29] Robert Winter concludes that he probably began *Rosamunde* in November, for first performance on 20 December ('Paper Studies and the Future of Schubert Research', in E. Badura-Skoda and Peter Branscombe (eds.) *Schubert Studies: Problems of Style and Chronology*, Cambridge University Press, London, 1982, pp. 228–29).

[30] He later replace this with the Overture to *Die Zauberharfe*, which is now known as the *Rosamunde* Overture.

Three objections to the proposition must now be countered. Maurice Brown points out that the papers used for the scores of the Symphony and the Entr'acte bear different watermarks: so 'the theory cannot be maintained against the facts', he claims.[31] But there is no real difficulty here. Having made a piano sketch of the scherzo of the Symphony, Schubert would have proceeded to make a piano sketch of the finale. He began to orchestrate the scherzo, which he is more likely to have done knowing that a finale was ready in draft form. That the sketch of the third movement ends half way through the trio does not necessarily signify that the symphony-sketch as a whole must end there. Schubert left no more undone in this third movement than he could have completed when orchestrating it. If this fact were not demonstrated by his beginning to orchestrate the movement in this unfinished state, it would be demonstrated by a study of his earlier symphonic sketches. When, having made his piano sketch of the finale, he then abandoned the symphony, he would have kept the piano sketch in his possession along with those for the rest of the symphony. When he later decided to orchestrate the finale sketch for *Rosamunde* late in 1823, he would only then have taken orchestral paper for this task. Robert Winter confirms this position: *Rosamunde*, Nos. 1 (the big B minor Entr'acte), 3a and 5, 'almost certainly represents his earliest usage of type IIa'.[32] If the Entr'acte was once the finale of the symphony, it was not scored during the period of work done on the symphony.

The second objection is Charles Osborne's: the theory that Schubert tore the movement concerned from the Symphony to use as an entr'acte cannot be maintained against the facts, he states, because whatever existed of the Symphony 'was already with Anselm Hüttenbrenner

---

[31] *Schubert: A Critical Biography*, p. 123.

[32] *Loc. cit.*, p. 229.

in Graz at the time when Schubert was composing his
Rosamunde music'.[33] This objection, also raised by
Maurice Brown, is obviously invalid if Schubert had
sketched the movement in piano score and retained this
piano score along with the sketches of the rest of the
Symphony. Third, Brown observes that the score of the
Entr'acte is headed, in Schubert's own hand, 'No. 1:
Entre-Act nach dem 1. Aufz'. He implies by this inscrip-
tion that if the movement had originated as part of a
symphony a crossed-out heading would betray the fact.
But if no full score of the movement had been prepared
at the time the Symphony was being worked on, then
clearly when one was prepared for the first time, for
Rosamunde, only the new title would appear.

A further note must be added on one of the internal
reasons already given for suspecting that the Entr'acte
began life as the finale of the Symphony. It was stated
above that the piece is cast in Schubert's usual finale form
(sonata-form). In fact, Schubert espoused two different
kinds of orchestral sonata-form. One was a full-blown
sonata-form used for symphonies, and the other a curtailed sonata-form for theatrical use, omitting the exposition-repeat and lacking a development section. The
Alfonso und Estrella Overture designated for *Rosamunde*
has merely an embryonic development which is really a
longer-than-usual link, doing little more than elaborating
a change of chord-position of the dominant seventh.
Would Schubert have specially composed, to share the
same theatrical scenario, an entr'acte with an earnest
sixty-bar development? (The *Zauberharfe* Overture which
later replaced *Alfonso und Estrella* completely lacks any
development.)

It is important in discussing this question not to con-
fuse a number of quite distinct issues. To propose that
the Entr'acte originated as the projected finale for the
Eighth Symphony is not necessarily to say that it is

[33] *Op cit.*, p. 94.

successful as a symphonic finale. Nor, even, is it to say
that Schubert himself considered it a successful finale. He
may have thought it so, or he may not. If he regarded it
as a failure, this judgement may have contributed to his
decision not to finish the symphony. Separate issues again
are the relationship of the scored Entr'acte to its (lost or
destroyed) piano sketch, and the relationship of that piano
sketch to what Schubert would have made of it had he
actually scored it as the finale of the symphony. Since the
Entr'acte may have differed in some significant ways
from the piano sketch made in the previous year – and if
Schubert had scored the piece for the symphony in the previous year he may have deviated from the sketch at times
(as he did when scoring the first two movements of the
symphony) and done so in different ways – it cannot be
assumed that by playing the Entr'acte in its known form
in order to complete a performance of the Symphony the
modern editor will have accurately deduced how Schubert would have ended the work. That the movement was
ultimately scored in haste may itself argue against Schubert's having made far-reaching changes. One possibility
is that the pauses and *ritardando* close to the beginning
were last-minute additions – an attempt to add a touch of
theatricality or at least to 'de-symphonise' the piece from
the outset by arresting the forward thrust which is typical
of the first subject of the symphonic finale.[34]

With the completion of *Rosamunde* and the dawning of
1824, Schubert probably put the 'Unfinished' out of mind,
especially if he had just made use of a residual sketch
from it. He was soon preparing, both psychologically and
practically, for the composition of an ambitious *grosse
Symphonie*, which was to come to fruition as his Ninth in
two or three years. For him, as for posterity, the production of the Ninth formed a climax to the aspirations of
these intervening two or three years, and to his entire
symphonic career. There is an element of falsehood

[34] A short note on the Entr'acte is given as Appendix 3, pp. 294–96.

in this view, of course. Normally, composers produce individual, self-sufficient works, not chains of preparatory 'exercises' paving the way for some notional ultimate masterpiece which may or may not ever come. Works succeed each other but do not supersede one another. Nowhere in Schubert's symphonic canon does this truth declare itself more emphatically than in the succession of the 'Unfinished' by the 'Great'. Whatever the failure of the 'Unfinished' as an entity, as a medium through which Schubert might communicate his new mastery to his contemporary public, or to that public's following generation, it is rightly recognised as a pinnacle in the history of the symphony and in the history of music, a supreme poetic vision in sound, sublimely unaffected by the existence of other, different masterpieces whether three or thirty or for that matter three hundred years distant from it.

XIII

Greatness Accomplished:
The Ninth Symphony

On 31 March 1824, Schubert wrote to Leopold Kupel-weiser:

> Of songs I have not written many new ones, but I have tried my hand at several instrumental works, for I wrote two quartets for violins, viola and violoncello and an octet, and I want to write another quartet, in fact I intend to pave my way towards a grand symphony in that manner.[1]

He had last completed a symphony six years earlier, and that work, the Sixth of 1818, he appears not to have regarded with much satisfaction. Since then he had finished only two symphonic movements. By his own standards of youthful productivity (six symphonies in six years from 1813 to 1818) he now lacked practice in symphonic writing. More especially, after a succession of four failures, he lacked the confidence to envisage a work of symphonic scope and stature, and see it through.

The *grosse Symphonie* soon to come was by no stretch of the imagination the work of one who lacked confidence. How, then did the other projects referred to in his letter help to pave the way and restore confidence? To a limited

---

[1] Deutsch, *Schubert: A Documentary Biography*, p. 339.

degree, any multi-movement instrumental piece (such as the String Quartet in A minor, D804, he had just completed) would serve his purpose. But in the event, two other works of 1824 probably sharpened his technique and developed his appetite still more. The Octet, for wind and strings, gave him fresh experience of handling a large ensemble in an extended but non-programmatic and non-vocal work. And the *Grand Duo* for piano duet (D812) involved large-scale structures hardly different from those to be expected in a symphony, applied to a medium not dissimilar to the octet combination in offering a textural compass and richness in some ways comparable to that of an orchestra.

Some, indeed, have followed Schumann in regarding the *Grand Duo* as a symphony in disguise. It has even been suggested (and Schumann himself implied it) that the work is a transcription for four hands of an original conceived as a symphony. There is no foundation for this view – no documentary support, nor any real internal evidence. Writers who propound the view tend either to justify their stance in general terms – for example, by alluding to 'the disconcerting nature of its orchestral style' – or to single out one example of what 'the pianoforte can *not* do'. The words quoted are, in both cases, Tovey's;[2] and the example of what is beyond the capacity of the piano is invariably the long-held unharmonised octaves near the end of the finale. It is undeniable that on a piano as soon as a note is struck its tone begins to decay, and that in asking for a note to be held *fortissimo* for two bars Schubert is being strictly unrealistic. Yet all other composers of piano music have tacitly accepted that realism in dynamic indications is unattainable, and those who see the long note in the *Grand Duo* as a sign of orchestral thinking do not claim that Schubert's last Piano Sonata in B flat (D960), whose finale begins with long-

[2]*Op. cit.*, p. 218.

held octaves, is orchestrally conceived, nor that his Piano
Sonata in A minor, D784, whose first movement abounds
with such sustained notes, is a piano transcription of a
symphony. The fact of the matter is that parts of the
Grand Duo may be orchestrated easily and effectively, and
others may not – at least, not within the constraints of the
orchestra Schubert had at his disposal. Certainly the work
is enriched by its composer's experience as a symphonist,
but it remains a successful work for piano duet, almost
certainly conceived for the two Countesses he was tutor-
ing at Zseliz in Hungary at this time. Even when Schubert
invents a line which begins, say, in the right hand of the
secondo player and is completed in the left hand of the
primo player, this measure is only an expedient all piano-
composers adopt, however many hands they are writing
for. When the would-be orchestrator finds that, in view of
the numerous sections in remote keys, he must either
used valved brass instruments not available to Schubert,
or use valveless instruments but ask them for many more
'false' notes than Schubert would have done, or accept
the constraints of Schubert's resources and style, thus
denying the presence of horns (and to some extent trumpets and drums) at places where they would obviously be
required, he realises that Schumann, Tovey and others
were being a shade over-fanciful.

For Tovey, the theory that the *Grand Duo* was orchestrally conceived fitted in conveniently with the widely-
held view that between the 'Unfinished' and the 'Great'
Schubert composed a symphony which was subsequently
lost. What Tovey did not know is that this so-called
'Gastein' symphony would eventually be proved never to
have existed. There is no purpose in discussing at length
here this disproved theory. But an outline of the case must
be given, so that references in the existing literature on
Schubert's symphonies may be better understood. Letters
which passed between members of the Schubert circle in
1825 referred to his working on a new symphony while

on holiday at Gmunden and Gastein in upper Austria during that summer. Sir George Grove, trying to reconcile this reference with the fact that none of the known symphonies was undated, or was dated 1825, concluded that the work written in that summer was lost.[3] Grove's hypothesis was disproved only in the 1970s and 1980s, when three separate strands of research converged on the same conclusion. First, John Reed put a new interpretation on well-known surviving documents;[4] then further archival research by Otto Biba[5] and paper studies by Robert Winter[6] clinched Reed's supposition that the symphony referred to in correspondence as having been written at Gastein and elsewhere was none other than the 'Great' C major. There was, then, no missing symphony – at least, not one from 1825.[7] The arguments are conclusive in spite of the apparent date of 1828 on the first page of the autograph score (a date which, being in Schubert's hand, was naturally taken at its face value by Grove, who had in 1867 been in Vienna studying the autographs of the symphonies). There have been several subsequent attempts to explain the '1828' on the autograph, and these are summarised in Robert Winter's essay. An attractive solution, although it raises certain questions yet to be answered, comes from John Reed, who points out that Schubert was in touch with two leading publishers early in 1828; if he had wished to interest them in the 'Great' Symphony he would have had a better

[3] Letter to the Editor of *The Times*, 28 September 1881 (*cf.* Deutsch, *Memoirs*, pp. 456–58).

[4] *Schubert, The Final Years*, Faber, London, 1972, pp. 71–92.

[5] 'Franz Schubert und die Gesellschaft der Musikfreunde in Wien', in Otto Brusatti (ed.), *Schubert-Kongress Wien 1978. Bericht*, Akademisches Druck- und Verlagsanstalt, Graz, 1979, pp. 23–36.

[6] *Loc. cit.*, pp. 209–275.

[7] But there was now a missing 1828 one, although musicologists were unaware of the fact: *cf.* chapter XV and Appendix 4, pp. 297–99.

chance of doing so if it appeared to be a new work rather
than a three-year-old one: 'an old symphony, and one in
the possession of the Music Society, was obviously a less
saleable property than a "new" one'.[8] The unusual circumstance that the autograph has no title page is thus
explained, by Reed: Schubert removed the title page with
its original date and dedication to the Vienna Music
Society, and post-dated the work before offering it to
Schott of Mainz.[9]

The Ninth Symphony itself was begun in 1825 and
completed in 1826. Some revisions were made, possibly in
both 1826 and 1827, but certainly not later than the
summer of 1827, for, as Otto Biba has demonstrated,[10] a
set of orchestral parts which accords with the final version
of the symphony had been copied out by August of that
year. Schubert was clearly given hope of a performance
in Vienna. In August 1825, when work was presumably
already well advanced, Moritz von Schwind replied[11] to a
letter (now lost) by Schubert:

> About your symphony we may be quite hopeful. Old
> Hönig is dean of the faculty of jurisprudence, and as such
> is to give a concert. That will afford a better opportunity
> of having it performed; indeed we count upon it.

This opportunity evidently passed Schubert by, and in
October 1826 he dedicated the symphony to the Gesellschaft der Musikfreunde, receiving in return a fee of 100

[8] *Op. cit.*, p. 196.

[9] *Cf.* Reed's preface to the Eulenburg miniature score of the Symphony (ed. Roger Fiske, Mainz, 1984), p. viii.

[10] 'Concert Life in Beethoven's Vienna', in *Beethoven: Performers and
Critics. The International Beethoven Congress Detroit 1977*, Wayne State
University Press, Detroit, 1980, pp. 77–93.

[11] Quoted in Deutsch, *A Documentary Biography*, p. 451. Von Schwind,
one of Schubert's best friends, was a distinguished Viennese painter
with a good knowledge of music.

*Badgastein, Upper Austria, in Schubert's day. He stayed here
and in Gmunden on the holiday during which he worked on the
'Great' C major Symphony. Engraving by J. Axmann after a
painting by Jakob Alt.*

guilders. Leopold von Sonnleithner tells[12] that it 'was
rehearsed by the Gesellschaft der Musikfreunde in the
practices at the Conservatoire, but it was provisionally put
on one side because of its length and difficulty'.[13] It was
left on one side until Schumann intervened in its fortunes
and secured a performance in Leipzig under Mendelssohn. Even this performance, in 1839, eleven years after
Schubert's death, was only a partial one, and when
further performances followed in Vienna and other
European capitals the length and difficulty of the symphony still precluded it being given complete.[14]

If the seeds of the 'Great' C major are looked for in
Schubert's earlier symphonies they will not be found so
much in the 'Unfinished' as in the preceding ones,
notably the Sixth and Seventh. The 'Great' is more Classical in conception than the 'Unfinished'. Schubert looks
back towards the roots of the mature Classical symphony.
He rediscovers Mozart's 'enjoyment of a sense of movement',[15] and re-interprets it. He emulates the scale of the
grand Beethovenian symphony, pioneered in the *Eroica*
and reaffirmed in the 'Choral', which Schubert heard in
Vienna in May 1824. Yet he produces a rich, well-
rounded and wholly Schubertian masterpiece that owes
little to any antecedents or models. The 'Great' is the last

---

[12] Quoted in Deutsch, *Schubert: Memoirs by his Friends*, p. 431.

[13] Biba states ('Schubert's Position in Viennese Musical Life', *19th-Cen-
tury Music*, III/2, p. 108):

> The widespread belief that the musicians preparing the Great C
> major for its premiere rejected it because of its unreasonable dif-
> ficulties is false. The well-preserved records of the Gesellschaft
> make it clear that the work was never planned for an official
> public performance.

He does not dispute, nor even mention, Sonnleithner's statement, but
he presents no grounds for questioning its accuracy.

[14] The history of performance is explored further in chapter XVI,
pp. 279–83.

[15] From Tovey's essay on the 'Linz' Symphony (*op. cit.*, p. 184).

Watercolour of Schubert by Wilhelm August Rieder (1825).
Several later likenesses of the composer, including the famous
copperplate engraving by J. N. Passini and a number of oil
portraits made by Rieder himself in later life, are based on this
painting, which is contemporary with the 'Great' C major Symphony.

symphony by a great Classical symphonist;[16] strictly it is
the only one in the 1820s, if to be truly Classical a symphony must argue its way from inception to culmination
in a purely instrumental medium. In that sense it stands
alone in its decade, although it shares that decade with
the *Symphonie Fantastique* as well as Beethoven's Ninth. If
at the beginning of the 'Great' the horns are heard to
open the door on Romanticism, that, along with other
Romantic elements in the work, is a symptom of a new

[16] Charles Rosen argues the case for regarding the 'Great' as a Classical symphony on premises of his own: *cf. The Classical Style*, Faber,
London, 1971, p. 459.

breadth of imagination and of vocabulary: Schubert cannot and does not set out to stand apart from the enrichment of utterance and vision that characterises the
meeting of Classical and Romantic ideals a quarter of the
way into the nineteenth century. The first symphony of
Berlioz is an altogether more thorough-going subscriber
to Romanticism. As for Beethoven's Ninth, it epitomises
the plight of the arch-Classicist who has pursued his
ideals to breaking-point and can extend a cherished tradition no more without, at a moment of crisis, jumping outside it. It also underlines the determination of Schubert
to remain faithful to Classical tradition, for while Beethoven the instrumental genius had recourse to Schiller and
an SATB chorus to crown his last symphony, Schubert
the song composer thought to admit neither a text nor a
voice to *his* Ninth.

It may be significant that on the one occasion when
Schubert seems in this symphony to be echoing Beethoven – in the middle of the finale – he is apparently alluding to a theme from the only vocal movement in all
Beethoven's Symphonies (the 'joy' theme in the finale of
the Ninth). If that is indeed the intended allusion, then
this 'joy' theme merely takes its place in a long procession
of unsung 'joy' themes in Schubert's score. Perhaps it is
through the song-like expression of their *joie de vivre*, as
much as anything, that these 'heavenly lengths' (as Schumann called them) uplift the spirit. Schumann, the first
real champion of the 'Great', was as alive as any latter-day
commentator to the impossibility of fixing its qualities by
allusion to parallel genres, or to specific emotions.

> Deep down in this symphony there lies more than mere
> song, more than mere joy and sorrow, as already
> expressed in music in a hundred other instances; it trans-
> ports us into a world where we cannot recall ever having
> been before.[17]

17 *Neue Zeitschrift für Musik*, 10 March 1840.

Schubert had never exploited the timbre of the horns as boldly as he does at the beginning of this symphony. To the two of them in unison, and unaccompanied, he entrusts the entire eight-bar theme (Ex. 80).

Ex. 80

Since the horn is evocative of Romanticism, partly on account of the use made of it after Schubert's death, and partly because its hunting associations evoke the world of Nature which was one of the obsessions of Romantic art, it is not surprising that many listeners have envisaged some Romantic vista opening up as the leisurely theme unfolds. This is not an obvious way to begin an intrinsically Classical symphony. Yet the theme has an orderly if unusual structure, based on principles that were good for, and since, Haydn. That is, the composer assumes an expectation of regularity in phrase-structure, to throw into relief his irregularity. But the irregularity is peculiar to Schubert. When he follows his first two-bar statement not with a two-bar response but with a rhythmic echo of the second bar, he appears to be doing what in many of his themes would merely postpone the two-bar response and, by the insertion of a redundant bar into the middle of a four-bar phrase, create a five-bar phrase.[18] But in the 'Great' the response reproduces all three bars. In the

---

[18] Instances of this internal expansion were noted above in three movements of the Seventh Symphony and in the finale of the A minor String Quintet – *cf.* pp. 177–78.

first two the substitution of only one note has a dispro-
portionate effect. The rhythmic echo takes a new melodic
shape, closing on the keynote; and to complete the
theme, this sixth bar is repeated in augmentation – that
is, with the note-lengths doubled. It seems quite incidental that the theme so constructed should run to exactly
eight bars, an ordinary enough span whose subdivision
here is extraordinary.

If this were a typical slow introduction in a typical
Classical symphony it might be extravagant to give so
much space to an analysis of its theme. Close attention to
the *Andante* theme of the 'Great' is desirable for three
reasons. It returns at the end of the *Allegro* proper, in
Allegro tempo, to form the last climax of the whole movement; it dominates the remainder of the *Andante* introduction for more than is usual in a Classical introduction,
where the tendency is progressively to liquidate the thematic content so as to clear the way for the *Allegro* theme; and
it lends its most prominent feature to the exposition, development, and recapitulation of the ensuing sonata-form
Allegro. In view of this it will be useful to attempt a survey
of the first movement that takes as its starting-point the
role played in it by this *Andante* theme – a new approach
which will reveal some interesting new perspectives.

The movement ends with two *fortissimo* statements of
the *Andante* theme.[19] Here, complete statements would
be prolix in effect, and Schubert duly shortens the theme
by omitting the fourth and sixth bars (of Ex. 80). One

[19] That Schubert re-introduces the *Andante* theme with its note-values
doubled in length would seem to argue a proportionate tempo relationship between the *Andante* and the *Allegro ma non troppo* (minim of
Andante equal to semibreve of *Allegro*). A similar proportion is implicit
in the E flat Piano Trio, D929, between the *Andante con moto* slow
movement and the *Allegro moderato* finale; in the course of the finale
the slow movement theme reappears, again with note-values doubled.
Among conductors who have observed this principle in recorded performances of the Symphony, thus obviating the need for an *accelerando*
into the *Allegro*, are Carlo Maria Giulini and Sir Charles Mackerras.

particular effect of this omission should be noted for later reference: since, in the theme's original form, the figure in bar 2 assumed special prominence by being the only figure re-used without change later in the theme (bar 5), then in the final form of the theme, when bars 4 and 6 are deleted but the fifth bar remains, this bar acquires even more proportionate importance.

In the introduction itself, the theme is repeated, then followed by a complementary second segment, richly scored with divided violas and cellos. This segment moves to E minor, closing on its dominant; the direct juxtaposition of this dominant with the home dominant seventh was cited in Ex. 49 (p. 136). The theme returns in strong bare octaves, but with two conspicuous changes. The third bar, described earlier as a rhythmic echo of the second bar, is now an echo in two additional senses: dynamically (it is *piano*), and melodically. It is a melodic echo in that it is now harmonised with a bass part identical with the second bar of the theme (Ex. 81).

Ex. 81

While this demonstrates that the third bar was, from the start, a potential descant to the second bar, more significant in this discussion is that in the restatement given in Ex. 81 the second bar, originally re-used as the fifth bar of the theme, is now re-used in the third bar too, thus becoming even more influential. The second change in this restatement affects the ending, which is harmonically 'open', allowing Schubert to proceed again to a dominant of E minor, followed as before by a dominant seventh of C.

The next segment of the introduction, the most important for its consequences later in the movement, is quoted in full in Ex. 82, if in skeletal form.

Ex. 82

The theme is here recast, initially, over dominant harmony. The third bar is now not so much an echo as a more affirmative statement of the second-bar motive. From the fifth bar onwards, this motive takes over. Its appearances multiply, in half-bar imitations in A flat major, and are then thinned out, upstaged by the harmonic drama of a remote D flat minor chord, moving unpredictably to one of F minor (the subdominant chord, minor-inflected, of C). Lastly, the motive is extended, blossoming into an arching cadence-figure so important later in the movement that it must be labelled (*xy* in Ex. 82). All that remains of the introduction is a further enunciation of the theme, extended

to allow for a dominant build-up and intensification of
rhythm in readiness for the *Allegro ma non troppo*.

The long-term significance of the passage just studied
will be seen by moving forwards beyond the first subject
of the *Allegro* and to a point midway through the second
subject group. This group is in G major, though it begins
in E minor. Extending the second subject itself, Schubert
settles on a chord of E flat major, and prolongs it, pat-
terning it with figures from the second subject and its
accompaniment. The three trombones enter softly in
unison (Ex. 83), and so begins a passage which has rightly
become a *locus classicus* of the use of trombones for
hushed, theme-bearing purpose.

Ex. 83

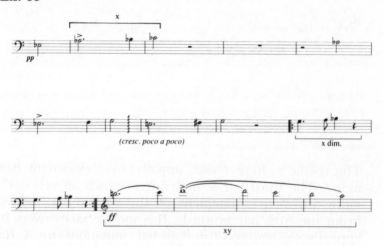

Two obviously striking features of this section of some
three dozen bars are the scoring and the harmony.
(Harmonically, this is a typical Schubertian excursion
away from and back to the prevailing key, but it is a
particularly venturesome example.) But the thematic
content is also noteworthy, for it centres on the second
bar of the introduction theme, just as Ex. 82 did. The

extra note preceding this motive may be understood by
analogy with the last note of the first bar of the symphony. This extra note is eventually dropped. The
motive is notated, of course, in values twice the length of
those in the introduction (Ex. 80), as the tempo is now
Allegro.

In the middle of the section (omitted from Ex. 83) a
long and gradual crescendo begins. As this approaches its
goal, Schubert adds further tension by quickening the
motive so that it appears in diminution (*x dim* in Ex. 83):
that is, the note-values are halved. Tension is then
released through the same arching cadence-figure (*xy*) as
closed the passage studied above in the introduction, and
this figure is now stated three times, with joyous variants
at the second and third hearing, to form the last main climax (and first triple *forte*) of the exposition. The re-entry
of *xy* at this point is a clue to the analogy of this whole
trombone passage with the section in the introduction:
both are pre-occupied with the second bar of the *Andante*
theme, both develop it obsessively, varying its time-scale
in the process, and both are huge harmonic excursions
whose homecoming is signalled by the triumphantly
expansive *xy*. Thus the second bar of the introduction has
assumed a major role in the exposition.

The use of both augmentation and diminution has
been observed in the above analysis. Both have a decisive
effect, respectively easing and increasing tension.
Maurice Brown's statement of Schubert, that 'his work is
completely devoid of such academic contrivances as augmentation, diminution, inversion and so on'[20] is simple
misinformation. More unfortunate is the misunderstanding he encourages by using the term 'contrivances'
and describing these as 'devices which, as one eminent
critic has said, belong to the nursery apparatus of

[20] 'Schubert', in *Grove's Dictionary of Music and Musicians*, 5th edition,
Macmillan, London, 1954, Vol. 7, p. 562.

composition'.[21] If one takes the trouble to discover what these procedures are, how widely they are used, and with what apposite and natural effect, one has no call impotently to blame the great (and the 'Great') in this way. Besides, 'contrivances' and 'devices' imply conscious manipulation, and the use of these terms suggests an unawareness of what a composer's subconscious mind may accomplish for him. The truth is that a composer is gifted with a hyperactive subconscious mind which does much of his composing for him. The work of his subconscious mind will probably be indistinguishable from that of his conscious mind. But whether relationships unveiled by analysis sprang from the composer's conscious of subconscious mind, they are all equally present – for the analyst or the listener – and equally to be acknowledged as functional constituents in the musical edifice. The Soviet composer Edison Denisov has written:[22]

> In analyzing any composition, we retrace certain moments in the creative process. It is wholly unimportant whether the work arose through the conscious application of some compositional principle, or purely intuitively (in which case we presume that the author himself 'didn't notice' it). If we can observe an underlying principle, it has an objective reality, and we are therefore fully justified in investigating it and regarding it as part of the compositional process.

The motive from the *Andante* theme plays the same part in the recapitulation as in the exposition. It is also the topic of the second half of the development. The first half of the development mixes elements from the first and second subjects. After protracted play on this material in A flat major, all *piano*, it moves off to other keys and a long crescendo begins, culminating in a *fortissimo*

[21] *Ibid.*, p. 562.

[22] 'The Compositional Process', *Tempo*, No. 105, 1973, pp. 2–11.

midway through the development. From this point, the
Andante motive is resumed. Ex. 84 outlines the whole of
this second half of the development, up to the recapitulation.

Ex. 84

The *Andante* motif is now given a sharper rhythmic
profile, with double dots. It is enunciated by the three
trombones, as before, but *fortissimo*. The tonality moves
through a cycle of major thirds (A flat, E, C), recalling the
first movement of the *Tragic* Symphony. A further step
restores A flat (shown in the 'first-time' bracket in Ex. 84),

where the motive is reduced to a diminution of itself, then repeated A flats. This cycle then repeats itself, though softly and with different scoring. Indeed, the repeat is so radically varied that one hardly notices that it is a repeat. Schubert is of course unable to use 'repeat-signs', which are used in Ex. 84 to clarify and simplify the structure. When the cycle is fulfilled the second time, the dominant of C is quickly attained, ready for the recapitulation. Thus the *Andante* motif is not only the last thing heard before the recapitulation begins (*cf.* the last two bars of Ex. 84), but provides the climax of the development just as it provided the main climaxes of the exposition and recapitulation; and, as was seen earlier, of the coda.

It is thus possible to plot the course of much of the first movement, taking account of its principal climaxes, by reference only to the introduction material. This ease of analysis indicates how far-reaching is Schubert's integration of the slow introduction into the first movement. It would be an exaggeration to say that in the light of these observations the first and second subjects are unimportant, although in relative terms there is a grain of truth in this statement. It would be hard to think of a Classical movement in which the 'subjects' have a less dominant role. In these circumstances, it is perfectly credible that Schubert should have completed the whole movement before he determined the finite shape of his first subject. After the movement was finished, he changed the subject (Ex. 85(a)), at every appearance, to Ex. 85(b). This change has been generally applauded as resulting in a more distinctive theme. Actually, neither version is particularly distinctive, as symphonic subjects go. But that is part of Schubert's scheme, which is to conceive a symphonic movement in which the thematic material of the introduction should not be eclipsed. It is in its attempt to strike a new balance in this respect that this movement is so innovative. Schubert's main concern, when he finished his introduction, drew his

Ex. 85

(a)

(b)

(c)

double-bar, and began his *Allegro ma non troppo*, was to
establish a 'sense of movement', to set up a momentum
that would provide the setting for his grand design.
The absence of any imposing thematic idea would not
hinder his purpose. An idea which incorporated useful
rhythmic modules, as potential units of energy, would
best serve his plan. In this light it will be appropriate to
give further consideration to the rhythmic character of
the movement.

A new spaciousness was noted as a feature which dis-
tinguishes the 'Unfinished' and 'Great' from Schubert's
youthful symphonies. In the 'Unfinished', space was
implied by, among other things, a new treatment of the
orchestral pitch-space. In the case of the 'Great', space is
implied by multiplication. Tiny rhythmic cells proliferate
in myriad repetitions, energising broad phrases which
themselves multiply into huge paragraphs. To this tireless
continuity is added a rhythmic drive that carries all
before it. The 'Great' is as much a celebration of rhythm
as Beethoven's Seventh is. Unlike the torso of the 'Unfinished', a slowish symphony in triple time, it moves
briskly in duple time, with a slow movement that is not
very slow at all and a three-in-the-bar scherzo throughout
which one may count a larger two (*one*, two, three, *two*,
two, three, *one* . . .).

Both Schubert's first and second subjects are more important as pools of rhythmic cells than for their melodic shape. It is for this reason that the second subject can so readily extend itself to become a continuing background texture for the trombone passage in Ex. 83, that the first and second subjects can so homogeneously interact in the first half of the development, that both can combine to create an animated ambience for the play on the *Andante* motive in the second half of the development, and that elements of the first subject can linger on to maintain continuity during the final reprise of the *Andante* theme at the end of the coda. The recurring patterns which, stemming from the first and second subjects, establish themselves as the energising units in this richly patterned score are one-bar patterns: they fill one bar and recur in succeeding bars. Schubert's original first subject (Ex. 85(a)) began with a half-bar pattern. It was probably to bring it into line with the prevailing pattern-length, as observed after completion of the movement, that he changed it to Ex. 85(b) – which exhibits a one-bar pattern. He had already forged a one-bar model from this theme in the development section, by placing a rest after its third note (Ex. 85(c)). It was logical to 'backdate' this reconsideration to the beginning of the *Allegro*.

Two other aspects of this movement require comment. Firstly, the transition to the second key for the second subject is even more abrupt than in the first movement of the 'Unfinished'. Schubert makes do with a harmonic shift which takes no longer than a single bar. Harold Truscott takes issue with this view. 'Another of these "sudden" transitions which are not. The E minor harmony is *not* the second key; it is the beginning of Schubert's transition passage, a transition in which the turn to the real second key, G major, comes with the wonderful passage with the trombone theme.'[23] This riposte has some point, but one could well refer to G major as the

[23] Letter to Martin Anderson, dated 22 October 1987.

third key and E minor as the second. Schubert could have remained in E minor for the rest of his exposition, and the listener would have been no less content than when Schubert actually did stay in his unorthodox second key, G major, to the end of the exposition in the 'Unfinished'. Moreover, G major arrives so late in the exposition of the 'Great' that it has a climactic function but no function as a medium for the exposition of thematic material. If the exposition is considered thematically rather than tonally, the 'second group' is virtually complete by the time G major arrives. The ear used to *Der Musensohn* and the 'Unfinished'[24] has no difficulty in hearing E minor as a Schubertian second-subject key, just as in the String Quintet in C the musical world at large accepts E flat as the second-subject key after, again, only four bars of transition from C, and calls the famous new theme in E flat the second subject. (Truscott presumably calls this theme, and what all other writers call the second subject of the 'Unfinished', the transition.)

Secondly, there is a particularly daring excursion in the coda, and Schubert amplified it on second thoughts so as to enhance and aggrandise the final advent of the introduction theme. The excursion is based on a new idea (Ex. 86(a)) which owes obvious allegiance to an earlier idea (Ex. 86(b)).

Ex. 86

Imitations of this idea seem to lead to the threshold of C sharp major and F sharp minor in no time at all, but

[24] *Cf.* p. 193.

the tonic C is soon re-approached by way of Ex. 86(a) in the bass.[25] Schubert subsequently added a varied and extended repetition of this excursion, lighting up other distant tonal areas and culminating with a threefold statement of Ex. 86(a) in the bass, the third time in augmentation – a fine rhetorical stroke imparting a fitting majestic breadth to the final throes of the movement. All that remains is a see-sawing between tonic and dominant harmony, with a quickening rate of change between the two, to set off the culminating reprise of the introduction theme. Schubert, unlike Dvořák in his *Carnival* Overture, has stopped just short of circling back – by different routes – to his tonic chord once too often.

As Schubert proceeds with his symphony and begins the second movement, it seems that he is not proposing to take the opportunity, even in such a big-boned work, to introduce an extreme contrast. In one respect at least – in the degree of rhythmic activity – he opts to draw the four movements together, unifying them by allowing each to maintain, in its own terms, the pulsating onward sweep of the first. As far as the second movement is concerned, duple time will help Schubert fulfil his vision, as will a tempo moderate rather than slow. His *Andante con moto* serves this purpose well with its march-like characteristics. It moves with a steady tread, and all its themes are 'downbeat' – beginning on a first beat, and having a rhythmic substructure that reinforces rather than offsets the pulse. It processes non-stop, with uninterrupted 'left-right' step; that is to say, there is no bar in the movement in which notes are not struck on both the two main beats. The only exception, apart from the last bar of course, is

[25] The first daring harmonic move of this excursion entails the mutation of a major triad by raising first its root, to create a diminished triad, and then its third and fifth, to produce a further major triad a semitone above the original (bb. 590–96). This exerted a seminal effect on later composers, notably Dvořák (in, for example, his Eighth Symphony, bb. 268–69 of the first movement).

the cataclysmic one-and-a-half-bar silence which forms the climax of the movement and is the more highly charged with tension because it is rhythmically exceptional.

The larger durational aspect – structure – is articulated as clearly as the smaller durational aspects, rhythm and phrase-structure. Figure 6 assigns a number to each theme and indicates the tonal plan: a short line is a transition and a plus sign denotes extended development of what precedes it.

								Figure 6										
A						F	A											
1	2	3	1	2	3	1	2	–	4	–	1	2	3	1	2	3	+ 4	coda

The well-ordered regularity with which theme follows theme reinforces the sense of 'procession', as does the steadfast consistency of key. Any attempt to relate the resulting form to traditional schemes will lead to the conclusion that it is a hybrid. The fourth theme in F major, separated on either side by short transitions, could be taken as the middle section of a ternary design. But this interpretation does not take account of the full reprise of the fourth theme later in the movement. Alternatively the scheme is a sonata-form. Theme 4 is the second subject, stated in F major and recapitulated in the tonic. As is customary in a slow movement, there is no real development. There may be some difficulty in reconciling with sonata-form the number of themes and repetitions in the first subject group and the fact that none of these repetitions develops into a transition: the first group is in fact a rounded, 'closed' section beginning and ending in A, with a mere four-bar transition following it, to prepare for the second subject. In this regard, the first group perhaps sounds more like the first section of a ternary structure. It should be borne in mind, though, that the short transition – merely a few linking bars – after a 'closed' first group is not alien to Schubert's sonata-form usage: it can be found in the first movements of both this symphony and the 'Unfinished'. The number of themes and repetitions is not usual in a first subject group; nor is it usual in the first section of a ternary movement. If Schubert was indebted to the second movement of Beethoven's Seventh Symphony, an idea that bears consideration, it could be that Beethoven's ternary scheme was in his mind.

Like Schubert's second movement, the *Allegretto* of Beethoven's Seventh is a not-very-slow slow movement in a symphony of tireless rhythmic elan. Both movements are in A minor and contain themes in A major (Beethoven's theme for his middle section, Schubert's second theme), and there are general rhythmic similarities. In spite of such likenesses, Schubert strikes his own path from the start. He begins by establishing a metronomic regularity in the upper strings and hinting, in the cellos and basses below, at particles of the first theme (Ex. 87), though in an almost casual order, with *b* preceding *a*. More important, the cellos and basses end this little preface with *c*, the two equal repeated notes, both accented – important, because this motive enjoys a motto-like universality of reference throughout the movement.

Ex. 87

It forms the third bar of the first theme, the last bar of the second theme, and the last bar of each of the four-bar modules that make up the third theme; it underpins the

subsequent transition to F major, providing its sole melodic reference; and, thus made prominent in so many
themes and theme-repetitions in the course of the movement, it becomes the exclusive topic of the last eleven
bars of the coda. This element of rhythmic continuity is
only one ingredient of the almost hypnotic motion that
preserves the movement from the risks of over-segment-
ation that must be apparent in Figure 6.

Schubert's F major theme (his second subject), which is
foreshadowed by the cellos and basses in the linking bars
that precede it, has an air of confiding emotional intimacies. This characteristic may be attributed in part to the
utter beauty and simplicity of its line (Ex. 88); and in part
to the fact that it is harmonised in three parts, with a
free-moving, expressive middle part. Was Schubert's pen
steered, wittingly or no, by the memory of an affecting
little tune from Mozart's Violin Sonata in E flat, к481
(Ex. 89)?

Ex. 88

Ex. 89

Schubert's harmony happens to be Mozart's, more or less,
but the texture, scoring, and continuation are Schubert's
own, as is the later segmentation of the tune and distribution of the segments among contrasting timbres: when
the melody is resumed beginning on a high F, its first two
notes are allotted to the strings and the remainder to the
woodwind, while at its last appearance the initial scale is

extended downwards and its segments assigned in turn to
trombones, high woodwind, and upper strings. This last
appearance merges into a transition back to A minor for
the recapitulation: a famous passage where, to quote
Tovey, the horns 'toll like a bell haunted by a human
soul'.[26] The reiterated Gs of the horns are re-interpreted
by changing harmonies coloured in by the upper and
lower strings in alternation, the whole adding up to a
Romantic sound-picture which surely moved Brahms to
similar effects in the first and last movements of his
Fourth Symphony. The wonderful turning-point is
reached at precisely that point where the horns cease to
do what a bell could do: the harmony moves on, obliging
the horns to fall by one degree, then by another. Thus,
by means of a pivotal Neapolitan sixth, A minor is
restored.

As the first theme returns, the trumpet speaks in new
counterpoint, with the intimacy of a woodwind instrument. This little enrichment is one of many imaginative
additions in the recapitulation, several of them involving
the trumpets and horns. But the most far-reaching addition is an extension added after the third theme, when it
comes round for the second time. It is a strenuous development, and it leads to a powerful diminished seventh
which carries more accumulated tension than most other
and later examples of this overworked tool of Romanticism. A charged silence follows, to be broken by a
plucked chord similar enough to be a near-echo, but different enough – by one mere semitone in an inner part –
to open up a new tonal vista. A further silence gives the
ear time to acclimatise to the likelihood that the key of B
flat major will take hold. The cellos enter, singing in con-
firmation of this allusion to Schubert's favourite 'Neapolitan' key, whereupon the oboe proposes the restoration of
A minor. The cellos point to B flat once more, with
enhanced accompaniment, and again the oboe insists on

[26] *Op. cit.*, p. 208.

A, but now its major mode; and all is then ready for the F major second subject to return in A major. The main climax of the movement is past, and its placing before the reprise of the second subject (to pursue the analysis of the movement as a sonata-form) suggests a new perspective in the treatment of the form, which Brahms was to embrace in the slow movements of his Second and Fourth Symphonies.

Two striking new developments are brought by the coda. The clarinet's obsessive reiterations of figure *d* from the first theme (Ex. 87) over shifting harmonies suggest an unlikely analogy with innumerable instances in the keyboard sonatas of Domenico Scarlatti. And later, the second theme, which has always been heard in A major, is 'resolved' to A minor and given a new circular completion which tells unmistakably that a chapter is closing and the end is in view.

The scherzo and trio combine weight with vitality in a manner new to symphonic writing. For the well-developed sonata-form there are precedents in the scherzo of the Sixth Symphony and the unfinished D708A (whose scherzo is complete in piano sketch up to the 'recapitulation'). For the weighty orchestration we can turn only to the scherzo of the Seventh, the first (finished) Schubert scherzo to include trombones, although it is largely for the imagination to determine how Schubert would have clothed a sketch which, although it obviously demands much *tutti* scoring, consists mainly of one line of music. The third movement of the 'Great' ventures heavier scoring than any equivalent movement in a Classical symphony. It is not simply a matter of the inclusion of trombones. In the scherzo itself, Schubert tends to throw the whole weight of the string section, in octave-unisons, against the massed wind forces: more than half of the strings' contribution is in octave-unisons. This technique was to become a valuable part of the orchestral style of later composers as diverse as Berlioz, Bruckner and Tchaikovsky. Moreover Schubert's trio from its very first bars makes no obeisance to the tradition that this section of the movement should offer a gentler contrast, with lighter scoring.

Schubert had already made extensive use of the one-bar motive which begins this scherzo (Ex. 90) in the scherzo of D708A.

Ex. 90

In this scherzo the second bar, the threefold C, is no less influential than the first. Apart from its regular use in harness with the first bar throughout the scherzo, it sometimes has a life of its own; and it forms the basis of the linking passage between the scherzo and the trio. The connection between that link and the original motive is made plain by what happens in the preceding last bars of the scherzo. The waltz-like second subject (Ex. 91) in the dominant provides a suitable *cantabile* foil for the first subject, which happily co-exists with it as part of its accompaniment.

Ex. 91

The ensuing offshoot of this second subject, which takes its third bar as a starting-point and continues to sweep

down and up the broken chord of D, the strings playing
en masse with two bars to a single stroke of the bow, even
more suavely offsets the continuing play on the first subject in the woodwind.

The development is in two distinct phases. The first
asserts A flat vehemently, and stays there to build a new
theme from the first-subject materials, to which the cellos
sing a new counter-theme built of second-subject materials. The second takes the broken-chord offshoot of the
second subject, inverts it so that it sweeps up then down,
and extends each cycle of it from four bars to six. These
huge waves on massed strings mark out, in their six-bar
blocks, the chords of D flat major, C sharp minor, A
major, D minor, and G major, the last being elaborated to
give it the flavour of a dominant, ready for the recapitulation. Between these two phases of development, a new
theme not unrelated to the second subject appears in the
flute, in C flat major, at once repeated by the violins with
a sudden, magical Schubertian shift up a semitone to C
major. The addition of an oboe to the violin line, one of
Schubert's favourite combinations, adds edge to the violin
tone and makes this second appearance of this new eight-
bar theme (which is never to be heard again) seem to
inhabit a quite different world from the first.

New in the recapitulation is the treatment of the first
subject. Originally presented in bare octaves, it is now
harmonised, then treated in soft scampering imitations
which are the nearest this scherzo comes to the delicate
counterpoint of its ancestor in D708A. The coda resumes
the new themes made from old materials which began the
development section, and leads to a resounding C major
close, whereupon the repeated Es (in the rhythm of the
second bar of the movement) pivot the music into A
major for the trio. (This tonal relationship between
scherzo and trio, and the method of transition from one
to the other, were anticipated in the third movement of
the Seventh Symphony.) Of all the significant departures
from tradition in the 'Great' C major, the character of the

trio is one of the most striking, and the most frequently overlooked. Even though the strict nominal implication of 'trio' as denoting an alternative minuet harmonised in three parts had only spasmodic influence after 1750, the early Classical symphonies of Haydn and Mozart tend to contain in their trio section more relaxed, shortwinded and uncomplicated invention than will be found in any other part of their symphonies. Beethoven aspired to grandeur in his Fourth and Seventh, rugged counterpoint in his Fifth, and more sophisticated contrapuntal play in his Ninth. Schubert in the 'Great' eschews counterpoint in favour of song; but his trio is a song of grander breadth, sonorous power, and sustained fervour than one may find in a comparable situation in any other symphony of Classical times. Nor do examples in the later nineteenth century come readily to mind.

The song is sung by the woodwind,[27] with the brass adding harmonic strength and rhythmic kick to the accompaniment in the strings. The immediate impression is of a daring largeness of phrase: although there is no change of tempo from the scherzo, the music flows more broadly, in longer conceptual spans. Where the scherzo proceeded in bars, or pairs of bars, here one feels pairs or fours. The first section seems to have all the time in the world to reach its destination of C sharp minor. The second is on the verge of returning to A major, when it is happily diverted to A minor, and thence to C major, where the trumpets add their timbre to the full-throated mixture. The theme returns in the tonic (A), but its fourth phrase is subtly deflected to the fresh territory of the 'Neapolitan' key, B flat major, seeming to add yet more size to the composer's vision. After the return to A

[27] It is typical of Schubert's liberated use of the trombones that for two whole phrases in the trio he uses a high alto trombone to act as a woodwind substitute, entrusting to it a middle part of three, between clarinets and bassoons (bb. 342–58).

and close in that key, this expansive second section is repeated in accordance with trio practice, the resultant overall dimensions of the trio obliging Schubert to provide a special transition back to the scherzo, a transition which like that from scherzo to trio makes use of the second bar of the scherzo.

This huge movement ends, after the reprise of the scherzo, with a resounding cadence in C major. The finale is naturally to follow in this same key. It cannot cap that foregoing cadence in weight or spread or orchestral sonority, and it makes its first points by means of energy and rhetoric as much as orchestral might. Is this opening the first theme, or is it an introduction in the tempo (*Allegro vivace*) of the finale proper? The answer is that it is neither to the exclusion of the other: its ambivalence is its strength. But its fragmentary, convulsive progress – its air of 'limbering up' – is to be set in a new perspective when it is recapitulated later.

The first subject group contains an abundance of ideas, all of them derived from the dotted rhythm with which the movement first sprang to life, or from its hushed triplet response. The tonic key holds sway for a long period, giving way to the dominant for the second subject only late in the day. The second subject itself is of decisive importance, both before and long after its arrival. It begins with four whole-bar notes (Ex. 92), which reappear sequentially throughout its course, and eventually bring it to completion (Ex. 93). These four notes strongly suggest a four-bar grouping – so much so that one could almost rewrite the music with bars four times as long: the four notes would then fall on the four beats of a single bar. The arrival of this theme could, then, be viewed as a further stage in the trend towards larger spans noted in the trio of the third movement. The spans are now so long that what strikes the ear is something infinitely more spacious than the fussy subdivisions that strike the eye. These four-bar groupings had already taken hold before the second subject arrived, and even

Ex. 92

Ex. 93

before the abandonment of the tonic key. The four long notes of the second subject themselves may be recalled as having been forcefully enunciated by woodwind and horns some fifty bars back (readers of the score should see bar 113), and from that point forwards the four-bar grouping was to remain unchallenged. Its effect on the later course of the movement will be seen as this survey progresses.[28]

Two other features of the second subject must be noted in passing. Parallel thirds (or their inversion, parallel sixths) were a familiar idiom of the Viennese Classical

[28] The setting-up of a regular bar-grouping was often an important strategy in Schubert, as in Beethoven. One of the most arresting moments in the String Quintet in C, D956, occurs in the scherzo where after 80 bars in four-bar groups Schubert dramatically cuts the next group short by planting a new first bar, *fortissimo*, where its third bar should have fallen.

style. They are particularly evident in orchestral writing,
a fact which may be connected with the presence of
woodwind instruments in pairs. But in this theme one can
almost sense Schubert using the technique as a means of
strengthening the line, as though paralleling the melody
in thirds is an alternative to, and has a comparable effect
to, 'doubling' the melody at the unison or at the octave. It
is fairly consistently applied here, as is the accompaniment pattern in the strings, a triplet figure repeated bar
by bar which no doubt tested the stamina and compre-
hension of those who first attempted to play the symphony and gave up the effort.

The span framed by Exx. 92 and 93, long as it is, is but
the 'A' section of an ABA presentation. The 'B' section contains phrases which seem to enshrine the soul of the
oboe, and the following 'A' is a fully scored reprise of the
first section. A codetta, mixing elements from the first
and second subjects, completes the exposition. Its climax,
marked by the only triple *forte* in the entire exposition, is
a crowning cadential statement of the first four bars of
Ex. 93. At the resolving tonic, the same four-bar idea falls
away in the bass, becoming the gradually fading substance of a long decrescendo and thinning-out of the
instrumentation. It is worth noting that when, immediately after this, the development begins with the two clarinets intoning in E flat major a theme which can be easily
associated with the joy theme of Beethoven's Ninth, that
theme is – in this context – a direct descendant of the
four-bar idea from the second subject (to be precise, the
first four bars of Ex. 93 which was sounded by the whole
orchestra in climactic triple *forte* to close the exposition).

Like other developments by Schubert, this one subdi-
vides naturally into two parts. The first is concerned with
the theme referred to above; the second is concerned
with the four long notes of the second subject. Indeed,
when those four long notes first interrupt the development, they are followed by the four bars which originally

followed them (in Ex. 91), and these are extended and developed. But when they are exhausted, all is reduced to the four notes alone. Against them are heard anticipations of the initial upward spring of the first subject, and soon the first subject takes the stage, with the four notes still being reiterated as backcloth to it, filling the gaps between its fragmented convulsions. Thus the all-important 'head' of the second subject now implants a background of four-bar grouping for the first subject, which is heard differently thereby; and the influence of that grouping is thus carried a stage further.

In the recapitulation, the first subject group is radically re-worked, and the four notes of the second-subject 'head' play a more explicit part than before in its closing stages. As before, the silence which precedes the second subject itself is broken first by an anticipation, in the horns, of the four long notes, sounding as a giant anacrusis to the theme. The second group runs as before, leading to the coda. The listener who knows Schubert's enthusiasm for the tonal excursion in a coda, which may have been kindled in the first place by Beethoven's Second Symphony, might expect this finale to have a particularly long and energetic one – and will not be disappointed. Schubert does not delay its commencement. As the last climax of the recapitulation subsides to a soft tonic chord of C major, and finally a bare bass C, he drops the bass by way of a B flat to an A, which supports an A major chord, and the excursion has begun (and the seed is sown of a passage in the first movement of Schumann's Second Symphony).

From this starting-point the excursion proceeds in four loosely sequential stages. Each stage begins with something resembling the accompaniment to the second subject, but without the theme: the focus is thus on the harmony, as in that seminal excursion in Beethoven's Second. The harmony moves in four-bar blocks, reflecting the four-bar grouping which is by now firmly implicit. The bass makes the leading move, to the dominant of a

new key, and the familiar cadence preparation which
originated in Ex. 93 (first four bars) brings a partial
resolution.[29] Schubert has been chided for reproducing
this process so that it is heard four times in all. The fact
of the matter is that only two of the four hearings are
harmonically identical, and the steady screwing-up of the
pitch coupled with an overall crescendo tends to conceal
such repetition; it is rather just a part of the inevitable
and unstoppable growth of one of the finest pieces of cli-
max-building in all music. At the climax itself, C major is
attained anew, and the thematic goal is reached – the first
four notes of the second subject hammered out, on the
home tonic, in bare octaves. The motive's urge for dominance is thus fulfilled, and a final development of it
brings all manner of new emphasis to it, demanding a
threefold reference to the cadence-approach figure from
Ex. 91 to make a fitting resolution. The main climactic
business done, Schubert returns to the energetic bustle of
the finale's opening and drives that hard to its own brilliant conclusion.

A well-known problem facing editors of Schubert
manuscripts is that of distinguishing his accent signs from
his hairpin *diminuendo* signs. Between the orthodox sign
for an accent (>) and that for a *diminuendo* (>) there is
to be found in Schubert's autographs a whole gamut of
minutely different variants. Sometimes, irrespective of
the context, the sign seems too elongated for an accent
and/or too short for a *diminuendo*. At other times it is not
so much that the length of the sign is ambiguous as that
the visually more plausible of the two interpretations
appears less appropriate to the musical context. There is

---

[29] A partial resolution, in that the keys of E flat major, F major, and G
major are successively implied – and quite unmistakably – but the
tonic chord of none of them is stated in a stronger form than the
second inversion. This subtle, tantalising technique of key-implication
is one to which Schubert became more and more addicted in his later
years. The piano prelude of the song *Bei dir allein*, D866, No. 2 (1828),
implies C minor, within its A flat major tonal frame, by this process.

still scope for fresh thought and new findings, although it is clear that a major undertaking would be required. Account would have to be taken of the performance practice of the musicians of the day in the playing of accents, the relative authority of the various manuscript sources, the meaning of the signs for exponents of different instruments, and Schubert's degree of observance of such differences. Other questions to be asked might be: did Schubert see the difference between > and ⟩ in performance as merely a difference of time-scale, one being a faster *diminuendo* than the other? Or is it the case, as many modern performers seem to accept, that the longer symbol is necessarily a dynamic inflection while the shorter one may be a colouristic one of another sort – a nuance of tone or intonation (for example, involving a certain kind and degree of vibrato) rather than of volume? Was Schubert careless in his use of the symbols, or painstaking? Or inconsistent in his attitude to them? Could it be, on the other hand, that he invested these markings with less significance for the performer than we now suppose: that they were addressed to the score-reading analyst, or to that person within Schubert himself – perhaps acting in some mysterious way as a compensation for a distance between the idea and the notation available to express it? Whatever the answers to such questions, there is hardly a more conspicuous instance of the dilemma than the marking on the last chord of the 'Great' C major Symphony.

Here the accent mark is so elongated that many conductors have favoured its interpretation as a *diminuendo*. Nicholas Toller suggests that the fact that Schubert seems to have retaken his pen to complete the (large) accent sign argues against it denoting an accent: it is as though he was determined that it should appear large.[30] This argument can be countered by the observation that this

---

[30] In *Gesture and Expressive Purpose in Schubert's Instrumental Music of 1822-28*, University of Hull, 1988 (unpublished thesis).

sign is only one of three of a kind (one at the top of the score, one at the bottom, and this one below the flute part) written by Schubert at this bar, and the other two, being unflawed, did not require a retake of the pen; Schubert enlarged the third one only to bring it up to the size of the other two. Whichever of the three he wrote first (presumably the top one) he wrote it with a flourish either to impart to it the weight and significance of a *final* accent, or because he tended in any case to use bold strokes of the pen at the end of a symphony (as in the florid, thick-ended final 'double-bar' signs on this same page of autograph).[31]

Klaus Tennstedt has proposed[32] a different reason for regarding this same instance as a *diminuendo*. Nowhere in music, he states, except at the last chord of the 'Great' is there both an accent *and sforzando*. 'That is why I perform it as *diminuendo*', he explains. It might be a compelling argument, were it not based on a faulty premise. For other examples of accent and *sforzando* combined, one has to look no further than bar 459 of this same finale, or bar 494 of the first movement of the same symphony, not to mention innumerable instances in works as unalike as the Octet and *Fierrabras*. (In all these cases, as in the last chord of the 'Great', it is a *forzato* (*fz*) rather than a *sforzando* (*sf*) that Schubert uses.)

Another solution – to the general issue of accent-versus-*diminuendo* rather than the particular case at the close of the 'Great' – has been ventured by Stefano Mollo in a booklet accompanying a Deutsche Grammophon recording.[33] There is no problem, Mollo states, for Schubert differentiated quite clearly between the two phenomena by writing accents above the notes concerned, while

[31] The last page of Schubert's autograph is reproduced in the Eulenburg miniature score, p. xix.

[32] In an interview in *Ovation*, December 1982.

[33] *Cf.* p. 109, note 12.

hairpins are written below the stave. Why, then, has such a simple answer eluded generations of Schubert scholars? Because it is not an answer at all. The first page of the autograph of the 'Great', which is reproduced in the same booklet for all to see, alone clinches the falsity of Mollo's claim six times. And Claudio Abbado, who conducts the recorded performance, wisely ignores Mollo's advice.

I attempted earlier in this chapter[34] to show that the four movements of the 'Great' are very much 'of a piece', although they share no common thematic material. There are, finally, some further indications of a unity of conception. The coda of the finale reaches a climax through the threefold repetition of a four-bar cadence-approach idea, the third statement reaching triple *forte* and resolving the high G of the first two in an even higher C. The description exactly fits the climax of the first movement's recapitulation (which in turn reflects that of the exposition). Moreover, a rare chord, which is even rarer when resolved as Schubert resolves it in the 'Great', plays a prominent role, appearing in three of the four movements at comparable junctures. The chord is an augmented sixth, of 'German' type, placed on the subdominant, and resolving in a first inversion of the tonic. Ex. 94 shows it as it first appears in the coda of the first movement. It occurs nine times in the symphony,[35] each

Ex. 94

---

[34] *Cf.* p. 219.

[35] First movement, b. 632; third movement, b. 378; fourth movement, bb. 189, 245, 325, 777, 833, 913 and 1045.

time at the approach of a cadence of major climactic import.

Until research in the 1970s proved otherwise, the 'Great' C major was thought of as Schubert's last symphony. Nobody would have questioned its fitness for that role. Had Schubert enjoyed Beethoven's life-span and been able to write symphonies for nearly thirty years more after the 'Great', it seems reasonable to suppose that none of them would have eclipsed it. It is a symphony *sui generis*, and within its own kind it is hard to imagine that it might be surpassed. It is now known that Schubert essayed a symphony once more, three years after this one. The Tenth was to comprise an exploration of new directions. It could not be a culmination of directions already pursued in the other symphonies of his maturity, for the 'Unfinished' and the 'Great' were themselves culminations of the two distinct directions the mature symphonist had so far opted to pursue.

XIV

Ink and Paper

Like other symphonists, Schubert relied on pen, ink and paper as the media through which to communicate the products of his imagination to performers, and through them, to listeners. He was probably unaware of the full significance of this fact for the future understanding of his work. Modern research is able to base important musicological decisions on the evidence of ink colour, handwriting, and paper types displayed in autograph scores. Such considerations count all the more in Schubert's case by virtue of the facts that the huge majority of his works survive in signed manuscripts in his own hand, and that he was active in the last decades before hand-made paper production was largely superseded by mechanised manufacture. It is possible to build up a picture of his year-by-year habits in the purchase and utilisation of paper, in his manner of laying out a score, in other aspects of his notation, and in his handwriting. Patterns emerge from which it is possible to assign dates to manuscripts left undated by the composer. Only in the second half of the twentieth century were techniques developed and research undertaken which enabled the available clues to be interpreted.[1]

[1] The role of paper studies in Schubert research is elucidated in an admirable essay by Robert Winter entitled 'Paper Studies and the Future of Schubert Research' in Badura-Skoda and Branscombe, *op. cit.*, pp. 209–75.

Symphonies are set down, of course, in a full score, which is a conflation – on as many staves as are required – of all the instrumental parts. An autograph full score is the customary textual source of any symphony. How does the composer commit this score to paper? Or, to put the question more precisely, what is the relation between the intellectual process of composing the symphony and the manner in which its final notated representation is reached? It is usually assumed that the composer separates two stages of the notation, first fixing the pitch and time elements in some sort of 'short' score or piano score, then orchestrating this 'sketch'. To some extent there may be a corresponding separation of the intellectual processes. The first draft may be a piano score, compressed on to two staves though not necessarily within the playing compass of a pianist, with no indication at all of the final instrumentation. More usually, since the music is ideally conceived orchestrally, the composer will have some broad idea of the orchestration at this stage, whether or not he writes in names of instruments here and there in the piano score. This method, or something like it, has prevailed since the early nineteenth century, not surprisingly since the full score normally comprises between one dozen and two dozen staves, and sometimes more.

Yet it was not an invariable method in the earlier days of orchestral composition. Schubert presents a particularly interesting case, and although there is not sufficient evidence to permit absolutely firm conclusions about his preparation of symphonic scores, there are several revealing indications. An almost automatic assumption is made by some commentators, when the only available source material of a work is an autograph full score, that the sketches must have been lost or destroyed. Schubert's Ninth Symphony is a case in point. Brown affirms: 'The sketches [. . .] for the C major Symphony [. . .] are lost'.[2] Reed makes a similar assumption: 'If the sketches for

[2] *Schubert: A Critical Biography*, p. 5.

the Great C major Symphony ever come to light [. . .] '.[3] The other possibility, which seems not have been seriously examined, is that there never were any sketches. True, Mandyczewski (in the *Revisionsbericht* – the editorial notes to the complete edition) and Deutsch[4] both made categorical statements to the effect that Schubert did not make preliminary sketches except in the case of the 'Unfinished' Symphony, but neither offered any supporting arguments: they seem to have taken the absence of such sketches for Nos. 1–6 and 9 as evidence in itself. The contrary point of view has been more thoroughly considered and presented, a leading advocate being Michael Griffel, who claims[5] that 'it was Schubert's normal practice first to sketch a work in piano score'. When he was convinced that his symphony was finished, 'he would discard his sketches for it and all the preliminary drafts'. While he is cautious about the status of his evidence *as* evidence, he is firm in his view. Yet the facts he marshals to support his contention are all compatible with Schubert's having made no sketches at all for his finished symphonies. Since sketches *may* indeed yet come to light, it would appear foolhardy to proffer the hunch – without incontrovertible evidence – that the 'Great' was composed directly into full score, without the help of sketches of any sort. Nonetheless, that is what I propose to do. What follows is a hypothesis, or rather a succession of hypotheses, covering Schubert's entire symphonic career.

Schubert finished seven symphonies. There are no known piano sketches for any of them. There are piano sketches of the 'Unfinished'. But it is the other unfinished symphonies that provide the most useful clues to Schubert's procedure. The earliest surviving page of a Schubert

[3] *Op. cit.*, p. 196.

[4] 'The Riddle of the Unfinished Symphony', *Music Review*, I, 1940, p. 38.

[5] A Reappraisal of Schubert's Methods of Composition', *Musical Quarterly*, LXIII/2, April 1977, pp. 186–210, and especially pp. 189–90.

symphony gives one such clue. Of the D2B symphony begun in 1811 the autograph comprises merely thirty bars, in full score. On the first page of this score[6] Schubert is found experimenting, on spare space at the foot of the page, with various numbers of 'beams' for the short notes which run up the scale from the first note of the introduction in the first violins. He is not at once sure how to notate the sound-image which has just presented itself to his inner ear, and has to test the possibilities before he can write the correct solution into his score. If there had been a piano sketch, that testing would probably have been carried out before the rhythm was written into the piano score. A temporary expedient may have been adopted at that stage, of course, and the solving of the problem deferred: but in that case when Schubert tested the notation before completing the full score he is more likely to have done his thinking-on-paper on a spare corner of the piano sketch than on the full score itself.

If Schubert composed D2B directly into score, there is no reason that he should not have done the same with all his youthful symphonies (Nos. 1–6), so long as there was no abrupt change of musical style, nor any deep compositional crisis, in the period concerned. An important clue may be found in the autograph score of the Fourth Symphony.[7] After completing 44 bars of the finale, Schubert extended his first violin part for a further fourteen bars, without adding in parts for the other instruments. He then had second thoughts, crossed out these fourteen bars, and replaced them with a different continuation. Having written in this substitute violin part, he proceeded to write in parts for the other instruments. Now the violin continuation he first thought of led him, in the course of the fourteen bars concerned, from C minor to E flat major, apparently in readiness for a second subject; but the substitute part (his final version)

[6]*Cf.* the facsimile on p. 25.

[7] Kept in the Gesellschaft der Musikfreunde, Vienna.

modulates to A flat major for his second subject. If, when he wrote his original violin part, he was working from a piano sketch, the remainder of that sketch would have been made useless when he changed his mind, for the sketch would have been based on a second subject in E flat, whereas the final version proceeds on the basis of a second subject in A flat. It is much more likely – and the 'correction' itself implies this deduction – that Schubert was actually composing the music as he wrote his score. Composing straight into full score would have been, at this stage in the development of symphonic style, a fairly exacting intellectual exercise, but by no means impossible for one endowed with a good head and first-rate musicianly skills. Nowhere in Schubert's first six symphonies are more than twelve staves required.

I have already suggested[8] that by the time Schubert had completed his Sixth Symphony he was aware that he had reached a stylistic crossroads and must now strike out in a new direction. The pursuit of a new direction would necessitate a more reflective approach to composing: the next symphony would therefore be sketched in piano score, to facilitate experiment and revision. Another advantage of this method was that Schubert could see entire extended sections, such as a complete exposition, on one or two sides of paper. This facility would help him too, as the new direction he sought would entail structural and tonal as well as textural and harmonic experiment. He sketched a new symphony in this way (D615), and a further one (D708A). In the latter there are signs that he did not have instrumental timbre, compass, or limitations sufficiently in view as he worked. This failing may have contributed to a decision to compose the next symphony directly into score. Certainly, in the very first pages of this Symphony No. 7 in E there is every indication that Schubert is thinking in clear orchestral terms,

[8] In chapter IX, pp. 124 *et seq.*

and relishing the sonority of his newly enlarged orchestral medium, with three trombones added.

Commentators who believe that the score of the
Seventh was preceded by a piano sketch overlook a
number of significant factors. On the first page Schubert
sets out the names of the instruments required, alongside
their respective staves. He specifies two horns, in E. In
the course of the second page he suddenly adds in two
additional horns in G, because the turn taken by the
music at this point necessitates their use. From this point
on, the four horns are retained for the entire first movement. Had Schubert been working from a pre-existent
sketch, he would certainly have known when first select-
ing his instruments on the first page that horns in both E
and G would be required. That the second subject is in G
major would have given him a decisive reason for setting
out with horns in the two keys.

When setting down his list of instruments for the
second movement, Schubert included all those used in
the first movement. But as the movement unfolds it becomes clear from the character of the music that there is
no place in it for the trumpets, trombones and drums,
nor, in all probability, for the second pair of horns.
There is no trace in this movement of the strong contrasts
found in some other Schubert slow movements, such
as might suggest here the retention of those instruments.
If Schubert had completed the scoring of the movement
himself he would undoubtedly have omitted them. Why
did he not omit them from his preliminary list of instrumental requirements? Because he had not already composed the movement when he began scoring it.

It is difficult, then, to agree with Reinhard van Hoorickx who, having discussed the sketches for D615, finds it
'very probable that his Symphony in E (D729) originally
consisted of similar sketches'.[9] It is almost certain that

[9] 'The Chronology of Schubert's Fragments and Sketches', in Badura-
Skoda and Branscombe, *op. cit.*, p. 315.

Schubert composed and scored the symphony in one
sweep, enjoying all the advantages of doing so. The
instance of revision, examined above, in the finale of the
Fourth Symphony suggests the possibility that Schubert
worked in sections, extending the first violin or another
leading part for a few pages, then returning to complete
the orchestration before commencing the next section.
That was possibly one of the methods used in the early
symphonies. In the Seventh, Schubert evidently found
that even going back to complete the scoring of each section at a time slowed the pace of his thinking adversely.
Instead, he sketched right through to the end of each
movement, stopping only to touch in skeletal indications
of harmony, texture, or counter-melody at certain critical
points. He may have adopted this procedure too, at
times, in the earlier symphonies. In the Seventh, one has
the distinct impression that it gives the composer the best
chance of preserving flow and continuity. Whatever faults
the Seventh may have, it exhibits no lack of symphonic
sweep. In this quality it anticipates the Ninth, which was
probably composed in a similar way.

That Schubert finished the Seventh Symphony, in the
structural sense, and had also managed to leave enough
clues to enable him to complete the filling-out of detail,
although he was subsequently diverted from doing that,
is a vindication of the method of sketching used. To this
extent at least, the Seventh was a success. He will probably have been aware of this success, if indeed he did
return to the method in his 'Great'. Meanwhile, he was
envisaging a quite different kind of symphony. In slower
music the problem of the pen keeping up with the pace
of the music is less acute, and the 'Unfinished', apart
from being easier in pace, was to explore a more intense
and searching lyricism, coloured by richer harmonic
detail. Schubert, apparently aware that he was breaking
new stylistic ground – to a degree unprecedented in any
of his symphonies – opted for caution and began work in
piano score. It cannot be said that the method let him

down, any more than the other method had done in the
Seventh, even though, like the Seventh, the Eighth was
left unfinished. In the Ninth Symphony, one clue to the
likelihood that Schubert reverted to the sketching
method favoured in the Seventh is provided by the ink-
colours and their pattern of use in the autograph score.
At places where the leading melodic part and the bass,
and perhaps important texture-determining parts at key
junctures, are in ink of a different colour from the
remainder, the impression is given that an orchestral
sketch was subsequently filled in. A detailed study of the
autograph with these terms of reference has yet to be
made. It may well yield interesting results, in relation to
the present issue as well as to those issues which were in
Robert Winter's mind when he too pointed to 'procedural
puzzles' yet to be solved in this autograph.[10]

Paper studies[11] have shown that some sections of
music were added to the score some time after completion of the orchestral draft. If Schubert had written a
preliminary piano sketch such additions would probably
have been made during work on that sketch; or, as at
places in the Eighth Symphony, the once-and-for-all orchestral score would have embodied them from the start,
without the change being indicated in the piano score.
The re-shaping of the *Allegro* theme in the first movement of the Ninth[12] after the movement had been
wholly composed is another clue. The change was almost
certainly made in the light of what transpires later in the
movement. A piano sketch would have given Schubert
the opportunity to view the entire course of the movement and to make such adjustments before writing the
orchestral score. He probably first notated an unsatisfact-
ory version of the theme for the reason that he was

[10] *Loc. cit.*, p. 267, n. 6.

[11] *Ibid.*, pp. 232–39.

[12] *Cf.* pp. 225–26.

writing it as it came into his head, without detailed foreknowledge of the subsequent course of events. Then there is the revision he made to the second subject in the finale. Schubert's original idea for a second subject, following the four prefatory long notes in the horns (and therefore at bar 169), was a fugato on a somewhat fussy neo-Baroque subject. He quickly replaced this idea, as the autograph shows, with the second subject as it was ultimately to be. Is it possible that Schubert had already sketched a finale in which this fugato second subject had been extended, developed, and recapitulated, and that only now did he conceive his true second subject? If so, much of the remainder of the piano sketch would now be rendered useless, for the remainder of the finale in the orchestral autograph is based on the *new* second subject – and more than half of the music that follows is based on second subject material.

It is known that Mozart sometimes composed works directly into orchestral score. Hummel, one of Mozart's pupils, recounted[13] that his teacher worked in much the same way as I believe Schubert did in the Seventh Symphony, and as it is now suggested he did in his Ninth also:

> It is no small advantage that with this method of writing the score grows fast and one can see something finished in a very short time, while by writing out one page after another in full one never seems to make any headway. Moreover this is of greater importance for the progress of the work than one would think. One is in good spirits and carries out one's task with greater ease and willingness. And in the long run, though it might seem to require more time to keep going back to the beginning again, the work in fact takes less time. Mozart could not have written so much without this method.

[13] Quoted by Adolf Bernhard Marx in *Die Lehre von der musikalische Komposition, praktisch-theoretisch*, vol. iv, Leipzig, 1847, rev. 1888, English transl. 1910.

It may be supposed that the speed of composition achieved by Mozart, using this method in his orchestral works, helped to ensure the spontaneity and unity of his music. It is known that he was able to compose complete works or movements and hold them in his head for days before committing them to paper. In this light, speed of transcription from mind to paper was obligatory and a preliminary piano sketch superfluous. Although Schubert probably set about his symphonies with a less clear detailed view of the whole work or individual movements, he may well have foreseen the shape and direction and much of the detail of sizable sections, while also relying heavily on a well-developed skill in 'symphonic extemporisation'. He had in common with Mozart that he could and often did compose with a magic combination of spontaneity and speed.[14] In the case of symphonic composition, this entailed dispensing with piano sketches, and it may be that the 'Great' C major represents the triumphant climax of this method's currency. One may easily reconcile with that the music's enormous onward momentum, its 'sense of ready self-growth and natural connection',[15] or the impression taken by Einstein[16] that 'Schubert is here still living or living again in that paradise of pure music-making from which Beethoven had been driven forth'. It is possible that never again in the history of the symphony was white-hot inspiration committed directly to orchestral score as it apparently was here.

Some two years after completion of the 'Great', when Schubert had only two or three months to live, he set to work on another symphony. Once more, as in the

[14] The unifying features in the Seventh Symphony observed in chapter XI (pp. 177–78) may well be a by-product of the speed of composition.

[15] William McNaught, in Hill, *The Symphony*, p. 142.

[16] *Op. cit.*, p. 329.

'Unfinished', he deviated from the line of stylistic evolution that connects the Seventh to the Ninth; and once more, he returned to the method of sketching adopted for the 'Unfinished'. His caution will be better understood when the unprecedented aspirations of this last symphony have been examined.

XV

Vision of Beyond: The Tenth Symphony

Many problems beset posterity's understanding of Schubert's last attempted symphony. The piano sketch is hard to decipher,[1] a problem aggravated by the exploratory style of much of the music contained in it; the composer's structural intentions are not wholly explicit in any movement, the difficulties being most acute in the first; there are no more than three dozen instrumental indications in the entire sketch; and the sketch is undated. The present study will focus on certainties and seek to make clear distinctions between fact and hypothesis. The question of identification of the sketch, which only in the 1970s was seen to be an attempt at a final symphony made in Schubert's last year, will be considered separately.[2]

To begin with the work's date, Robert Winter has adduced strong evidence, on the basis of paper-types, that 'sketching on the symphony could scarcely have

---

[1] In parts of the sketch, Schubert's physical control of his writing seems diminished, as though by a combination of ill-health and impatience. Noteheads are at times less carefully formed and placed than in earlier sketches. Dots are more elongated. Some dynamic markings, accents, slurs and other symbols are so carelessly shaped or sited that it requires a prolonged and very close study to distinguish them from one another and from noteheads, stems, tails, and beams. Crossings-out and corrections create further difficulties.

[2] In Appendix 4, pp. 297–99.

258

commenced before September 1828, and more likely in October'. Schubert died on November 19, and this being the only incomplete work of that autumn, Winter declares that 'there can be little doubt that Schubert carried these drafts with him to his deathbed'.[3] Another aspect of the sketch would seem to corroborate this view. Schubert began the second movement on a sheet of paper which already bore some counterpoint exercises in his own hand, and the third movement incorporates a quantity and kind of counterpoint quite unprecedented in his symphonies and other orchestral music. It is known that he arranged to take lessons in fugue and counterpoint with Simon Sechter, the Viennese theorist, later to be Bruckner's teacher, in November 1828, with Josef Lanz as his fellow-pupil.[4] 'We had had only a single lesson', Sechter recalled: 'the next time Herr Lanz appeared alone, to tell me that Franz Schubert was very ill'.[5] The lesson with Sechter, according to Lanz,[6] took place on 4 November, fifteen days before Schubert died. It is possible that the exercises had been worked at Sechter's suggestion, or in unsolicited preparation for the lesson. The third movement of the symphony would appear to have been a by-product, if not of the first encounter with Sechter on 4 November, then of the impulse which took

[3] *Loc. cit.*, p. 255.

[4] Simon Sechter (1788–1867) was an Austrian theorist, composer, conductor and organist who held important musical posts in Vienna from 1810 until his retirement from the Vienna Conservatoire in 1863. He was famed as a teacher of music theory, and especially of contrapuntal technique. He is said to have composed a fugue a day, and his own diary of compositions lists over 8,000 pieces. His later pupils, after Schubert, included Vieuxtemps, Nottebohm and Thalberg.

[5] Letter to Ferdinand Luib, dated 21 August 1857, published in Deutsch, *Schubert: Memoirs by his Friends*, p. 106.

[6] Letter to Ferdinand Luib, 1857, now in the Wiener Stadt- und Landesbibliothek. *Cf.* Christa Landon, 'New Schubert Finds', *Music Review*, XXX/3, August 1970, p. 227.

Schubert to Sechter. Whether Sechter saw any of this movement, or knew of its existence, is not recorded. But Schubert's good friend Eduard von Bauernfeld, who was among the last to visit him shortly before he died, certainly knew of the symphony's existence, and referred to it in a press article a few months later.[7]

The symphony begins with a strong diatonic theme (Ex. 95), clearly intended to be announced in octave-unison, which bears an obvious resemblance to the first themes of the unfinished Piano Sonata in C (*Reliquie*), D840, of 1825, and the unfinished *Klavierstück* in C, D916B, of 1827.

Ex. 95

Clearly implied by the sketch is a masterly postponement of full harmony until the rousing 'Italian sixth' in the fourteenth bar. The theme is re-announced in full but hushed harmony, and the listener soon becomes aware that the functions of thematic restatement and transition are being merged, as happened in some of the earlier symphonies. But here the manner of transition is intensely chromatic. The customary motions of closing a transition are gone through, but the end – on the dominant of F sharp minor – is a false one. From it a solo oboe emerges, reflecting on the position with short phrases of rare pathos and beauty, and the violins respond on a similar emotional plane, veering to the dominant for the second subject.

[7] Bauernfeld's article is considered further in Appendix 4, pp. 288–89.

The second subject, in the tenor register and to be assigned to the cellos, one imagines, is a broadly arching lyrical melody (Ex. 96) with unobtrusive accompaniment.

Ex. 96

At the seventh bar, a questioning minor-key interpolation briefly postpones the affirmative major close. The theme is extensively and lovingly treated – so much so that it dominates the entire exposition from this point forwards. Not even an emphatic resumption of the initial rhythm of the first theme, implying the onset of 'codetta', can dislodge it. One particularly characteristic treatment of the theme deserves comment: Schubert extends it internally by repeating its second bar to form a new and supernumerary third bar, a procedure reminiscent of several themes in the Seventh Symphony.

After the end of the exposition comes a double shock. Following the last A major chord, the development begins abruptly in the minor key on the note one semitone higher – B flat minor. Implicit in this move is a disturbing change of meaning, for the major mediant of A (C sharp) now functions as the minor mediant (D flat) of B flat. While this note is the pivot note in this sudden shift of key, the change of meaning thrust upon it lends instability even to what is theoretically a plausible 'pivot-modulation'. It is a key-relationship that haunted Schubert in the ripe masterpieces of his last year: one has only to compare the beginning of the second section (*Largo*) in the F minor Fantasy for piano duet (F sharp minor, in the context of F major), the middle section (F minor) of the E major slow movement of the String Quintet in C, or the beginning of the development (F minor) following the E major exposition-end in another work for piano duet, the *Allegro* in A minor ('*Lebensstürme*'), D947.

The other shocking aspect of the beginning of Schubert's development in the symphony is the sudden relaxation of tempo from *Allegro maestoso* to *Andante*, another dislocating factor. A change of tempo at this point in sonata design was not unprecedented, if the purpose was to re-introduce a slow introduction (*cf.* Beethoven's Piano Sonata in C minor, Op. 13). Schubert is entering a brave new world by venturing at this point a slower tempo which is fresh and unknown, not retrospective. What he presents in this tempo, and in this remote new key, is the trombones (specified here by Schubert) intoning a variant (Ex. 97) of the second subject (Ex. 96) so subtle that one

Ex. 97

may plot the exact line of the original second subject (but now turned minor) by picking out the first note of the third trombone, the second note of the second trombone, and so on, finding the theme thus shared among all four trombones. Or rather, one should say 'three trombones', for although Schubert writes 'Tromboni' over his four-part harmony, he would not have used four trombones in a symphony. He would have scored this passage as he did certain comparable passages in the Masses and operas, using a bassoon on one of the inner parts, masquerading as a trombone. The listener is unlikely to notice that the ensemble is not a homogeneous, one-family foursome.

It is possible that Schubert's 'double shock' was theatrical in inspiration. On 25 October 1823 he had attended the opening night of Weber's *Euryanthe* at the Kärntnertor

Theatre.[8] In the overture, Weber inserts a *Largo* between two *Allegro* sections. At the close of the first *Allegro*, in E flat major, the dominant note (B flat) is suddenly converted into a 'leading-note' (as A sharp) and the *Largo* follows at once in B minor. The change of key and change of tempo are virtually the same as those chosen by Schubert. The Weber model had possibly affected him no less directly in the E flat Piano Trio, D929, where after a minimal transition from the home key of E flat major the second group begins in B minor (Weber's keys exactly), the switch of key being articulated with the aid of trills and scales distinctly theatrical in manner.

From this beginning of the development, all that Schubert sketched of the remainder of the first movement is contained on one page. The *Andante* appears to lead directly to a *Presto* in D major, which ultimately leads to a conclusion, with double-bar.[9] Towards the end of the *Presto* are several short 'modules' (sections of from two to six bars) which have to be re-shuffled into their correct order with the help of Schubert's not altogether explicit connective signs. These 'modules' all fit into a continuous *Presto* which stays firmly rooted in D major. Schubert would not, of course, have written an extended passage like this in the tonic key as part of a development. What then is its role? It appears that Schubert has compressed on to this page elements of both development and coda. Between them he would have inserted a recapitulation, which would have been readily devised at a later stage. The *Andante* would lead, as it is or with additional material, not to the *Presto* but to the recapitulation; and the coda would have incorporated the entire *Presto*, possibly first retracing the later stages of the *Andante*. Schubert would

---

[8]*Cf.* his letter to Schober (30 November 1823) and Bauernfeld's essay on Schubert. Schober's letter appears in Deutsch, *Schubert: A Documentary Biography*, pp. 300–1; the relevant part of Bauernfeld's essay appears in the same volume, p. 892.

[9]*Cf.* the facsimile on p. 265.

have been content to relinquish his first movement in this state for the time being, provided that he himself had a fairly clear view of its ultimate contents. He would have been inclined to do this especially if he already had ideas for a second movement waiting to be set down. Whatever the ultimate shape of the movement was to have been, it obviously displays a new kind of multi-tempo sonata design, embracing both an inset in a slower tempo and a conclusion in a faster tempo. It is tempting to see this structural trend as a reversion to the impulses of Schubert's early youth, when he wrote several fantasy-like pieces comprising numerous tempi and keys. More truly it may echo the structural experiments of third-period Beethoven, to be found in that composer's string quartets and piano sonatas rather than orchestral works.

The second movement has claims to being the most remarkable movement in the symphony. It is an *Andante* in triple time and in B minor. Reverting to the key of the 'Unfinished' Symphony, Schubert resumes its vein of intense lyricism. But he extends this vein, entering a new expressive world which both echoes the bleak desolation of *Die Winterreise*, written in the previous year, and looks forward to the mourning Mahler of parts of *Kindertoten-lieder* and to the idiosyncratic atmosphere and procedures of Bruckner. There is a certain restraint in the texture of the sketch, at times a bareness, which must severely test the judgement of anyone who seeks to discover how Schubert might have scored it. Is the bareness that of a sketch, which would have been filled out when the music was orchestrated? Or is it a calculated bareness, an essential aspect of the expressive intention which must be left intact in any realisation? Prolonged study of this music leaves one unable to resist inclining to the second of these conclusions. And this verdict only increases the difficulty

Opposite: The last page of the first movement of the Tenth Symphony, D936A, in Schubert's piano score (Wiener Stadt- und Landesbibliothek).

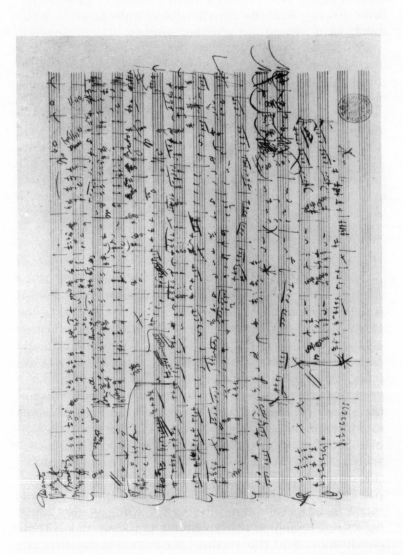

of envisaging the orchestral sound Schubert might have been groping towards, for there is so little precedent for this kind of writing in his earlier works.

The movement begins with four bars of unaccompanied *pizzicato* bass (Ex. 98) prefacing a theme of initially constricted range, for which Schubert's only accompaniment is a counterpoint in the tenor register.

Ex. 98

It may be surmised that this accompaniment is to be filled out by at least a continuation of the plucked bass. Thus the texture as well as the key brings to mind the last song of *Die Winterreise*, 'Der Leiermann', as does the tendency of the melody to lean heavily on the second beat of the three-beat bar. Much weight of expression is concentrated within the confined ambit of the theme's first two bars. The first bar is foreshadowed in the *pizzicato* preface: the second bar is at once reproduced as third bar, and so these few meagre steps spread their influence. Even the *forte* contrast soon presented by the horns and taken up by the full orchestra is but a variant form.

When the dominant is reached Schubert introduces as second subject nothing other than the original 'tenor' counter-melody, now sung by the violins as a melody in its own right; and the exposition of material is completed when minor yields to major (the rare key of F sharp major) for a melody which, once heard, is never forgotten.

It is extraordinary to think that this melody was added by Schubert as an afterthought, when he had not only completed the first draft of the movement but sketched the third movement too. There is a short development; and a passage whose eloquence resides in pure, Romantic harmony melts into a reprise of the opening.

There follows one of Schubert's most radically reworked recapitulations, which leads the ear ever deeper into this movement's own new world of experience. The homecoming to B minor, through short solo woodwind phrases that blossom from long held notes, is particularly affecting, and the spare-textured coda uncovers still further implications in the first theme of the movement and especially in the triplet figure of its second bar, laying the movement finally to rest with a hauntingly poignant cadential use of the augmented sixth on the flat supertonic (Ex. 99) which inevitably recalls the close of the recently composed String Quintet in C, D956. What generates this harmony is, appropriately, an eleventh-hour intensification of the oppressive quality of the constricted first theme, as its first upward step is now narrowed from a tone to a semitone (*cf*. the bass of Ex. 99).

Ex. 99

From this account it might appear that the movement is complete. It virtually is, but with two vexatious reservations. The F sharp major tune which closes the exposition and is undoubtedly one of Schubert's most sublime creations never returns; and the entire coda is crossed out. Is it possible that Schubert, who was not noted for under-employing his best tunes, deliberately withheld the

F sharp melody from his recapitulation? And is it possible that on reflection he deemed his coda to be of inferior quality to the rest of the movement? This second possibility is unthinkable. The coda must have been crossed through for some other reason. As for the F sharp major theme, Schubert could – in a movement as novel and forward-looking as this – have taken the novel step of presenting his sole heart-easing, consolatory idea once and once only, frustrating the expectations of its return. That remains a possibility, if a remote one. But an alternative hypothesis invites consideration.

After finishing his third movement, a complex and demanding project whose completion must have given him enormous satisfaction, as a result of which any idea of abandoning the symphony would have been even further from his mind than it already was, Schubert looked back to his slow movement. He decided that the later part of the exposition required amplification, a process he began by adding in a counter-melody in a passage already present in the sketch. This counter-melody was written on a spare stave at the foot of the page, but had to be continued elsewhere, on spare staves at the foot of a page already used for part of the third movement. The counter-melody now opened up into the F sharp major melody referred to above; and at the end of this complete 26-bar theme Schubert finished this last-minute insertion. He then considered what effect this added material should have on the recapitulation. He found the last stages of the recapitulation already so perfectly conceived and sewn together that there was no scope for adding in a reprise of his newly-devised theme. It would be possible, though, to incorporate it within the coda. So he crossed out his coda. . . . And he would have proceeded to re-draft the coda embodying a B major restatement of his new theme, but he was interrupted – presumably by some external factor such as a worsening of his final illness. The crossing-through of the coda was possibly the composer's last creative act before the death intervened.

Schubert began his third movement with the heading 'Scherzo'. The first page of sketch represents what was doubtless one of the most testing compositional tasks he ever undertook. After only a line or so of work it is clear that he gave up thinking of this sketch as a true beginning of his scherzo, and used the rest of the page as a 'worksheet'. The music is contrapuntal to a degree unprecedented in a Schubert symphony, and the worksheet is concerned with ascertaining the true finite shape of the themes, testing their compatibility in combination, and investigating the scope for applying to them various time-honoured contrapuntal 'devices'. Having done all this he broke off, tried a few unconnected episodes on the reverse of the same sheet, then made a fresh start. But in making this fresh start he did not write anew the heading 'Scherzo'. The fresh start was to be the real beginning, and from this point one can trace the course of an elaborate and extended movement which skilfully applies and develops some of the findings of the preliminary sketches while jettisoning others. Table 1, to be considered in conjunction with Exx. 100 and 101, will clarify the structure and enumerate the contrapuntal procedures.

Traditionally, a scherzo and trio exhibits a modular form, all its music being contained within well-defined, repeatable sections. Schubert here departs from that tradition. His scherzo, if it is right to continue to call it that, behaves like a rondo, with a rondo theme returning periodically, always in the tonic key, and episodes between. It is true that when Beethoven extends the traditional scherzo scheme to embrace two or more hearings of the trio, a loosely rondo-like pattern emerges: in Beethoven's Seventh, scherzo-trio-scherzo-trio-scherzo-trio (truncated)-scherzo (five bars). The important difference is that while Beethoven retains the usual modular manner of progress through the whole of this scheme, Schubert writes a through-composed piece: that is, it has the continuity of, say, sonata-form, rather than being an assemblage of small or medium-sized blocks.

		Table 1
R	D major	Rondo theme (Ex. 100) in middle voice (*a*), with triplet descant *b* and characterful bass *c*: all presented in a binary construction with repeats.
		Canonic treatment of *b* leads at length to
E	B flat major	Chorale-like theme *d* with *pizzicato* bass (Ex. 101). Binary construction.
		Re-statement of same in E flat major (and back to B flat major).
		Link to
R	D major	Reprise of rondo theme with counterpoint inverted (*c* transferred from bass to treble).
	D minor	*a* in augmentation in bass (Hungarian dance?).
E	F major	Reprise of *d*.
		Link to
	A minor	fugato on *a*, leading to
R	D major	Tonic statement of *d, fortissimo;* at the repetition of each segment, *d* has *a* added in simultaneous combination.
Coda	D major	Canon on variant of *b* over tonic pedal, punctuated by hints of *a* (first two notes).
		Final cadential statement of four bars of *a*.

R = Rondo theme	E = Episode

Ex. 100

Ex. 101

The question arises of whether Schubert was then pioneering a new kind of scherzo. Or had he, as the movement took shape, ceased to think of it as a scherzo at all?
The omission of the title 'Scherzo' from the second draft
does not necessarily settle the issue. It may be significant,
but not necessarily: it could simply not have occurred to a
composer in a hurry that he must write anew the title
already affixed to a first draft of the same movement on
an adjacent sheet of paper. An answer must be looked for
in the music itself. If it is a scherzo, it is a scherzo in
duple time. Schubert selects two-four time, and the six-
eight overlay is only spasmodically present. It is true that
Beethoven had written a duple-time trio in his Ninth
Symphony, while his String Quartet in C sharp minor,
Op. 131, has as its third movement a scherzo (not so
called) with four crotchets to each one-beat bar. But there
are other factors to be taken into account in Schubert's
movement. Its form is one traditionally associated with
finales. Counterpoint, too, is more a feature of finales
than of scherzi; at least, the thorough-going kind of
counterpoint found here is. Moreover, whatever the
Beethovenian would-be precedents in scherzo-writing
noted above, the time-signature here chosen by Schubert
is his favourite for finales. It is possible, then, that as
Schubert composed his scherzo it became a finale.

Is Schubert's Tenth Symphony, then, a three-movement symphony? It may never be possible to answer this
question with certainty. Three possibilities have to be considered: that the third movement remained a scherzo or
scherzo-equivalent and Schubert would have added a
separate finale; that the third movement was eventually
seen as a finale and Schubert would have inserted a new
scherzo as third movement; or that he regarded the
three-movement work as complete. The last of these
possibilities is hard to accept, because it would constitute
such a radical departure from tradition. Would Schubert
have ventured to do what Beethoven never did in a field
in which he was arch-innovator? It should be remembered that in the parallel multi-movement genres of
chamber music, and especially in the chamber works of
that composer to whom Schubert was particularly
indebted, Mozart, the three-movement scheme was not at
all uncommon. It is to be found in various ensemble-
pieces, such as the Oboe Quartet and Horn Quintet, not
to mention many duo-sonatas by Mozart as well as some
by Beethoven. When Beethoven answered Mozart's Quintet for piano and wind with his own Quintet, Op. 16, one
of the features of the model he appropriated was its
three-movement scheme. In the symphonic field there
was another Mozart work, and one apparently well
known to Schubert from his schooldays – the 'Prague'
Symphony. Whatever Mozart's reasons for omitting the
minuet in the 'Prague', reasons of which Schubert may or
may not have been aware, the precedent of a three-movement symphony existed, within a repertory which had
been influential on Schubert's early development as a symphonist. Within the realm of solo keyboard music, another
kind of precedent can be identified. Beethoven closes his
three-movement G major Piano Sonata, Op. 14, No. 2,
with a finale remarkably akin to Schubert's – a scherzo
(thus entitled) in rondo form. With these precedents in
his consciousness, would he have been less likely to do the
unconventional thing of settling for three movements

in his Tenth Symphony than to do the unconventional thing of beginning the development of his first movement with an *Andante?*

Whatever one's conviction on this issue, the third movement has a number of striking incidental features. Its first theme is buried inside the texture, coincidentally posing a question ('Which part is the theme?') which is posed for only slightly different reasons by the first theme in the first *Allegro* of the 'Prague' Symphony. And Schubert's theme springs into action with two successive upward leaps of a fourth, a decidedly un-Classical formation that seems to prefigure certain melodic predilections of the early twentieth century. The counterpoint, throughout, has a perky lightness quite new in Schubert's orchestral writing. It inhabits a different world from the sober, more conventionally fugal counterpoint of the Masses. This quality makes it difficult to envisage how he would have orchestrated the movement, since any search for true analogies in other works by Schubert will be a vain one. It also keeps the listener ever aware of the scherzo origin of the material, which in turn facilitates an interpretation of the movement as a combination of scherzo and finale. This characteristic of the counterpoint is especially evident at the first reprise of the rondo theme, and again in the buoyant coda (where, if anywhere, familiar Viennese hedonism dares to surface). The section in augmentation is, on the contrary, a heavy-footed dance, perhaps *all'ongarese*, riotously incongruous but for the germane foundation-line.

The fugato, which comprises a complete four-part fugal exposition with further entries besides, is perfectly judged for its purpose, the later entries following one another at decreasing time-distances (that is, in progressively closer stretto) to accumulate excitement as the climax approaches. That climax is the full-throated reprise of the episode-theme (*d*), 'resolved' to the tonic key, D major, for the first time. But equally climactic, in a contrapuntal sense, is what follows, although it is

contrastingly *piano*. This combining of the two themes, a
technical trump-card reserved until the last stages of the
movement, looks forward to a favourite practice of
Bruckner's, although Schubert's is not so much a grand
Brucknerian apotheosis as an unassuming, Mozartian
drawing together of threads.

One thing this finale, if finale it be, makes clear is that
Schubert had little need of Sechter's advice. His decision
to go to Sechter was a symptom of his realisation that a
concentrated study of contrapuntal technique might add
a valuable dimension to his ever-developing style. Sechter
would have provided a stimulus of one sort, but another
stimulus – and a potent one – was the composer's own
urge to widen his expressive range by extending his technique. Although the success of this movement was hard
won, for it entailed a preliminary period of experiment
and refining of material perhaps akin to that which
Mozart admitted to in the preparation of his 'Haydn'
Quartets (к387, к421, к428, к458, к464 and к465), it
betrays no weakness of contrapuntal technique or imagination. Rather, it offers the promise of a new era in the
composer's voyage of self-discovery, just as the slow
movement raises the question as to what new aesthetic
visions – whether in symphony or other media – his still-
evolving lyricism would have opened up had he been
given a few more years on earth.

The success of a composition is not necessarily in proportion to the effort it cost its composer. The notion of
Schubert as a spontaneous, intuitive creator who did not
have to filter what the Muse offered him, in contradis-
tinction to Beethoven the inveterate chiseller of raw
materials, dies hard – but it is certainly dented by
instances such as this Tenth Symphony. It was not only
the third movement that required more paper than the
final version actually covers. There were also problems in
the first movement, for the first attempt at a first subject
group was scrapped and Schubert wrote a new opening
on the same theme which would connect up with the

second group already fully charted. It is not surprising that he chose to work in piano score. He was clearly aware that the symphony he was embarking on was, if the exaggeration can be risked, contrary to his nature. At least, it beckoned him down an unexplored avenue, which he could only tread with some uncertainty. The same situation had obtained in the last symphony he had sketched in piano score before this one, the 'Unfinished'.

How successful, then, is the Tenth Symphony? In one sense, it is impossible to answer this question. As a symphony – such as the Ninth, which is gloriously whole and carries the composer's authority and conviction from first note to last – it does not exist. It exists only as a project on paper, which may be translated into sound by means of a 'performing version' by another hand. In making a performing version, one is obliged to engage in a degree of cautious speculation, but beyond a certain limit one may not go. A composer who himself makes his own final version on the basis of his own sketches is naturally at liberty to 'improve' as he orchestrates, and is usually inclined to do so. 'Improvement' may involve melodic or harmonic changes, but more probably it will also entail structural changes. A line must be drawn short of this point by anyone acting on the composer's behalf. Structural change would lead him dangerously far down the path of speculation towards the abyss of falsification. If he adheres strictly to all that is ordained or may reasonably be seen to be implied in the sketch, he may produce a performing version that represents the composer's view of the work at one point in time. If, on the other hand, he 'improves' the structure on the basis of his own perceptions of any weaknesses it may have, the chances are that he will be fabricating something that represents the composer's view of the work at no point in time. A performing version, if sensitively done, must therefore remain something of a sketch itself, in this sense. Its purpose is to present to listeners the actual contents of a sketch which may otherwise go unheard. Since orchestras do not play sketches, the material of the sketch itself must be added to in order to provide a minimal context of completeness. 'Minimal' is the key-word here: the more an editor adds of his own material, the smaller proportionate part the notes of the sketch will play in the resulting version, and the larger will be the risk of reducing the authenticity of the work. If it is not possible to appraise the Tenth fully as a Schubert symphony, it is possible at least to assess its more fully-sketched sections, and to evaluate its implications for the development of Schubert as a symphonist, both within and (hypothetically) beyond his lifetime.

If he had completed the symphony himself, the movement in which he is most likely to have modified the structure is the first, although he would have had little reason to change anything from the arrival of the second subject to the end of the exposition. Perhaps it was here, of all places, that Schubert felt most at ease. The second subject itself can readily be reconciled with the manner of other works of his final years, such as the Piano Trios in B flat and E flat, the last three piano sonatas, and the String Quintet. Once announced, this theme returns in various keys and guises (and, to hazard a guess, instrumental colours), doing so with an air of relaxed expansiveness one associates with Schubert when he reaches this particular point in his mature sonata expositions. Although the later part of the exposition is chequered with crossings-out and changes of mind, the final thoughts represent an apposite and imposing culmination. Indeed, the second subject itself achieves a grandeur in the closing stages which is brought about by a gradual mutation of character which is truly symphonic. But it is not appropriate to look here for the elan or vociferous joy of the 'Great' C major, any more than a reprise of the poetry that is peculiar to the 'Unfinished'. A symphony *sui generis* demands a response *sui generis*. In particular, the Tenth is not founded on a preponderance of heavyweight scoring. Of all Classical symphonies, the 'Great' merits the epithet '*tutti*-symphony'. In no other symphonic work of the period do all the orchestral participants work so hard so continuously. By contrast, it is implicit in the sketch of the Tenth that the busy, robust scoring of the 'Great' is alien to it, which is not to say that it lacks moments of orchestral grandeur.

The slow movement speaks of affairs of the soul not touched in music before. Schubert is no more afraid of restricting himself to a fairly circumscribed emotional scenario, and seeking depth and intensity of expression within it, than he was in the later songs of *Die Winterreise*. There is accordingly less contrast, on the face of it, than in the slow movement of the 'Great' or, for that matter, that of the Fourth Symphony. Yet a spell is cast, and sustained; and it is impossible to escape its influence, thanks to the clarity of the artistic vision and the musical certainty with which it is portrayed. The third movement, which so tested the composer, tests the listener's preconceptions no less. It is astonishing as a product of the year 1828: yet it would be astonishing whatever the moment in history in which it was created. For anything comparable in Beethoven one would have to look to the chamber music, not the symphonies. The counterpoint has the lightness of touch to be found in Beethoven's Op. 18 Quartets, rather than the sturdiness of the contrapuntal excursions in the Symphonies, although the fugati in the finale of the *Eroica* grew from similarly airy beginnings. For examples of the thorough-going application of contrapuntal techniques within the framework of a Classical form one would have to go back further – to Mozart's G major String Quartet, к387, for example. Mozart's finale, like the Schubert, employs within a form of the day (sonata-form in Mozart's case) fugal writing, invertible counterpoint, stretto, and combination of themes, and ends by making a succinct cadential epigram of its first theme. Yet Mozart's finale, happily suited as it is to the quartet medium, is somewhat neo-Baroque in its more frequent reliance on fugue, and its use of double fugue as the means of combining themes. Schubert's

counterpoint, its character and its application, is not pal-
pably Baroque in any way. Whereas Mozart, like Haydn,
re-introduced counterpoint into Classical forms conscious
that it was a Baroque phenomenon he was reviving (he
knew his Bach, thanks to Baron von Swieten), Schubert,
who knew his Handel from the complete edition in his
brother Ferdinand's possession, and certainly paid homage
to the earlier composer in certain vocal works, derived
more for this last symphony from the instrumental counterpoint of Beethoven. With Beethoven, counterpoint became less a Baroque throwback, more an
absorbed element of Classical style. To Schubert in his
Tenth, counterpoint is a timeless resource rather than an
archaism. In that it is one weapon in a campaign to push
back the frontiers of expression, it is a symptom of his
determination to move forwards into a fruitful future.

An audience confronted with this finale in 1828 would
have found it baffling, hard to get to know, and perhaps
obscure in intention. But no audience heard it before the
last quarter of the twentieth century, when it elicited in
milder form the same response. Today, the latest Babbitt
or Takemitsu is perhaps more readily assimilated than
Schubert's last symphonic movement, which has to be
reconciled with the so-familiar furniture of a much-
played Classical repertory. A long-pondered tradition of
responses to that repertory is, after all, the inheritance of
modern society. But to some extent the whole symphony
poses this fascinating problem, the first movement with
its new structural perspectives, the slow movement with
its unique emotional concentration.

Schubert's position in history, in terms of chronological
placement, is that he stands at the end of the Classical
period, as Bach stood at the end of the Baroque era. But
between the two there is a poignant distinction to be
drawn. Bach, his *œuvre* the final exalted resting-place of
accumulated Baroque tradition, departed the world an
aging anachronism. Schubert, having had not half so
many years to amass an *œuvre*, was snatched in his prime
with his sights resolutely on the future.

XVI

Epilogue

It cannot be said with certainty that more than two of Schubert's symphonies were performed in his lifetime. The Fifth and Sixth Symphonies were given private performances in 1816 and 1818 respectively in the 'music salon' hosted by Otto Hatwig. The First Symphony, written while Schubert was at the *Stadtkonvikt*, was probably performed by the school orchestra: and the Second may have been performed at Hatwig's – at least, sets of parts of both the First and Second (those of the Second copied in 1816) were presented to the Gesellschaft der Musikfreunde in 1828 by Josef Doppler, who had taken part in Schubert family music-making since 1814 and was also a member of Hatwig's group. There were no chronicled performances of the Third and Fourth, although the meetings at Hatwig's premises continued until 1818 and these works may well have been played there.[1] There were, however, no public performances of any of these early symphonies in Schubert's lifetime.

The lack of performances scarcely impeded Schubert's development as a symphonist. In the six works which

---

[1] Noting that contemporary performance materials of all the first six symphonies except No. 4 survive in the archives of the Gesellschaft, Otto Biba observes that 'there is every indication that they were used then'. He then states firmly that these materials were used in performances at salons of Otto Hatwig, without spelling out the evidence ('Schubert's Position in Viennese Musical Life', *19th-Century Music*, III/2, p. 109).

279

occupied him till his 21st year he acquired, with little or
no help from those around him, a youthful assurance
which enabled him to evolve a symphonic manner of his
own while thoroughly assimilating the influences of those
composers and works that most fired his imagination.
The ability to draw from the repertoire he played, knew,
and loved, without losing his identity, was not only
remarkable – it was necessary. His teacher in these early
years was Salieri, the same as had enjoyed other-than-
friendly relations with Mozart. Salieri (b. 1750) was not
young, and was not drawn to Mozart's operas and Beethoven's instrumental music as Schubert was, but did
devote himself to the production of vocal works, now
largely forgotten, rooted in old Italian practice. As
Leopold von Sonnleithner relates, he 'understood singing
and the older operatic forms but of instrumental music
(sonata, quartet, symphony) he had as little idea as he had
of true church music'.[2] The young Schubert rightly con-
sumed the first-hand guidance implicit in the scores of
Haydn, Mozart, and Beethoven, choosing his mentors
with unerring good judgement (for there were numerous
composers of the second and third ranks in the current
repertoire in his school and in the city), and so made up
the deficiency. Such was his fecundity and fluency that in
this way he was able to produce movements as attractive
and sophisticated as the finales of the Second and Third
Symphonies, and the slow movement of the Fourth, not
to mention the whole of the Fifth, all before his twentieth
year, at which age Beethoven was still destined to wait ten
years before giving the world his First.

Having completed six symphonies in as many years, he
managed to complete only one in the remaining ten years
of his life. Yet that one symphony was not performed. It
was given nothing more than a private rehearsal by the
Gesellschaft der Musikfreunde. One cannot imagine, in

[2] Quoted in Deutsch, *Schubert: Memoirs by his Friends*, p. 112.

view of Sonnleithner's witness[3] and the difficulties experienced in the preparation of performances later in the century, that Schubert, if he was present, found justice done to his piece; it is not even certain that the whole work was played, rather than parts of it. Thus it appears that Schubert heard, in satisfactory circumstances, none of his truly mature symphonic music, and the fulfilment he derived from his long-cherished ambition to write a *grosse Symphonie* was the fulfilment of undertaking, composing, and completing it. The Viennese public, which was aware of Schubert as a composer of songs and dances, and to a lesser extent of smaller instrumental works, knew little or nothing of what he had achieved in the medium he declared to be one of the 'highest forms of musical art'. Nor, in the years after his death, was the Viennese musical establishment quick to put matters right. The story of the dawning of world recognition of the Ninth Symphony – a story which runs into the second half of the nineteenth century, if not beyond – is central to the story of dawning recognition of his whole symphonic *œuvre*.

Not until a quarter of a century after its composition did Vienna hear what Schubert wrote as his 'Great' C major Symphony. In the interim, there is no record of any of his other symphonies having been publicly performed in the city, with one exception. The Sixth Symphony was played by the Gesellschaft der Musikfreunde less than a month after Schubert's death. Following that concert, on 14 December 1828, another performance of the Sixth was given on 12 March 1829 at a 'Concert Spirituel' in the Landhaus-Saal. After that, no Schubert symphony received its due in his native city until 1850. Whether the picture would have been any different if the work played in the 1828/9 performances had been the Fifth, or the Third or Second, is a matter for conjecture.

There was a performance of half of the Ninth

[3]*Cf.* chapter XIII, pp. 213–14.

Symphony in Vienna on 15 December 1839. Mendelssohn,
Following the intervention in Schubert's posthumous
affairs by Schumann, had given a performance earlier
that year at the Leipzig Gewandhaus. Vienna followed
suit, but only two movements were played, with an aria
from Donizetti's *Lucia di Lammermoor* between them, as
though to sugar the pill. A successful performance followed in Frankfurt on 22 January 1841. In Paris in 1842
Habeneck failed to persuade the orchestra to perform
the work, and two years later Mendelssohn had a similar
problem with the Philharmonic Society in London. But
Prince Albert is reported to have arranged a performance
with his private orchestra at Windsor later in 1844.[4] Boston
then heard the work, in 1849, before the first complete
Vienna performance conducted by Josef Hellmesberger on
1 December 1850. By this time Breitkopf und Härtel had
published the orchestral parts (1840) and score (1849).

The momentum now set up was not as cumulative as
may be expected. True, New York heard the symphony
in 1851 and on 23 November in the same year Habeneck
finally secured a hearing for the work in Paris. But the
second French performance was not given until 1897. In
Vienna, meanwhile, seven years elapsed between the first
performance there and the second (1857, under Karl
Eckert). And when August Manns introduced the work to
the English public at the Crystal Palace in 1856 (Prince
Albert's performance had been a private one) he gave it
in two overlapping instalments, with the first three movements on April 5 and the last three on April 12. It is not
clear whether he thought he should spare his audience
the whole work at one sitting; more likely, he was sparing
his orchestra. One problem for orchestras all along had
been the stamina required of the string players. The
problem was acutely posed in the finale, where the violins
reiterate a triplet figuration for nearly ninety bars in

[4]John Reed cast doubts on the validity of this report in a paper de-
livered to the Schubert Institute UK at Oxford in October 1991.

accompaniment to the second subject. To some extent the difficulty will have been intellectual as well as physical. 'All this effort in a subservient role, while the wind sing their hearts out!', one imagines being the secret thought at many of the string desks.

It was in the wake of this slow acceptance of the 'Great', which was not truly a repertory piece until the twentieth century, that the early symphonies received notice. The 'Unfinished', once released by Hüttenbrenner, was heard first in Vienna under Herbeck (17 December 1865 and 4 November 1866), then in Leipzig (1866, under Reinecke) and London, where on 6 April 1867 the B minor Entr'acte from *Rosamunde* was added as finale. The first four symphonies remained unperformed, in the care of Schubert's brother Ferdinand, until he sent them to Breitkopf und Härtel in Leipzig in 1843. The previous year he had sold the Fifth to the music-dealer Whistling, also in Leipzig. The Fourth was premiered in Leipzig in 1849, and the Sixth was played there shortly afterwards. In due course these early symphonies found their way to London, where performances were arranged (No. 6 in 1868, Nos. 4 and 5 in 1873, No. 2 in 1877, and No. 1 in 1880), and in 1881 at the Crystal Palace August Manns gave the first cycle of all the Schubert symphonies. Shortly afterwards, in 1884, Breitkopf und Härtel embarked on a critical edition of Schubert's works which principally involved Brahms (who edited the symphonies and acted as chairman of the editorial board) and Mandyczewski. This project was completed in 1897; but only in the twentieth century, and with the advent of broadcasting in particular, did the entire symphonic *œuvre* become widely known.

The symphonies exerted an influence on nineteenth-century composers in spite of their slowness to enter the concert-hall. They did so because it was largely composers who championed the cause of these sadly overlooked works as the century progressed. Schumann was

*The house at Kettenbrückengasse 6 where Schubert lived with his
brother Ferdinand in the last months of his life. It was here, in the
apartment on the top floor fronted by the last three windows on the
right, that Schubert worked on his last symphony (D936A) and
died (photographs by Ken Thomson).*

the prime mover. After arriving in Vienna in 1838, seeking a more congenial milieu for himself, he visited
Ferdinand Schubert on 1 January 1839 and was shown a
chest full of manuscripts, including the symphonies.
Impressed especially with the Ninth, he had it sent direct
to Mendelssohn in Leipzig, who immediately arranged
performances. Schumann himself was in Leipzig that
December and wrote to Clara after a rehearsal of the
Ninth:

If only you had been there. It is not possible to describe it
to you; all the instruments are human voices; it is gifted

beyond measure, and this instrumentation, Beethoven notwithstanding – and this length, this heavenly length, like a novel in four volumes, longer than the Ninth Symphony. I was completely happy and wished for nothing but that you might be my wife and that I, too, could write such symphonies.[4]

Other composers echoed the enthusiasm of Schumann and Mendelssohn. Berlioz wrote that 'this Symphony [. . .] is, to my thinking, worthy of a place among the loftiest productions of our art'.[5] Bruckner's admiration for the Ninth Symphony, among Schubert's other works, is reflected in his own symphonies, which owe as much to Schubert as to Beethoven, if not more.[6]

[4] Quoted in Deutsch, *Schubert: Memoirs by his Friends*, pp. 399–400.

[5] *Journal des débats*, 27 November 1851, p. 2.

[6] *Cf.* Franz Grasberger, 'Schubert and Bruckner', in Brusatti (ed.), *Schubert-Kongress Wien 1978 – Bericht*, pp. 215–28.

Brahms' general debt to Schubert[7] is also self-evident, as to a lesser extent is Dvořák's. An article written by Dvořák in 1894[8] contains a heart-warming appreciation of the symphonies, and especially the Eighth and Ninth:

> I do not hesitate to say that, greatly as I esteem Schubert's songs, I value his instrumental works even more highly. Were all of his compositions to be destroyed but two, I should say, save the last two symphonies.

But he pleads also for more performances of the earlier symphonies: 'the more I study them, the more I marvel'. Two musical pilgrims who left Britain for Vienna in 1867 in search of Schubert's orchestral music were Arthur Sullivan and George Grove. Sullivan's debt to Schubert is known to all who are familiar with the 'Savoy operas' or his more serious compositions. Grove recalled that in the year before their visit August Manns had conducted the 'Great' at the Crystal Palace. It was, he later wrote, 'the only one of his orchestral works then known in England; at that time, too, believed to be his only Symphony'.[9] On arrival in Vienna, Grove and Sullivan quickly traced scores of the earlier symphonies (Nos. 1–4 and 6) and a set of parts of the Fifth.

Schubert's legacy to these later composers of the nineteenth century was an original, pioneering harmonic idiom; a flair for orchestral colouring which, while initially an extension of Mozart's practice, ultimately came close to the sound-ideals of the nascent Romantic age; and a novel, personal extension of tonal resource and application. Under this last heading belong, first, the

[7] Brahms' interest in Schubert and the influence of Schubert on his music is analysed in some detail in James Webster, 'Schubert's Sonata Form and Brahms's First Maturity', *19th-Century Music*, II/1, July 1978, pp. 18–35, and III/1, July 1979, pp. 52–71.

[8] Dvořák and Henry T. Finck, 'Franz Schubert', *The Century Magazine*, XLVIII, July 1894, pp. 341–48.

[9] Quoted in Deutsch, *Schubert: Memoirs by his Friends*, p. 450.

development of key-relations, and particularly the juxtaposition of keys a third apart which was absorbed into the
symphonic practice of both Brahms and Bruckner, the
'Great' C major being notably seminal in this respect;
second, the distribution of tonal planes over a large-scale
construction, crystallising, for example, in the three-key
exposition which was later adopted on its own account
and as a model for the diversification of other major
structural spans within existing forms; and third, the
mode of travel between successive keys, by means of a
magical variety of modulations, shifts, and shocks.

When the colouristic aspects of Schubert's music are
considered, whether in respect of harmony, orchestration, or key, it is appreciated that he moved not merely
with the times but even ahead of them, to such an extent
that he may be reckoned to belong with the Romantic
composers. But if Romanticism implies more than an
enriching of the purely musical means, then Schubert was
merely the nightwatchman of the Classical symphony.
And only months after his death, the night was to yield to
the dazzling dawn of the Romantic symphony, with the
emergence of the *Symphonie Fantastique* of Berlioz. This
newcomer brought about no permanent eclipse of the
Classical symphony as a foundation for the future development of the genre, for while the worlds of literature,
travel, religion, pageant, folklore, theatre, and even ballet
spilled over into symphonic music in the remaining years
of the century, the symphony as left by Beethoven and
Schubert was intermittently sustained, by Schumann, for
example, in his Second Symphony, and later by Brahms,
pending the more wholehearted renewal of its principles
in the twentieth century.

This pattern of evolution might have been clearer if
Schubert had been granted Beethoven's relative longevity
and lived to compose symphonies into the 1850s. For it is
possible that he would have remained loyal to the species
of symphony that had so far occupied him, and would
have changed the balance of symphonic development in

these three further decades. Not that the Ninth would
have dictated the nature of additional symphonies that
Schubert might later have written: the Tenth suggests a
new outgrowth. If he had died at Beethoven's age, in
1854, he would have had the chance to hear all the symphonies of Berlioz, the entire *œuvre* of Mendelssohn and
Chopin, *Tannhäuser*, *Lohengrin*, and Liszt's Piano Sonata.
There is perhaps nothing here that would have persuaded him to try to change his essentially lyrical nature.
The later interest in counterpoint which brought a new
dimension to the Tenth Symphony would have posed
more of a challenge. Would the Tenth have purged his
contrapuntal ambitions? Or would it have acted as a stimulus? Would counterpoint have been reconciled with
Schubert's innate lyricism to new advantage? In the light
of innovations, not merely contrapuntal ones, in the
Tenth Symphony, might Schubert have proceeded to
treat the symphony as a crucible for experiment rather as
Beethoven treated the piano sonata in his third period,
with fugal excursions one of the major strands of that
experiment?

Such questions burn to be asked because the composer
was silenced in his prime. As Tovey remarked when discussing the Fifth Symphony, every work Schubert left is
an early work. It is usually possible to view a composer's
early works in relation to the works of his maturity, or
those of two or three phases of maturity. Schubert had
barely reached his first maturity. Haydn used to say that
he could think of no more suitable epitaph for himself
than the three words 'vixi, scripsi, dixi!' – which may be
translated 'I lived, I wrote, I said what I had to say!' As
Anton Schindler later pointed out,[10] the first two words
alone would have been applicable in Schubert's case. The
world possesses a portion of what he had to say. Yet in
quality, and almost in quantity, he seemed to be striving
to compensate in advance for an early demise. To have

[10] Quoted in Deutsch, *Schubert: Memoirs by his Friends*, p. 320.

offered such a towering monument to his life as the Ninth, the 'Great' C major Symphony, when at a comparable age Beethoven had not yet composed his First, and to have bequeathed in addition a whole cycle of symphonies rich in accomplishment and a sizable appendix of unfinished symphonies rich in implication and promise, is an artistic *tour de force* for which generation upon generation can only be profoundly thankful.

Appendix 1

Chronological List
of Schubert's Symphonies

Symphony in D major, D2B (fragment of one movement in orchestral score)	1811?
Symphony No. 1 in D major, D82	1813
Symphony No. 2 in B flat major, D125	1814–15
Symphony No. 3 in D major, D200	1815
Symphony No. 4 in C minor (*Tragic*), D417	1816
Symphony No. 5 in B flat major, D485	1816
Symphony No. 6 in C major, D589	1817–18
Symphony in D major, D615 (fragments of two movements; piano sketch)	1818
Symphony in D major, D708A (fragments of four movements; piano sketch)	1820–21
Symphony No. 7 in E major, D729 (structurally complete sketch on orchestral paper)	1821
Symphony No. 8 in B minor ('Unfinished'), D759 (two complete movements; piano sketch of scherzo and part of trio, with two pages of orchestral score of scherzo)	1822
Symphony No. 9 in C major ('Great'), D944	1825–26
Symphony No. 10 in D major, D936A (materially complete sketches of three movements in piano score)	1828

Appendix 2

The Numeration of the Symphonies

The numbering given in Appendix 1 is that generally observed today. A number is assigned to any symphony which Schubert left in such an advanced state of composition that it may, through whatever process or agency, have a life in the performed repertory.

The practice of referring to the 'Great' C major as 'No. 7' goes back as far as the 1830s, when Ferdinand Schubert thus designated it. Whether Ferdinand was ignorant of the real Seventh and Eighth Symphonies, or simply disregarded them for this purpose, is not clear. He did have the Seventh (the E major, D729) in his possession at this time, whether he realised it or not. Ferdinand's numbering was adopted in the thematic catalogue of Schubert's works prepared by Alois Fuchs (in consultation with Ferdinand) in the 1840s. The E major Symphony (the Seventh) was now entered as 'No. 8', and space was left after this for a further entry. John Reed assumes that this space was left for the 'Unfinished' – an interesting indication that even at this time its existence was known.[1] Ferdinand had, however, presumably never set eyes on the 'Unfinished', which had for many years been in the hands of the Hüttenbrenners, where it still was. It is just as likely that the last space in the Fuchs catalogue could have been for the symphony written in Schubert's last weeks. It had after all been accorded an entry in the list of lesser-known works by Schubert with Bauernfeld published in a Viennese journal in 1829, where it appeared as '1828 – Letzte Symphonie'.[2] The existence of this symphony

[1] *Op. cit.*, p. 78.

[2] *Cf.* Appendix 4, pp. 297–99.

could thus have come to the notice of Ferdinand, who probably did not take a close enough interest in his brother's productions during his lifetime to have known about either the 'Unfinished' or the Tenth as a matter of course. That Ferdinand did not make reference to this 'last symphony' in the letters exchanged with publishers in the decades after Schubert's death does not necessarily indicate that he was ignorant of its existence. He naturally would not have referred to incomplete works in such correspondence. The numbering of the E major Symphony as 'No. 8' in Fuchs' list is, incidentally, reflected in the fact that to this day the autograph sketch in the Royal College of Music bears, in the top left-hand corner of its first page, the inscription 'No. 8' in a hand other than the composer's.

It was George Grove who, in the second half of the nineteenth century, brought logic and clarity to the situation by making the 'Great' known in England as No. 9, thus leaving room for the E major sketch as No. 7 and the B minor torso as No. 8. Since then this numbering has been almost universally observed. Yet there remain two challenges to its sovereignty. The old numbering of the 'Great' as 'No. 7' persists even now – in the last quarter of the twentieth century – in some parts of Europe. And now Walter Dürr and Arnold Feil, the editors of the revised Deutsch catalogue (1978), expect us to accept 'No. 7' for the 'Unfinished' and 'No. 8' for the 'Great'. Thus, if the Deutsch revision be heeded at all, there will soon be in circulation three different numberings of the 'Great': it will be No. 7 (old-style), No. 9 (since Grove), and No. 8 (revised Deutsch).

The purpose of numbering is to enable the musical public to identify works which are widely performed and discussed, and to relate them chronologically to one another. If Ferdinand's idea was to lump unfinished works together at the end of the number-sequence, as though to treat them as a class of their own, he was clearly undermining the chronological purpose. The Deutsch revision will be open to question on other grounds, the more widely the true Seventh (in E major) is performed and discussed. In all honesty, the influence of the Deutsch revision on the world of concert promotion and musical debate is limited, and it is a hopeful sign that numerous major organisations (such as the BBC, most major publishers, and nearly all record companies), knowing of the challenge from the revised Deutsch, have responded by maintaining the *status quo*. One can only hope now that the New Schubert Edition, when it comes to issuing the later symphonies,[3] will decide not to perpetuate 'revised-Deutsch policy'. One can understand and indeed applaud Dürr and Feil and the New Schubert Edition taking a puristic line in most areas of their decision-making; that they should adopt a scholarly rigour is not in question. But the requirements of numbering are generated largely by the musical world outside the ivory tower of pure scholarship. Moreover, well-grounded traditions cannot be overthrown without decades of confusion and inconsistency. Even in the case of Dvořák, whose symphonic number-sequence was enlarged in a rational revision akin to Grove's of Schubert's, the old numbering has not been totally superseded a quarter of a century after the revision. With Schubert, if works known to the public in performances, broadcasts, recordings, and the Schubert literature are to be squeezed out of the 'official canon' and deprived of their handy and familiar means of identification, this conflict between ultra-purism and practicality is not likely to be resolved in the purists' favour.

[3] Nos. 1–3 only have appeared (1967) at the time of writing.

Appendix 3

The Entr'acte in B minor from *Rosamunde*

The Entr'acte is cast in sonata-form, which is Schubert's usual form for a symphonic finale. This fact has been obscured for some listeners by idiosyncrasies in the musical material and the way in which it behaves in the short term. The first subject group begins after a six-bar 'curtain' whose initial run up the scale from fifth to tonic suggests a close relationship with the very end of the scherzo of the 'Unfinished' Symphony, as Gerald Abraham has pointed out.[1] This first group is launched by a theme which behaves in a singularly indecisive manner, for all its air of rhythmic resolve. The short-winded ideas, the hesitant repetitions, the *ritardando*, and the impression of cadential or quasi-cadential formations at every bar or two – these all contribute to the indecisive effect. It is as though the theme is incapable of fulfilling itself. That is, of course, entirely appropriate, as self-fulfilling themes have no place in sonata-form thinking. But the way in which this particular theme achieves this effect has no doubt prompted some listeners, when considering this movement as a possible finale of the 'Unfinished' Symphony, to the involuntary reaction that it betrays the loose, rhetorical construction of theatre music, and so belongs more obviously to *Rosamunde* than to the symphony.

Fulfilment comes, in the first instance, with the B major theme that follows (Ex. 102). This theme has the character and build of a second subject, but is in fact a second theme within the first group, and it acts as a lyrical resolution of the first theme. It has the same rhythmic ingredients – two long notes with anacrusis and the decorative twirl which

[1] 'Finishing the Unfinished', *The Musical Times*, cxii, 1971, pp. 547–48.

Ex. 102

is now postponed till the fourth bar – but now these are moulded into a continuous and perfectly proportioned theme where before they were presented as a pithy, disjunct assemblage of modules. One finds encapsulated in this theme Schubert's personal approach to harmony. Ex. 102 shows, in в1, a serviceable bass of the sort a competent *Kapellmeister* might have provided for the theme. Straightforward in its harmonic implications, it affords an early-Beethoven harmonic balance, with the opening of the first phrase underpinned by the tonic chord, and the opening of the second (bar 5) by the dominant; and just as the two melodic phrases begin sequentially, so do the two bass phrases. Schubert's bass is в2. At [a] his G sharp creates an unorthodox second inversion in the harmony. At [b] a seventh on the flattened leading-note lends an extraordinary distance to the opening of the second phrase, exploiting the homely logic of the melody's sequence to offset the ear-stretching remoteness of this harmonic deviation. And at [c] a characteristic second inversion of a secondary dominant seventh permits a continuation of the stepwise ascent in the bass. This stepwise ascent contrasts strikingly with the expressive leaps of the first bass phrase, which seem calculated to invest the rather stay-at-home immobility of the upper melody with a richness of meaning the *Kapellmeister* could not have imagined.

The theme is played by the strings only, but is repeated at

once with an oboe doubling the first violins. But the oboe diverges from the violin melody to add a descant in the third bar of each phrase – a touch of pure poetry which, taken with the poetic richness of the harmony, helps to identify the Entr'acte with the special poetic world of the 'Unfinished' Symphony. The following boldly imaginative transition, short in duration but expansive in its harmonic and orchestral colour, tends to reinforce this identity, as does the intense second subject (in F sharp minor) which then begins in an atmosphere of charged quietude. Through the remainder of the exposition, poignant harmonic inflections and magical deviations of key sustain the spirit of the 'Unfinished'.

The development, like many of Schubert's, contains two main strands. One is a new *cantabile* idea in the wind which, as it becomes more dance-like, comes more to resemble the first theme: the other, thus prepared for, is the first theme. The recapitulation then begins not with the first theme, but with Ex. 102, the second theme of the first group. This irregularity is not unexpected, for the development ends with a protracted discourse on the first theme which amounts to a kind of re-interpretation of the original function of that theme at the beginning of the movement as a preparation for – and setting out of material for – the B major theme. After the recapitulation there follows a coda harmonically adventurous enough, rhythmically emphatic enough, and on a scale grand enough to serve as culmination – in Schubert's mind in 1822 – of a progressive and special symphony. The final blazing chord of B major, at the close of a long B minor coda, may be heard as an apotheosis of the gentler minor-to-major mutation in the course of the first subject group.[2]

---

[2]For an excellent account of the origins of the *Rosamunde* music, and the possible relationship of this Entr'acte to the drama, see the Preface to the miniature score of the Entr'acte and Ballet Music edited by M. J. E. Brown in 1969 and published by Eulenburg, London.

Appendix 4

The Identification of the Tenth Symphony

A volume of piano sketches by Schubert, bearing on its first page the title 'Sinfonie' and the date 'May 1818', was assumed by Otto Erich Deutsch to represent an attempt at a symphony in D major. In his 1951 Thematic Catalogue of Schubert's Works, Deutsch numbered this supposed symphony D615. The manuscript was more fully described by Maurice Brown in an article which appeared shortly before the Catalogue.[1] Brown, like Deutsch, took the sketches to be the incomplete remains of a single symphony.

The sketches in fact consist of nine different movements, most of them unfinished. In that all the movements are in D or keys closely related to D, and were bound in the one volume, one may see grounds for Brown's supposition. The quantity of material and the stylistic disparity of the movements seem to have sown no doubts in musicological minds. But when the volume in question was re-examined by the staff of the Wiener Stadt- und Landesbibliothek, where it is kept, in preparation for the Schubert anniversary celebrations of 1978 and with the help of new dating techniques based on developments in paper study and handwriting research, it was established that three different works from different periods were contained in it. Ernst Hilmar dated the three works, which are all sketches for symphonies, as belonging to 1818, 1820–1, and 1828,[2] and the sketches were subsequently published in facsimile. Separate Deutsch-numbers were accordingly assigned to the three sym-

[1] 'Schubert's Unfinished Symphony in D', *Music and Letters*, XXXI/2, April 1950, pp. 101–9.

[2] 'Nachwort' to *Franz Schubert: Drei Symphonie-Fragmente*.

phonies in the second edition of Deutsch's catalogue in 1978. Since that time, fresh research has led to a challenge to Hilmar's view of the date of the 1828 work. Robert Winter has established beyond reasonable doubt that Schubert began sketching it no earlier than September 1828, and more likely in October,[3] as against Hilmar's spring-summer dating in the Deutsch revision. On this account the catalogue number D936A requires upward revision.

Thus it was determined only 150 years after Schubert's death that he had begun work on a Tenth Symphony.[4] Curiously, two long-standing clues had been overlooked. One clue is offered by the volume of sketches itself. The library cover is inscribed 'Zwei Sinfonien in D', implying that a librarian of the late nineteenth or early twentieth century thought there was too much material in the volume for one symphony. If Brown had inspected this cover his suspicions might have been aroused. But he admits in his article describing the sketches that he was working from photocopies, and it may be supposed that the photocopies sent him from Vienna did not include a copy of the cover-board. The facsimile edition likewise omits the cover, and Hilmar's note makes no reference to it.

The second clue is a documentary one almost as old as the manuscript itself. Schubert's friend Eduard von Bauernfeld, the dramatist who was collaborating with him on the opera *Der Graf von Gleichen* in 1827 and was one of the last people to visit him in his dying days, wrote an appreciation of the composer some seven months after his death,[5] in which he included a list of works by his friend 'bisher noch nicht zur allgemeinen Kenntniss gekommenen' (not widely known about). The list included:

1825   Grosse Symphonie (Great Symphony)
1828   Letzte Symphonie (Last Symphony)

---

[3] *Loc. cit.*, p. 255.

[4] The other two symphonies in the volume, D615 and D708A, are earlier works, discussed in chapter X, pp. 138–58.

[5] In the *Wiener Zeitschrift für Kunst, Literatur, Theater und Mode*, 13 June 1829.

Only now can Bauernfeld be given due credit for his accuracy. For only in the last part of the twentieth century has research established that the 'Great' C major (Schubert's 'grosse Symphonie') was indeed composed in 1825 rather than 1828, and that a further symphony was undertaken in his last year – a last symphony known about by Bauernfeld but either unknown to or ignored by the many other survivors of Schubert's circle in the years and decades after his death.

Appendix 5

Autographs and Performing Versions

The autograph scores of all Schubert's finished symphonies except No. 5 are in the library of the Gesellschaft der Musikfreunde in Vienna. The Fifth Symphony is listed by both editions of the Deutsch catalogue as 'Berlin Stadtbibliothek', although its home for many years has been Uniwersytet Jagiellónska, Kraków (Poland).[1] There are good photocopies of all of these, including No. 5, in the Photogramm-Archiv at the Nationalbibliothek, Vienna.

The D2B fragment is in the University Library at Lund in Sweden; D615 and D708A at the Wiener Stadt- und Landesbibliothek; the sketched Symphony No. 7 in E (D729) at the Royal College of Music in London; the score and sketches of No. 8 in B minor at the Gesellschaft der Musikfreunde; and the sketch of No. 10 (D936A) at the Wiener Stadt- und Landesbibliothek. The autograph score of the B minor Entr'acte from *Rosamunde* is in the Nationalbibliothek, Vienna.

Among editions, realisations, and completions of the unfinished works are:

Symphony in D, D2B – Brian Newbould (1981);
Symphony in D, D615B – Peter Gülke (1978), Newbould (1981);
Symphony in D, D708A – Gülke (1978), Newbould (1981);

---

[1] A fascinating account of the evacuation of large numbers of precious manuscripts by Bach, Mozart, Beethoven and others from Berlin to Grüssau during the Second World War, and the subsequent appropriation of these by the Poles for political purposes, is given by Nigel Lewis (*Paperchase*, Hamish Hamilton, London, 1981). Schubert's Fifth Symphony was one of the autographs involved, although Lewis wrongly lists this work as the 'E-flat major symphony' (p. 37).

Symphony No. 7 in E, D729 – John Francis Barnett (1880–1), Felix Weingartner (1934), Newbould (1977–8); Symphony No. 8 in B minor, D759 (scherzo) – Geoffrey Bush (1944), Denis Vaughan (c. 1960), Gerald Abraham (1970), Florian Hollard (1976, rev. 1977–8), Stephen Casale (1978), Newbould (1982); Symphony No. 10 in D, D936A – Newbould (1979–81).

Appendix 6

Bibliography

1. Catalogues, Facsimiles, Special Issues and Editions

CHUSID, MARTIN, (ed.), *Schubert: Symphony in B minor ('Unfinished')*, Norton Critical Score, Norton, New York/Chappell, London, 1968.

DEUTSCH, OTTO ERICH, *Schubert. Thematic Catalogue of All His Works in Chronological Order*, J. M. Dent, London, 1951.

———, second edition, ed. the Editorial Board of the Neue Schubert-Ausgabe and Werner Aderhold, Bärenreiter, Kassel, 1978.

HILMAR, ERNST, *Verzeichnis der Schubert-Handschriften in der Musiksammlung der Wiener Stadt- und Landesbibliothek*, Catalogus Musicus, viii, Kassel, 1978.

——— and BRUSATTI, OTTO (eds.), *Franz Schubert – Gedenkausstellung 1978: Ausstellung der Wiener Stadt- und Landesbibliothek zum 150. Todestag des Komponisten*, Universal, Vienna, 1978.

LANGEVIN, P.-G. (ed.), 'Franz Schubert et la Symphonie', triple numéro 355–7, *La Revue musicale*, Paris, 1982.

SCHUBERT, FRANZ, *Drei Symphonie-Fragmente*, Bärenreiter, Kassel, 1978.

2. A Selection of Germane Studies, Biographical, Generic and Analytical

ABRAHAM GERALD, (ed.), *Schubert: A Symposium*, Lindsay Drummond, London, 1947 (rev. 1969).

BADURA-SKODA, EVA, and BRANSCOMBE, PETER (eds.), *Schubert Studies: Problems of Style and Chronology*, Cambridge University Press, London, 1982.

BRENDEL, ALFRED, *Musical Thoughts and Afterthoughts*, Robson, London, 1976. :

BROWN, MAURICE J. E., *Schubert: A Critical Biography*, Macmillan, London, 1958.

——, *Essays on Schubert*, Macmillan, London, 1966.

——, *Schubert Symphonies*, BBC Music Guide, BBC, London, 1970.

DEUTSCH, OTTO ERICH, *Schubert: A Documentary Biography*, J. M. Dent, London, 1946.

——, *Schubert: Memoirs by his Friends*, A. and C. Black, London, 1958.

EINSTEIN, ALFRED, *Schubert*, Cassell, London, 1951.

FEIL, ARNOLD, *Studien zu Schuberts Rhythmik*, Munich, 1966.

FRISCH, WALTER, (ed.), *Schubert: Critical and Analytical Studies*, University of Nebraska Press, Lincoln, 1986.

GÁL, HANS, *Franz Schubert and the Essence of Melody*, Gollancz, London, 1974.

——, *The Golden Age of Vienna*, M. Parrish, London/New York, 1948.

HANSON, ALICE M., *Musical Life in Biedermeyer Vienna*, Cambridge University Press, London, 1985.

HELLBORN, HEINRICH KREISSLE VON, *Franz Schubert*, Vienna, 1865 (English transl. 1869).

HUTCHINGS, ARTHUR, J., *Schubert*, J. M. Dent, London, 1945.

KUNZE, STEFAN, *Franz Schubert: Sinfonie h-moll: Unvollendete*, W. Fink, Munich, 1965.

LAAFF, ERNST, *Franz Schuberts Sinfonien*, H. Rauch, Wiesbaden, 1933.

LEWIS, NIGEL, *Paperchase*, Hamish Hamilton, London 1981.

MCNAUGHT, WILLIAM, 'Franz Schubert', in Ralph Hill (ed.), *The Symphony*, Penguin, London, 1949.

MANDYCZEWSKI, EUSEBIUS, (ed.), *Revisionsbericht, Franz Schuberts Werke: kritisch durchgesehene Gesamtausgabe*, Breitkopf und Härtel, Leipzig, 1897.

OSBORNE, CHARLES, *Schubert and his Vienna*, Weidenfeld and Nicolson, London, 1985.

REED, JOHN, *Schubert: The Final Years*, Faber, London, 1972.

RIEZLER, WALTER, *Schuberts Instrumentalmusik*, Atlantis, Zurich, 1967.

SMITH, A. B., *Schubert, i: The Symphonies in C major and B minor*, Musical Pilgrims Series No. 15, Oxford University Press, London, 1926.

TOVEY, DONALD FRANCIS, *Essays in Musical Analysis*, Volume 1, *Symphonies 1*, Oxford University Press, London, 1935.

WECHSBERG, JOSEPH, *Schubert*, Weidenfeld and Nicolson, London, 1977.

3. Articles

ABRAHAM, GERALD, 'Finishing the Unfinished', *The Musical Times*, cxii, 1971, pp. 547–48.

ANDRASHKE, P., 'Die Retuschen Gustav Mahlers an der 7. Symphonie von Franz Schubert', *Archiv für Musikwissenschaft*, xxxii, 1975, pp. 106–16.

BADURA-SKODA, PAUL, 'Possibilities and Limitations of Stylistic Criticism in the Dating of Schubert's "Great" C major Symphony', in E. Badura-Skoda and P. Branscombe (eds.), *Schubert Studies: Problems of Style and Chronology*, Cambridge University Press, London, 1982.

BARNETT, JOHN FRANCIS, 'Some Details concerning the Completion and Instrumentation of Schubert's Sketch Symphony in E', *Proceedings of the Royal Musical Association*, xvii, 1890–1, pp. 177–90.

BAUERNFELD, EDUARD VON, 'On Franz Schubert', *Wiener Zeitschrift für Kunst, Literature, Theater und Mode*, 9/11/13 June 1829.

BIBA, OTTO, 'Franz Schubert und die Gesellschaft der Musikfreunde in Wien', in Otto Brusatti (ed.), *Schubert-Kongress Wien 1978. Bericht*, Akademisches Drück- und Verlagsanstalt, Graz, 1979, pp. 23–26.

——, 'Schubert's Position in Viennese Musical Life', *Nineteenth-Century Music*, III/2, pp. 106–13.

BROWN, MAURICE J. E., 'Schubert's Unfinished Symphony in D', *Music and Letters*, xxxi, 1950, pp. 101–9.

CARSE, ADAM, 'Editing Schubert's Unfinished Symphony', *The Musical Times*, xcv, 1954, pp. 143–45.

COLLES, H. C., 'Categories', *Music and Letters*, IX/4, 1928, pp. 336–40.

CONE, EDWARD T., 'Schubert's Beethoven', *The Musical Quarterly*, vi, 1970, pp. 779–93.

COREN, D., 'Ambiguity in Schubert's Recapitulations', *The Musical Quarterly*, lx, 1974, pp. 568–82.

DEUTSCH, OTTO ERICH, 'The Discovery of Schubert's C major Symphony', *The Musical Quarterly*, xxxviii, 1952, pp. 528–32.
——, 'The Riddle of Schubert's Unfinished Symphony', *Music Review*, 1, 1940, pp. 36–53.

GOLDSCHMIDT, HARRY, 'Eine weitere E-dur-Sinfonie', in Otto Brusatti (ed.), *Schubert-Kongress Wien 1978. Bericht*, Akademisches Drück- und Verlagsanstalt, Graz, 1979, pp. 79–112.

GOOSSENS, EUGENE, 'The Symphonies of Schubert', *The Chesterian*, 10/74, November 1928.

GRASBERGER, FRANZ, 'Schubert und Bruckner', in Otto Brusatti (ed.), *Schubert-Kongress Wien 1978. Bericht*, Akademisches Druck-und Verlagsanstalt, Graz, 1979, pp. 215–28.

GRAY, W., 'Schubert the Instrumental Composer', *The Musical Quarterly*, lxiv, 1978, pp. 483–94.

GRIFFEL, L. MICHAEL., 'A Reappraisal of Schubert's Methods of Composition', *The Musical Quarterly*, LXIII/2, April 1977, pp. 186–210.

GÜLKE, PETER, 'Neue Beiträge zur Kenntnis des Sinfonikers Schubert: Die Fragmente D.615, D.708a und D.936a', in Heinz-Klaus Metzger and Rainer Riehn (eds.), *Music-Konzepte: Sonderband Franz Schubert*, Munich, December 1979, pp. 186–220.

HAMBURGER, P., 'Schuberts "Ufuldente": kendsgeminger og formodninger', *Dansk musiktidsskrift*, xl, 1967, p. 37.

HILMAR, ERNST, 'Neue Funde, Daten und Dokumente zum symphonischen Werk Franz Schuberts', *Österreichische Musikzeitschrift*, xxxiii, 1978, pp. 266–76.

HOLLANDER, HANS, 'Die Beethoven-Reflexe in Schuberts grosse C-dur-Sinfonie', *Die neue Zeitschrift für Musik*, cxxxvi, May 1965, pp. 183–95.

HOORICKX, REINHARD VAN, 'Schubert's Reminiscences of His Own Works', *The Musical Quarterly*, lx/3, July 1974, pp. 373–88.
——, 'The Chronology of Schubert's Fragments and Sketches', in E. Badura-Skoda and P. Branscombe (eds.), *Schubert Studies: Problems of Style and Chronology*, Cambridge University Press, London, 1982.

LAAFF, ERNST, 'Schubert's grosse C-dur-Symphonie: erkennbare Grundlagen ihrer Einheitlichkeit', *Festschrift Friedrich Blume*, Bärenreiter, Kassel, 1963, pp. 204–13.

——, 'Schuberts h-moll Symphonie', in F. Blume (ed.), *Gedenk-schrift für Hermann Abert*, M. Niemeyer, Halle, 1928, pp. 93–115.

LANDON, CHRISTA, 'Neue Schubert-Funde', *Österreichische Musik-zeitschrift*, xxiv, 1969, pp. 299–323 (English transl. *Music Review*, xxxi/3, 1970, pp. 215–31).

LEIBOWITZ, RENÉ, 'Eine verlorene Symphonie Schuberts', in Heinz-Klaus Metzger and Rainer Riehn (eds.), *Music-Konzepte: Sonderband Franz Schubert*, Munich, December 1979, pp. 221–26.

——, 'Tempo und Charakter in Schuberts Symphonien', in Heinz-Klaus Metzger and Rainer Riehn (eds.), *Music-konzepte: Sonderband Franz Schubert*, Munich, December 1979, pp. 167–86.

McKAY, ELIZABETH NORMAN, 'Rossinis Einfluss auf Schubert', *Österreichische Musikzeitschrift*, xviii, 1963, p. 17.

MACKENZIE, COMPTON, 'On Finishing the Unfinished Symphony', *A Musical Chair*, Chatto & Windus, London, 1939, pp. 110–17.

NEWBOULD, BRIAN, 'Schubert's Other Unfinished', *The Musical Times*, cxix/1625, July 1978, pp. 587–89.

——, 'Unfinished Schubert', *The Listener*, London, 13 January 1983, p. 30.

——, 'Completing Schubert's Unfinished Orchestral Works', *Ovation*, v/11, December 1984, pp. 22–25.

——, 'Looking at what might have been . . . and deciphering the intentions', *The Times Higher Education Supplement*, London, 8 March 1985, p. 13.

——, 'Schubert's Last Symphony', *The Musical Times*, cxxvi/1707, May 1985, pp. 272–75.

——, 'A Working Sketch by Schubert (D.936a)', *Current Musicology*, No. 43, 1987, pp. 22–32.

NEWMAN, ERNEST, 'Schubert: A Point in the "Unfinished" ', *More Essays from The World of Music*, Calder, London, 1958, pp. 110–12.

NEWMAN, W. S., 'Freedom of Tempo in Schubert's Instrumental Music', *The Musical Quarterly*, lxi, 1975, pp. 528–45.

PEYSER, HERBERT F., 'The Epic of the "Unfinished"', *The Musical Quarterly*, xiv, 1928, pp. 639–60.

PRITCHARD, T. C. L., 'The Unfinished Symphony', *Music Review*, iii, 1942, pp. 10–32.

REED, JOHN, 'How the 'Great' C major was written', *Music and Letters*, 1vi, 1975, pp. 18–25.

——, 'The "Gastein" Symphony Reconsidered', *Music and Letters*, xi, 1959, pp. 341–49.

ROUSSEL, ALBERT, 'Schubert the Symphonist', *The Chesterian*, 10/74, November 1928.

SAMS, ERIC, 'Schubert's Illness Re-examined', *The Musical Times*, cxxi, 1980, pp. 15–22.

SCHUMANN, ROBERT, 'Die 7. Symphonie von Franz Schubert', *Neue Zeitschrift für Musik*, xii, 1840, p. 81.

TOVEY, DONALD FRANCIS, 'Tonality', *Music and Letters*, ix/4, 1928, pp. 341–63.

TRUSCOTT, HAROLD, 'Franz Schubert', in Robert Simpson (ed.), *The Symphony*, Penguin, Harmondsworth, 1966-7, Vol. 1, pp. 188–208.

WALTER, FRANZ, 'La symphonie inachevée en mi de Schubert ou les avatars d'une partition', *Schweizerische Musikzeitung*, Vol. XCIV, 1954, pp. 445–49.

WEBSTER, JAMES, 'Schubert's Sonata Form and Brahms's First Maturity', *19th-Century Music*, II/1, July 1978, pp. 18–35, and III/1, July 1979, pp. 52–71.

WHAPLES, M. K., 'On Structural Integration in Schubert's Instrumental Works', *Acta Musicologica*, xl, 1968, pp. 186–95.

WHITTALL, ARNOLD, 'The Sonata Crisis: Schubert in 1828', *Music Review*, xxx, 1969, pp. 124–30.

WINTER, ROBERT, 'Paper Studies and the Future of Schubert Research', in E. Badura-Skoda and P. Branscombe (eds.), *Schubert Studies: Problems of Style and Chronology*, Cambridge University Press, London, 1982.

4. Dissertations (Unpublished)

RICH, ALAN, *Formal Practices in Schubert's Larger Instrumental Works*, University of California, 1952.

TOLLER, NICHOLAS, *Gesture and Expressive Purpose in Schubert's Instrumental Music of 1822–28*, University of Hull, 1988.

WEBER, R., *Die Sinfonien Franz Schuberts im Versuch einer Struktur-wissen-schaftlichen Darstellung und Untersuchungen*, University of Münster, 1971.

Index

Max Rostal

BEETHOVEN

The Sonatas for Piano and Violin

*Thoughts
on their Interpretation*

With a Preface by
The Amadeus Quartet

**With a Pianist's Postscript
by Günter Ludwig**

**and a History of Performance Practice
by Paul Rolland**

In this book Max Rostal, one of the world's most renowned teachers of the violin, distills sixty years of experience to provide a guide to these perennial favourites, both for the performing musician and for the general reader. This is the first full-length study of these works in English since the beginning of this century.

'What Rostal has produced here is a highly detailed, intelligent and immensely thorough guide through all ten sonatas'
Robert Dearling, *Classical Music*

219pp, illustrated, 207 music examples, bibliography, index

0 907689 05 1; £12.95 (cased)
0 907689 06 X; £6.95 (paperback)